D0319505

THE SCALE MODELLER'S HANDBOOK

THE SCALE MODELLER'S HANDBOOK

CHRIS ELLIS

HAMLYN

LONDON · NEW YORK · SYDNEY · TORONTO

A QUARTO BOOK

Published by
The Hamlyn publishing Group Limited
London · New York · Sydney · Toronto
Astronaut House, Feltham, Middlesex, England

ISBN 0 600 38399 7

This book was designed and produced by
Quarto Publishing Limited
32 Kingly Court, London W1
Art Editor: Roger Daniels
Editor: Christopher Pick

Phototypeset in Britain by Tradespools Limited.
Printed in Hong Kong by Leefung-Asco Printers Ltd

Frontispiece finely-detailed replica of an 18th century British first rate battleship, typical of the good wood kits.

Contents

INTRODUCTION

The world of small scale models has always held a fascination for the young – and the not so young. Models of a kind have been found dating back thousands of years – miniature boats and chariots in a Pharaoh's tomb, for instance – and through the centuries scale models have been much in evidence. Beautiful model warships made by French prisoners of war in Napoleonic times are among the best known and most treasured of all, but there are many other examples which are now collectors' pieces, such as the promotional models of Citroen cars produced in the 1920s. In turn, most of the more popular toys are, in effect, models. Pushalong cars and dolls are two good examples of miniature versions of full-size objects which appeal to children. In this century the distinction between toys and scale models has become blurred, for many modern toy aircraft, trains, boats, cars and so on today are so detailed and accurate that they qualify as scale models as well as toys.

Modern technology has had considerable effect; mass production and the use of cheap adaptable materials, notably plastics, have made scale models of all sorts a viable commercial proposition. The days when the embryo model-maker had no option but to buy expensive sets of parts or work from raw materials are now over. Today scale models are an industry in themselves. Hobby stores stock an ever-increasing selection of kits, parts and ready-made models at every price from the 'pocket money' level up. An enthusiast for scale replicas can now follow his hobby without needing to be a skilled craftsman; for, although many people still make models from raw materials, parts and accessories (popularly known as 'scratch building'), others build from kits and yet others simply collect ready-made models.

This book sets out to show both beginners and more experienced modellers the potential of some of the most popular model subjects. Since it would take a much larger book to give full technical coverage of every aspect of each subject, the intention is to show what is currently available, what to look for, and what sort of approach might enable you to get the best out of your chosen subject. Each of the subjects covered in this book has enormous ramifications; which aspects you follow up will depend to a large extent on your own inclinations, abilities and pocket.

If accurate scale replicas, complete in every small detail, are your particular favourites, then you will be happy with the many wood, plastic, metal or card construction kits on the market. Depending on how complex they are, they will take anything from five minutes to five months to make with perhaps as much time again in preliminary research and reference work. The requirements for making the simpler models may be no more than a tube of cement, a craft knife and a sheet of glasspaper. But, conversely, the serious and skilled maker of complicated kits may perhaps need power drills or even a lathe and a fully fitted workshop.

For something more active you may prefer a working model which can get to grips with the elements like its full-size counterpart – a model boat which sails, a model battleship with a motor, a flying model aircraft and so on. Often (but not always) these models make some sacrifices to scale fidelity in order to work satisfactorily. For example, a sailing boat may have simplified rigging and a false keel; a flying model aircraft, even if a scale replica, will probably have an oversize propeller and an enlarged undercarriage.

A good many enthusiasts do not always have either the time or the inclination to make models. Their tastes are catered for handsomely by a good selection of ready-made models. Everything from a pre-painted miniature metal aircraft to a fully equipped radio-controlled model aircraft can be purchased

During the 1920s and 1930s, the French Citroen company produced constructional toys as publicity for the full-size versions. Shown here are the parts of a 1929 Citroën C6 chassis ready for assembly and the box in which the toy was marketed.

Above 1:25 scale Centurion Mk III Tank; completely detailed inside and out, it has been sectionalized to show the interior.
Left an extremely detailed early Boeing YB-17 Flying Fortress made from a vac-form kit.
Below a Japanese 2-6-0 live steam locomotive in gauge 1 (1:32 scale) with oil-fired boiler and complete working parts.
Opposite page highly realistic 1917 period Fokker Triplanes shooting down a British reconnaissance machine.

ready-made over the hobby counter, though admittedly the price may be higher than that of the equivalent item in kit form. Ready die-cast models (sold either primarily as toys or as specialist high-price items) form a substantial part of the entire model car hobby and have a vast following. It is possible to be a model car enthusiast and never get involved in constructional work.

Which subject you choose and how much you participate is a personal decision and largely depends on your own interests, time, tastes and financial position. It's no good taking up the construction of large scale model aircraft or boats, for instance, if you cannot afford the considerable cost of the kits for large scale models. If your time for modelling is restricted,then models from simple plastic kits are a better proposition. Even complicated plastic models are too ambitious if you are never going to have the time to complete them. Remember that a model does not have to be complex or expensive to provide you with a lot of fun.

In this book we show what to look for in the model world, possible follow-up avenues, some representative hobby projects and further possibilities within each of the fields covered. If you are a complete beginner, you will be able to choose which type of modelling activity to take up; if you already have some experience, then you may well find yet more interesting projects and developments. One thing is for sure: it is no bad thing to try more than one type of modelling, whether to see which interests you most or merely to enjoy the interest that variety can offer.

WHICH KIT AND WHAT MODEL?

Almost everyone today gets a first taste of scale modelling from the ubiquitous plastic assembly kits. We could go further and say that their widespread availability from the 1950s onwards is the reason why the modelling hobby is so strong today. Plastic kits have been frequently derided (usually by those who've never really studied them) as 'childish', 'simple', 'pointless', 'rubbish', and so on, this dismissive attitude implying that such kits are of limited value. Yet they sell in millions, are popular with all age groups from young children upwards, and, most important of all, they put model making within the reach of everyone. Take a simple example: if, before the days of plastic kits, you wanted to make a model of a motor torpedo or PT boat, you either made it from scratch – that is, starting with raw materials such as wood or tin – or you bought an elaborate and relatively expensive kit of wood parts. Even with this kit you needed to be very skilled, and have a lot of time to spare, for the model had to be made up almost literally plank by plank from roughly finished components.

You can still buy this sort of kit today, and very good it is too, but there is also a great choice of plastic kits of MTBs or PT boats, depicting vessels of several nations, in several scales and varying in comlexity and price from the very simple to the very sophisticated; often motors are included too. All the plastic kits are relatively cheap, and because they consist of ready moulded and detailed parts they can be assembled quite readily even by a youngster.

This is really the secret of the plastic kits' universal appeal: anyone can take up the model making hobby simply by choosing an approach that meets his individual skill level, and experiments or adventures will not result in financial ruin!

Plastic kits bypass the most important but, let's face it, the most boring and time-consuming parts of the work. All the key components come in ready-to-assemble form; so the long chore of shaping the parts accurately is taken out of your hands and you are left with assembly, detailing and finishing – all of which are very much more interesting.

Just about everything has appeared in plastic kit form over the years – aircraft, tanks, ships, cars and motor-cycles, varying in size from tiny to giant. Often the more elaborate kits are motorized. Some of the other subjects which are or have been available in plastic kits include figures (eg soldiers) and animals of all types, birds, houses, factories and other buildings, eyes and other anatomical models, guillotines and ghouls, spaceships (real or imaginary) and many others including oddities such as pagodas and musical instruments. Tracking down this vast output of kits and seeking out the oddities is almost a full-time hobby in itself.

Spin-offs from the plastic kits moulded in polystyrene are vacform kits (almost entirely limited to aircraft) and combi kits which comprise both plastic and card-printed parts. These are most often limited to building models – houses, stations etc.

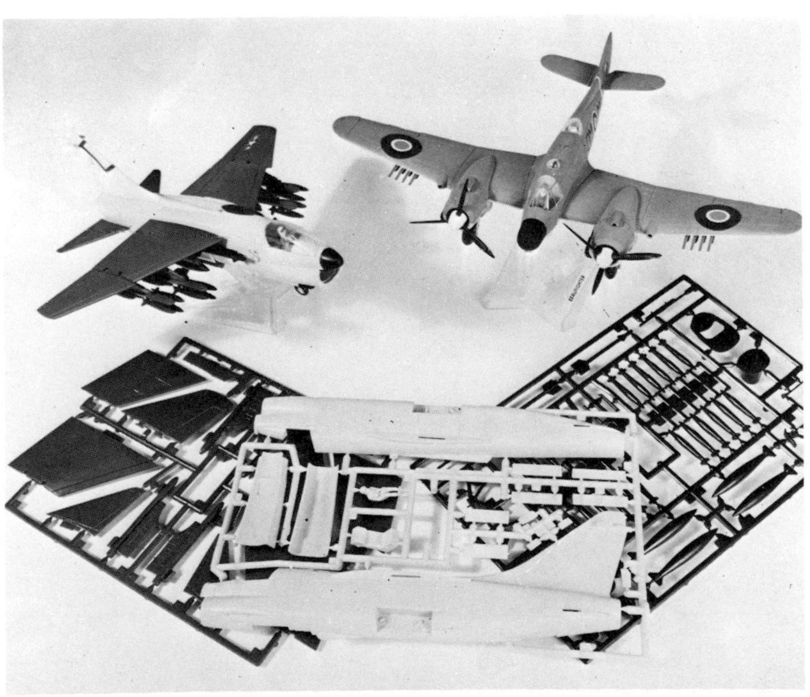

Above all-metal kits are usually sets of parts, some intricate, which must be cleaned up with a file and assembled with glue or low-melting point solder (not the conventional kind).
Right a typical plastic kit of parts, producing the type of models shown.
Opposite page two examples of the elaborate, motorized models now on sale as plastic kits. In front is a 1:72 Japanese torpedo boat, behind a 1:72 Vosper fast patrol boat.

815

Wood kits have survived the plastic kit revolution. Though wooden scale model aircraft kits long ago gave way to plastic, there are still many kits available for ships and boats and occasionally for other transport items such as farm carts. Nowadays wood kits largely depict subjects made of wood in real life; they demand a fair degree of true craftsmanship for, though most parts are machined to shape, they require final shaping and finishing to match the plans provided, while some small parts may have to be carved completely from wood blanks.

In aircraft kits wood is only found now in flying models. These only just come within the scope of this book, for most flying models are non-scale – they are simply miniature flying machines. However, there are some very impressive scale flying kits to be had, mostly intended for radio-control and covering the fields of gliding and powered flight. Radio-control and powered-flight models are subjects in their own right, though it is worth mentioning that small ready-to-run radio-control models of cars, trucks, tanks and aircraft are a recent development. All of them are very nicely produced and well finished in plastic.

Of course there is nothing to stop you buying one of the large wood scale aircraft kits intended for powered radio-control flight and assembling it as a static super-detailed model, adding masses of interior fittings and making a true replica of the real thing. Using this approach you could make a most imposing non-flying model with a wingspan of up to 6 feet.

The smaller scale flying models with a wingspan of up to 2 feet are altogether cruder. They are constructed in sheet balsa or by the conventional tissue on balsa framework method. Some of the smaller models of this type purport to be scale but are in fact considerably simplified.

Traditional wooden flying model kits, powered and unpowered, are produced for modellers of all ages. They make a good introduction to the idea of scale modelling.

Card, another material very popular in past generations, is still used in commercially produced kits, though, like wood, its popularity has been usurped by plastic. The very first scale aircraft kits were card, and a few good and well detailed kits of this type are still available today, mostly from Germany, Austria and Eastern Europe. Model buildings are the card kits most widely sold; their standard is generally good, and a properly made up model is both realistic and strong. In fact, when it comes to depicting the subtle colouring of building materials, colour printing on card can look more realistic than painted plastic, which undoubtedly helps the popularity of this type of kit. In Germany, traditional makers of card cutout kits continue to offer a delightful range of items, including fairgrounds, traction engines, ships, walled cities, airships and much else. Indeed, collecting and making these card models is a complete hobby in itself. A fair amount of skill and time is needed to make the most complex card kits, but others are extremely simple. Card is also a very convenient material for scratchbuilding, either on its own or with balsa wood as an integral part of the structure, or for bracing.

Above and left St Paul's Cathedral and a 1919 Leyland van in 1:76 scale, both made from a pre-coloured printed card sheet.
Below American-style hotel in 1:76 scale made entirely from pre-cut, pre-coloured card parts.

Various other materials can also be used for modelling. In the nineteenth century bone was extensively used, being carved and shaped most intricately to produce beautiful models, mostly of sailing ships, which now command high prices in the antique market. More recently, unlikely materials such as matchsticks and discarded ball pens have been used for model making. Indeed the largest ball pen manufacturer in the world runs an annual international competition for models made from his products, and remarkable models are made from matchsticks.

When plastic kits first appeared in large numbers, it looked for a time as if the days of metal, previously the main modelling material, were numbered. But recently metal kits have made a big comeback, mainly because relatively unsophisticated rubber moulds are used in their manufacture; these are very much cheaper than the heavy steel dies used for injection-moulded plastic kits. Plastic kits need to sell in millions to recover the high cost of the dies and are therefore restricted to popular subjects. Kits made from rubber moulds, on the other hand, are relatively cheaper to produce, and so small production runs are possible; this means that a greater variety of model kits can be produced. Many of the metal kits are produced by smaller companies.

Originally railway subjects – locomotives, rolling stock signals and many accessories – were the most common of all, and in fact they probably still are. However, cars, trucks, steam rollers, traction engines, buses, warships, model guns and model soldiers as well are all produced in abundance in cast metal form in a wide variety of scales. The metal used, an alloy of tin and lead, is soft, malleable and easy to work.

A recent development has been the release of home casting kits, mainly for model soldiers. With these you get a crucible, ingots of 'tin', rubber moulds and in some cases a burner. Limited only by your supply of 'tin' (which can be purchased separately), you can produce many figures from one mould, which makes these kits ideal for building up a wargames army or making an impressive battle diorama. Most of the commercial casting kits are for flat or 'half round' figures such as the old traditional 'toy' soldier. If, however, you are skilled enough, you can literally create an original model from scratch by making your own master figure and building up a mould from cold casting resin compound and silicon rubber. Some modellers whose skill does not run to producing original figures nevertheless use home-made moulds to produce other small items and accessories.

Opposite page Roman auxiliary cavalryman cast in metal and made entirely from scratch.
Below large-scale 1930 Bentley made entirely from metal with real wire wheels and real leather upholstery.

TOOLS

In general,the sort of tools you need for scale model making of the sort discussed in this book are not too expensive and are readily available. Models made in plastic, wood, card or cast metal all demand the same sort of tools, though you may use some more than others, depending on the work in hand or the material in use.

Almost everything required is sold at the bigger hobby stores which sell kits and materials, though hardware or 'Do-it-yourself' stores are also a source of most tools. Certain tools are essential for any sort of model work, others less so.

Let's start by looking at the essential tools first, as these are also the least expensive. Your first essential is a good modelling knife. Among other things, this is used for trimming the components off the sprues, removing the moulding 'flash', general trimming and cutting out materials (e.g. plastic sheet, balsa wood, card or even paper) you may be using in the model. A modelling knife can also be used as a simple plane when a large quantity of plastic or wood has to be scraped away, but more on this later.

There are many makes of craft or modelling knife available at various prices, with spare blades also readily available quite cheaply. You can get straight-edge, round-edge and hook-shaped blades, plus gougers and reamers. Several makers of modelling knives have complete sets featuring a handle and a full selection of blades – worth getting if you can afford that little extra.

As a general rule I always ensure that I have at least two brand-new spare blades in addition to the one in the knife. There are two reasons for this. First of all, if a blade breaks it does so when you do most of your modelling – in the evening – so lack of a spare blade may hold up progress till you can buy another. Second, there are many instances in model work when very tiny parts must be trimmed; a brand-new blade is desirable for this rather than the blade already in your knife, which may have a slightly worn edge. If you ever try trimming a small plastic part with a less than perfect blade, you'll find it only too easy to splinter the plastic if your blade isn't sharp. Don't discard old blades, however.

Conserve blades by using older ones for general cutting, hacking and scraping and keep new ones for very fine cutting and trimming where absolute precision is required. As a blade ages, so it can be transferred to an 'old blade' box, a small tin of the sort used for cough sweets.

The next most important tool in most model making is a file, plus associated 'abrasives' such as emery paper and the like. For most model making you need a very fine 'rat tail' or small half-round file, or both. This sort of file should have a point at one end, which is very useful for opening up locating holes or enlarging apertures like the inside of wheel hubs. Most of the other filing you need to do involves eliminating mould marks or casting marks such as the 'join' round the rim of a tyre – getting rid of 'flash', or filing down cemented edges to give a smooth finish. A very fine file will do all these things admirably without causing more than the minimum of abrasion to the surface of the plastic. More important, if the file should accidentally slip, it'll

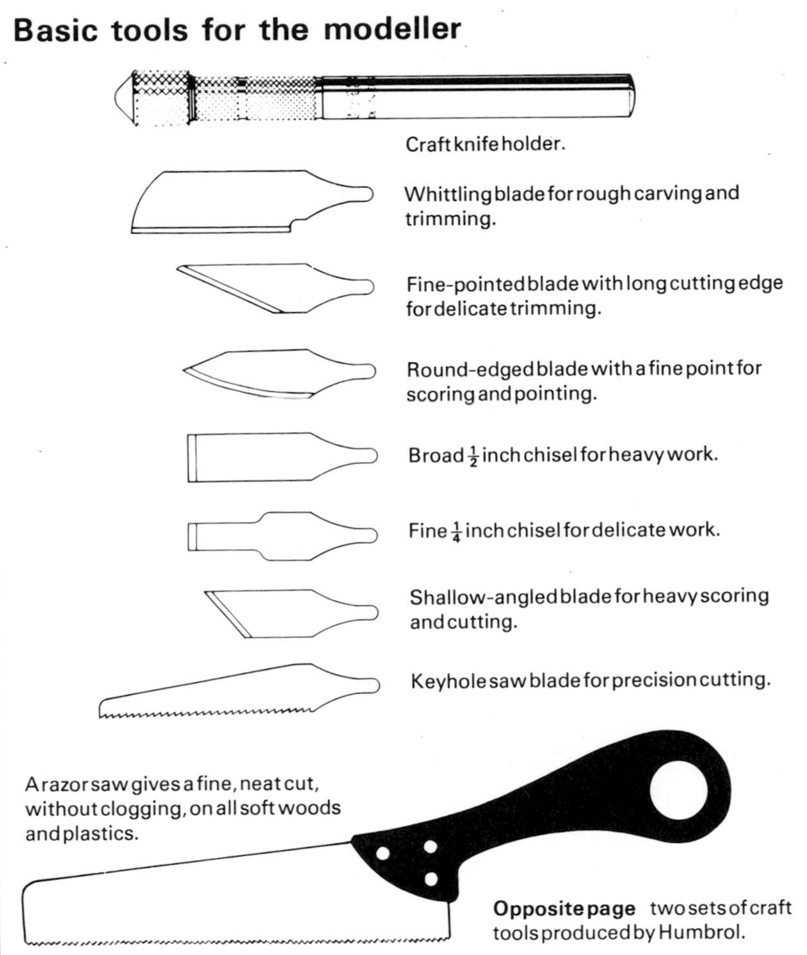

Opposite page two sets of craft tools produced by Humbrol.

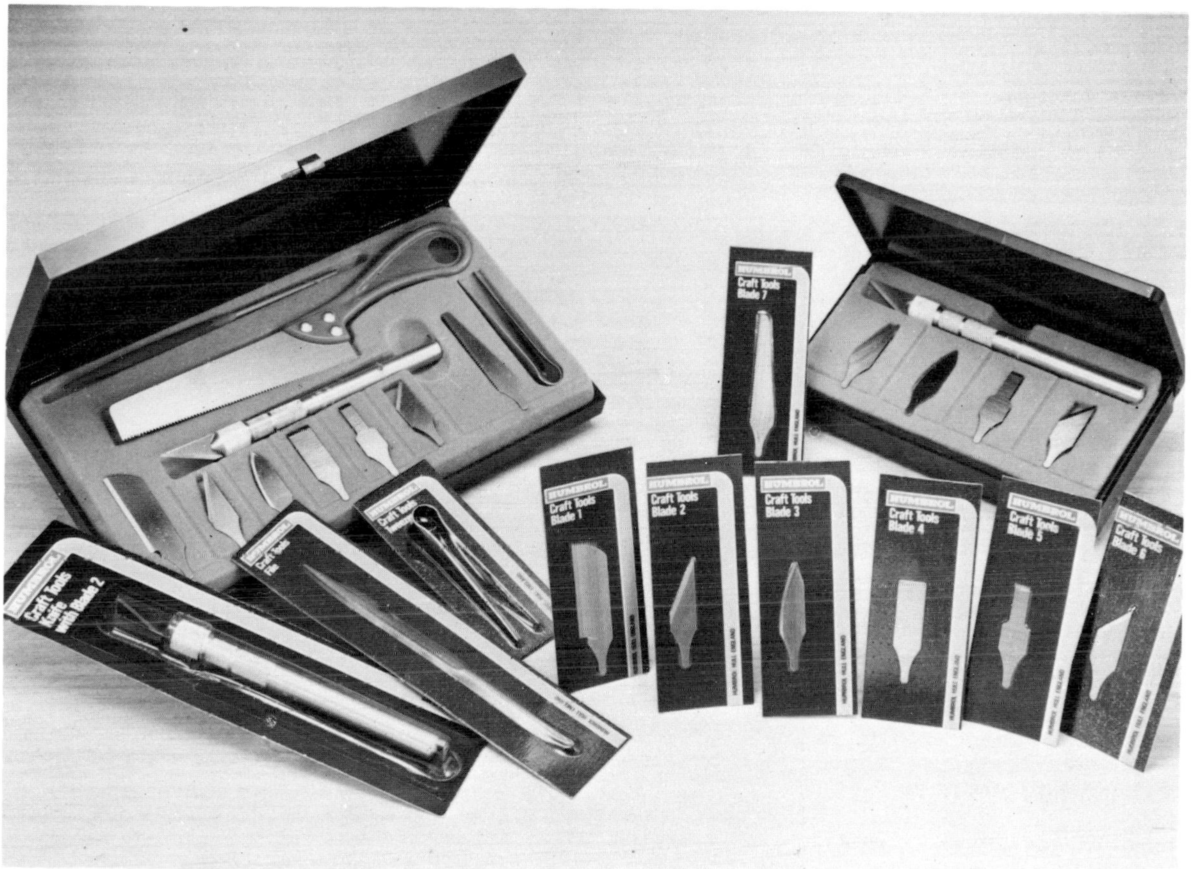

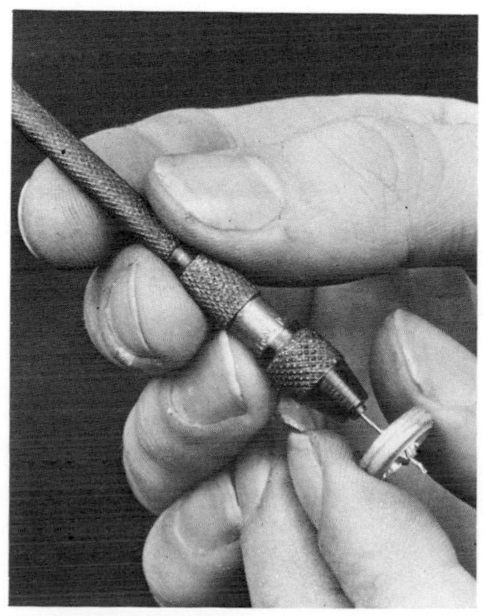

A pin drill for fine holes.

do the minimum of damage. A very good substitute for plastic models, or, indeed, additional acquisition, is an old nail file, or, better still, an emery board.

Just as important as a file is some sort of abrasive paper. Anything from the finest grade of glass paper down to 'wet and dry' paper is useful. The 'wet and dry' papers are especially good for a final finish on seams and join lines.

Another essential is a razor saw such as the type made by X-Acto. This is specially useful for conversion work and for cutting.

Also important are very small pin-drills 1/64 inch up to 1/16 inch or even 1/8 inch. The small ones, in particular, are extremely useful for drilling rigging holes, holes to take radio aerials, etc. If you are only drilling plastic, you'll find that you can work quite well simply by rotating the drill between finger and thumb, but this can lead to slipping when drilling harder materials like cast metal. So a pin chuck – is very well worth having. Last of all, a small screwdriver, which makes an excellent spatula for inserting blobs of cement into inaccessible apertures and a useful scraper for hooking filings out of odd corners and holes during assembly.

Lastly, for both cutting and measuring you need a dimensional steel ruler, while for handling tiny parts a pair of tweezers is essential.

A small vice is possibly the most useful 'extra' of all. This can be used to hold components while you work on them, thus giving the benefit of an extra hand to devote to modelling. A vice might come in handy, for instance, where a lot of filing has to be done along the top of an aircraft fuselage. Similarly, you may wish to drill out a lot of rigging holes in a wing or sailing ship mast, so you just clamp the part in the vice and away you go. It is important to remember, however, that a vice can crush fragile parts or damage details if used without due precaution. Thus cloth, corrugated card or felt should be used to pad or pack the area gripped by the jaws.

Next is the ordinary carpenter's D-clamp which comes in various sizes. These are sometimes useful for holding large parts together while they set. However, with most simple models ordinary clothes pegs or even rubber bands or masking tape strips will do the job just as well.

Small pin drills have already been mentioned. However, investing in a power drill is a worthwhile idea. There are various makes and models; all hold fine drills but can also hold polishing or grinding heads. Dremel is a major manufacturer in this field. Another handy tool to have is a soldering gun. There are several makes featuring assorted tips and cutters.

For ordinary model making from kits in such materials as wood, card, plastic or cast metal there is, in truth, very little need for a soldering iron – you may never have cause to use one. However, from time to time electric wires may need to be incorporated in a model; it is possible to solder cast kit components together but care and practice are needed as the cast metal kits are made from an alloy with a low melting-point.

Above a mini-vice in use. It is clamped to the edge of a work bench and holds a cast metal wheel which is being cleaned with a fine drill.
Below small cordless soldering iron, ideal for modelling.

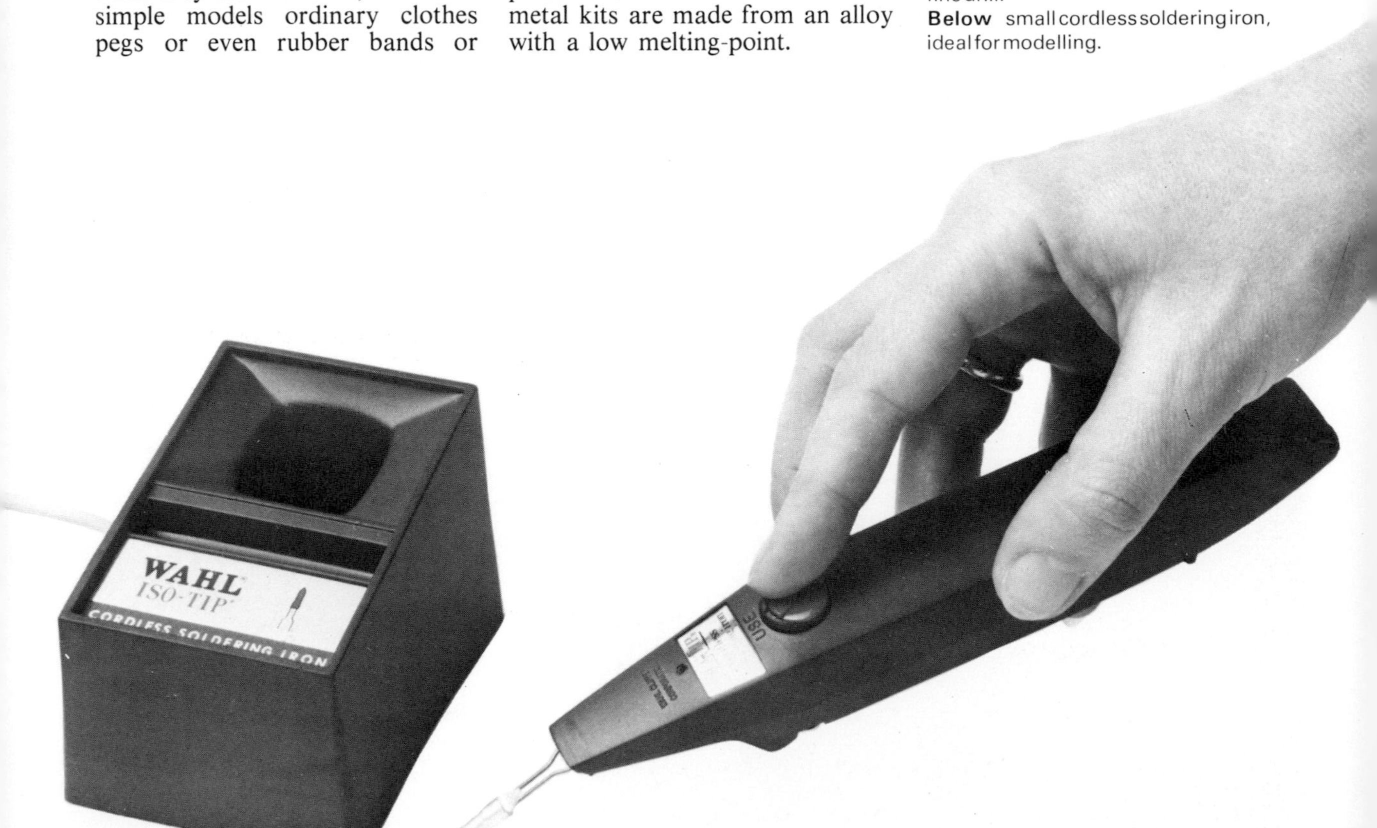

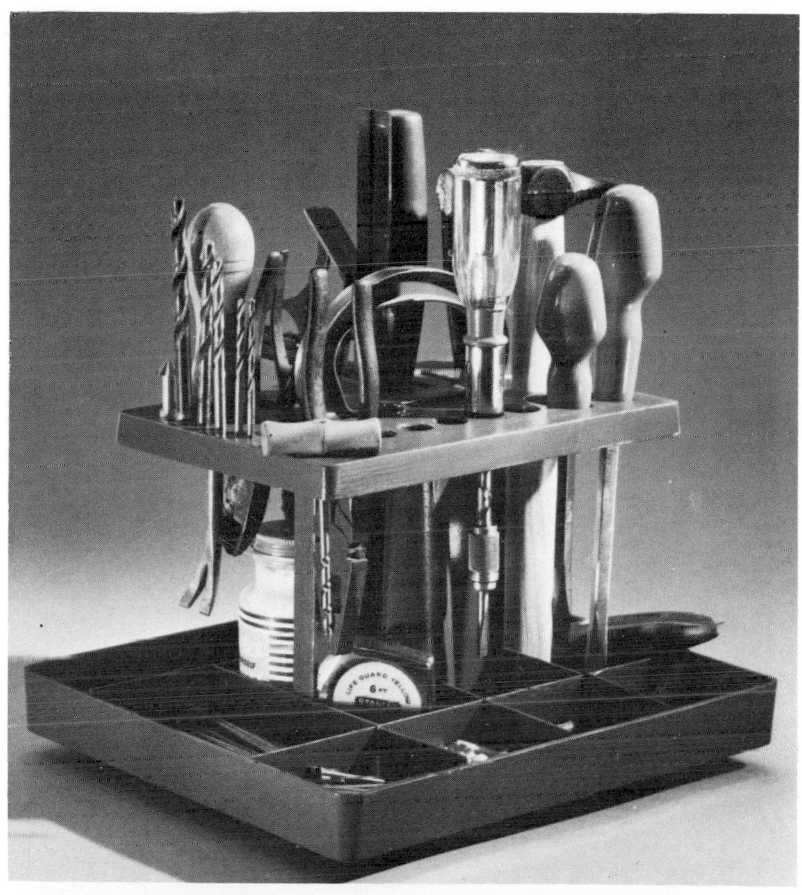

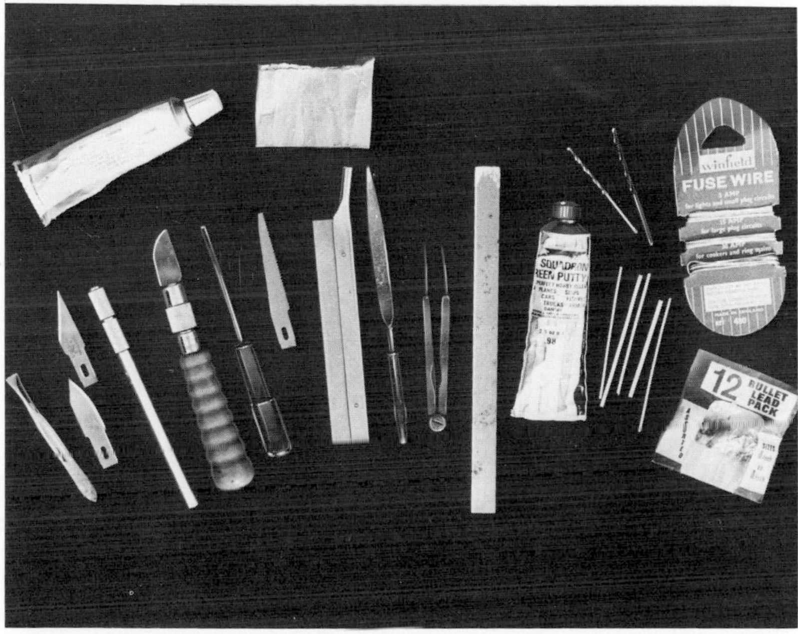

Finally it is worth stating that quite a few general purpose tools can be used for modelling. Among these are set squares, protractors, small hacksaws, chisels, small hammers, pliers, spirit levels, calipers, dividers, compasses, small planes, scribers, hand drills and bradawls. Of these, the pliers are the most often used, particularly in fine work where you might be making radio masts or handrails from wire or pins.

An old wood box or tin with a lid should be procured to hold all these tools neatly and safely. Don't forget that tools can be purchased over a period of time, the most important ones first.

All that remains is to consider the working surface. Few modellers have a fully equipped workshop built in, with all facilities like power points, tool racks, work benches, and lockers. If you have one you are lucky. So you need a substitute which could be either of the following:

1 A modelling tray: an old tea tray of the wooden variety with a handle at each end and a rim all round it. At the end of a modelling session it's simply stowed away with everything left on the board.

2 A modelling board: similar to the tray, this is an old drawing board, with a small vice screwed on one end. As it has no rim, this can only be used successfully on a rigid surface like a table, and an old newspaper should be put under the board to collect all the filings and cuttings which will inevitably stray over the edge.

3 A sheet of plywood or hardboard. The important thing is that your working surface should be capable of protecting the surrounding furniture.

When you come to painting your models – dealt with later – your working surface can be your painting surface as well.

Top left small portable tool rack. Small compartments hold spare items.
Left made up home tool kit and materials suitable for most kit work.

MATERIALS AND ADHESIVES

There are a number of essential materials that are likely to be useful at some time for your work in modelling, whether for detailing, improving or converting. Some items are so basic that they tend to be overlooked.

Adhesives
Polystyrene cement for assembling plastic kits is the most basic of all modelling aids, sold everywhere from chain stores to specialist hobby shops and under a big variety of trade names. Use it sparingly, apply it with a pin or matchstick unless vast areas are to be covered and keep the nozzle clean. Don't leave the tube where you are likely to squash it inadvertently and if you do drop cement on a moulded plastic surface don't attempt to wipe it off immediately – leave it to dry and then scrape or sand the surface clean with emery paper. Polystyrene cement is a solvent and its indiscriminate use with plastic kits will ruin a perfectly moulded model surface.

A variation is liquid cement, also for plastic kits, which comes in bottles. This can be applied with a brush in very small quantities and is ideal for cementing small detail parts in addition to general use. Most 'liquid' of all is Mekpak, which doesn't mark a moulded plastic surface so badly as cement from a tube. Brushes used with liquid cement must, however, be kept clean in turps and the bottle lids must be replaced whenever the cement is not in use, both to retain its properties and avoid spillage.

Polystyrene cement can sometimes be used as a 'filler' along join lines; the excess which is squeezed out when the parts are held together is left to set really hard, then filed or sanded down.

Card and small pieces of balsa can be cemented to polystyrene in conversion work using ordinary polystyrene cement, but larger chunks of wood mated to plastic sometimes require the use of impact adhesives – many brands are now available from hardware shops or chain stores. Another cement, Uhu, is a good general purpose adhesive for cementing non-compatible materials in modelling work. It remains 'fluid' long enough for small adjustments to be made to the set of a particular part, another property commending it to the modellers. Also, it is transparent and ideal for affixing cockpit canopies or other transparencies, as mentioned elsewhere in this book, where polystyrene cement might cause unwanted clouding. Uhu tends to 'string', however, and should be applied carefully and sparingly.

Balsa cement is self-explanatory, if you are working in balsa or similar light woods. Another very useful glue when working with wood or card is White PVA adhesive.

Five Minute Epoxy is the other essential glue every modeller should have, for it sticks all manner of non-compatible substances quickly and effectively. It is particularly good for assembling cast metal kits.

Putty and Filler
Known variously as plastic filler, body putty or customizing body putty, this material can be used for most re-shaping and major reconstruction work involved in kit conversions; at the same time, it has numerous minor but important applications in straightforward kit assembly.

Moulding faults – such as dimples or shrinkage – can be corrected by filling in the areas concerned and obtrusive join lines can also be eradicated by filling gaps etc. with putty and sanding or filing away the excess after allowing time for setting. Unwanted locating holes can be filled, ailerons or panel lines obliterated, cowlings built up, and gun mantlets or fairings shaped by judicious use of plastic putty.

Remember that plastic putty shrinks slightly on setting, so apply more than you need to cover any given area; don't attempt to file or sand it before it is thoroughly set and preferably leave it overnight (or even longer if possible). When large areas are to be built up, apply the putty in layers, allowing each layer to set before applying the next – putty applied in large quantities takes longer to set and tends to disintegrate more easily; if your filing or sanding causes cracks to appear or fragmentation, simply apply more putty in the appropriate area and leave it to set once more.

Plastic putty sets with a texture almost indistinguishable from polystyrene and I find that it makes an excellent filler or covering for any wooden parts used in a plastic kit conversion. When dry plastic putty is slightly porous, however, it must have at least one undercoat of flat white or grey before any finishing coat is applied. If this is not done the area of putty will show through.

Other putties which can be used with all models – wood, plastic, metal – originate in domestic requirements rather than in the modelling world. These include Milliput, Brummer Stopping and similar products mainly intended for motor car or general repairs. They can be used as described for plastic putty. However they dry rock hard and can then be sanded, carved and drilled at will. Milliput is rather more malleable than others. Some gifted modellers have made complete model soldiers from it, applying it over wire armatures to give both strength and shape.

For working in wood, there are well-known fillers like plastic wood, and if you work with balsa or light woods you may need to use sanding sealer to conceal the grain before undercoating or primer is applied. Lastly, there is plastic metal, also sold in tubes, which is useful to anyone making models from cast metal.

Plastic Card
Another aid to good modelling, and certainly to any kind of plastic kit conversion, is the sheet polystyrene known as plastic card and sold under a variety of brand names.

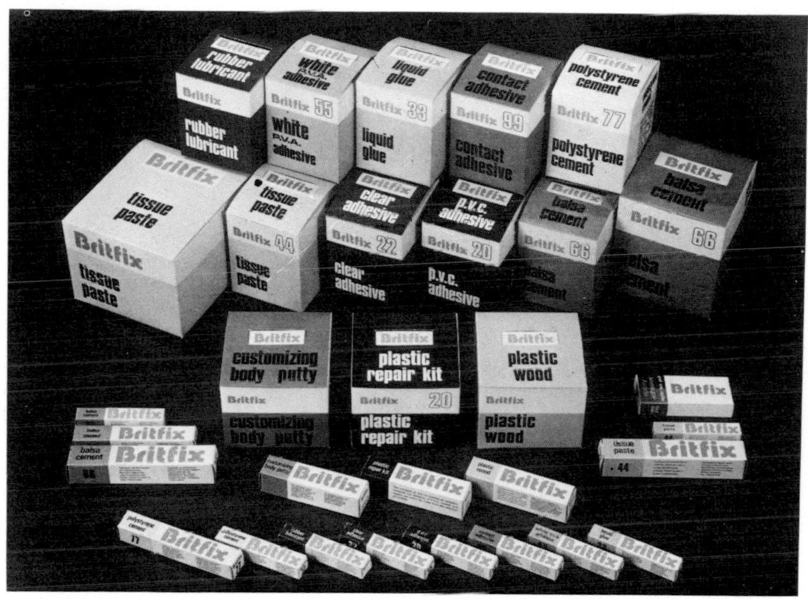

Above liquid polystyrene cement, an essential aid for the modeller.
Left the range of adhesives manufactured by Britfix

This comes in various thicknesses starting at ·01 inch (10 thou) and going up in 10 thou sizes to 40 thou or even thicker. You may also find it sold in metric equivalents to these sizes. Plastic card has the properties of the polystyrene used in plastic kits, can be sawn, filed, cemented and painted in the same way, and is suitable for everything from undercarriage doors of scale thickness (in place of those supplied in kits) up to complete models made from scratch. There is also a transparent plastic sheet with similar properties which is perfect for making windscreens or windows.

Another plastic card product is 'Microstrip', which consists of finely sliced plastic sheet in varying thicknesses. The applications are numerous – stump masts, window framing, girdering, ladder rungs, spoilers and so on.

A limitation of plastic sheet is its reluctance to curve: bend it too far and it is likely to snap; though it can be curved permanently by binding a strip round a suitable former (such as a broomstick) and holding it in hot water for a few minutes.

A related product of great value is plastic rod. This comes in assorted small diameters from about 1/32 inch upwards. Plastic rod has hundreds of uses and can simulate drainpipes, masts, exhaust stacks, handrails, gun barrels, rocket tubes and many other detail fittings.

Card and Paper

While plastic card is a fairly modern development, modellers should not scorn card, that age-old material. This is actually one of the cheapest and most readily available modelling materials to be had. Indeed, if your budget is severely limited and you can't afford or obtain kits of any kind, you can still do plenty of modelling with scrap card. It is all around you – post cards, business cards, shirt stiffeners, food cartons and toiletries provide plenty of free material. Or you can buy top quality card or board in sheet form from art supply shops.

Virtually anything can be built in card. We talk more about the possibilities in a later chapter, but suffice to say that card is also quite suitable for use as an accessory for ordinary kit construction, used instead of plastic card and for very much the same thing. For example, minor restructuring, flaps, replacement scale thickness wheel well doors and chimney stacks can all be made from card, even on a plastic model. Card can also be used in conjunction with wood.

It is important to care about quality. Business cards and good quality post card are generally suitable for fine work. Old food packets and the like often yield soft, 'one-sided' card, suitable for rough work or model buildings with a stucco finish, for example.

Paper, such as cartridge paper, also has its uses in model work, and, indeed, paper cut-out models can sometimes be found. At least one ingenious modeller has used paper to make realistic palm trees by cutting it into fine strips and bundling it together, then wrapping brown paper tightly in spiral fashion round one end of the bundle to make the trunk.

Because they are absorbent, neither card nor paper stand up well to damp. Shellac painted over the model or the card/paper area is the answer here, provided the model is to be painted afterwards. A good Shellac coat (Shellac is sold in hardware stores) will give a good model a wood-like finish and stiffness.

Above 1:35 scale T-34 tank, greatly enhanced by extra equipment, such as the unditching logs (made from twigs) and the rolled tarpaulin (from paper).

Opposite page Sd Ktz 250 German half-track. The palm tree is made of finely-stripped paper tightly wrapped together.

Balsa and other woods

Whatever types of model you make, you are likely to use some sort of wood sooner or later. Wood can be used in its entirety, of course, to make models. But it is often used to supplement some other material. For example card can be combined with wood in model work, while many aircraft, ship or tank conversions from plastic kits use wood for modified parts required in conversion work. A good example of this occurs in some aircraft models. The Avro York (for instance) can be made by carving a complete fuselage from balsa and endowing it with wings, tail and other fittings from a plastic Lancaster kit.

Balsa is cheap and easily obtainable from almost all model shops. But you can also use obeche and other fine woods.

There are many instances where wood on a full-sized subject can be reproduced equally successfully in miniature by using wood as well. Tank fascines, unditching beams, ship's spars, wheel chocks, support cradles, wooden bridge supports and the like are all items that can be made in miniature from balsa wood. Most model shops sell balsa in cheap handy packs and you can buy sheets and strips in all sizes. You'll find it very well worth having by you for the odd occasions when wood can be pressed into use.

Another useful material is the sort of veneer which is sold for marquetry work.

If wood is mixed with plastic in a model it needs very careful and precise finishing to make its texture compatible with the adjacent plastic. Graining will most definitely show unless you take time and trouble to get a perfect surface. I find that painting with a mixture of clear dope and talcum powder is certainly the best treatment. You need several coats, and will have to sand down between each, but a satin smooth surface rewards the labour involved. Take care, however, to keep the 'neat' dope from the plastic surface, as dope is cellulose and corrosive on plastic. Once the talcum powder is mixed in, however, this corrosive 'sting' largely disappears from the dope.

Finally it is well worth pointing out that many other household materials can be used in modelling–among them tin foil, tin plate, transparent film, adhesive tapes etc.

SCALES

Scale is simply a way of expressing how far the model has been reduced from full size. It is usually written as a ratio (1:72) or as a fraction (1/72); both mean that the model is scaled to one seventy-second of the original or that one unit, eg a centimetre, equals 72 units of the original.

The wide range of common model scales may on first encounter seem rather confusing. In practice, however, they offer to modellers a rich variation in size, detail and intricacy of construction. Defined scales add interest to any collection by giving a true comparison between several different models and their full-size originals.

This variation allows the modeller to choose between taking a year to make a large scale kit that may involve motorization or even fitting remote controls or an evening to produce a small but faithful replica. Choice, as in most things, may be dictated by time, finance, storage possibilities, skill and experience – though rigging a sailing ship like the Cutty Sark or building a Walschaerts valve gear to go in a locomotive will certainly add to the latter! Collections can be centred on a theme in one particular scale; for example, World War Two German aircraft, modern jet liners, Napoleonic soldiers, Grand Prix cars. Models to constant scales are produced by more than one manufacturer, and any one manufacturer's kit will be compatible with the kit of the same scale from another source.

Ship scales

1:600, 1:700, and 1:1200
These are the generally accepted scales for model ships, with the exception of sailing ships and merchant steam vessels which, unfortunately, are often produced in odd scales. Airfix and Aurora have models in 1:600, and Airfix also has a 'Waterline Series' of 1:1200. Tamiya, Hasegowa, Aosima and Fujimi provide a range of 1: 700 scale World War Two vessels ('Waterline Series) with optional waterline hulls.

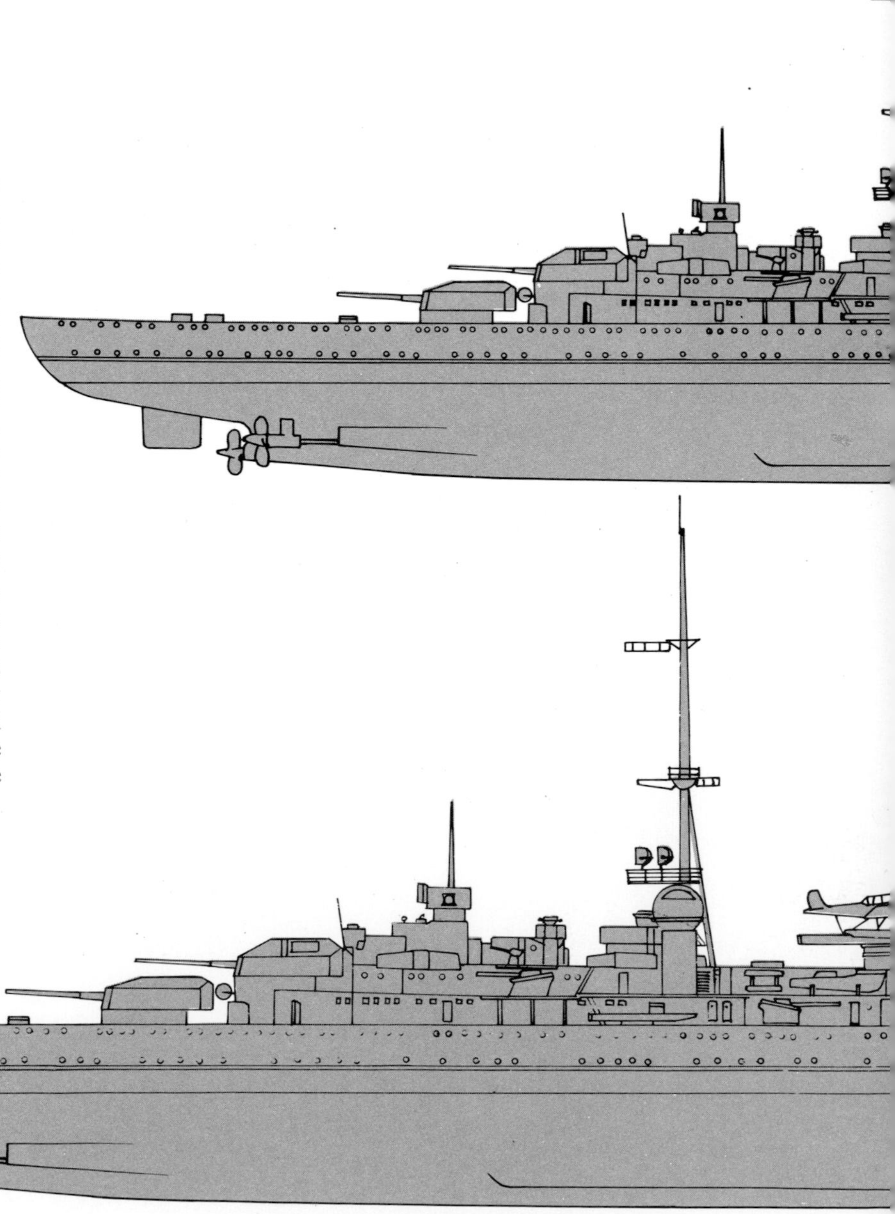

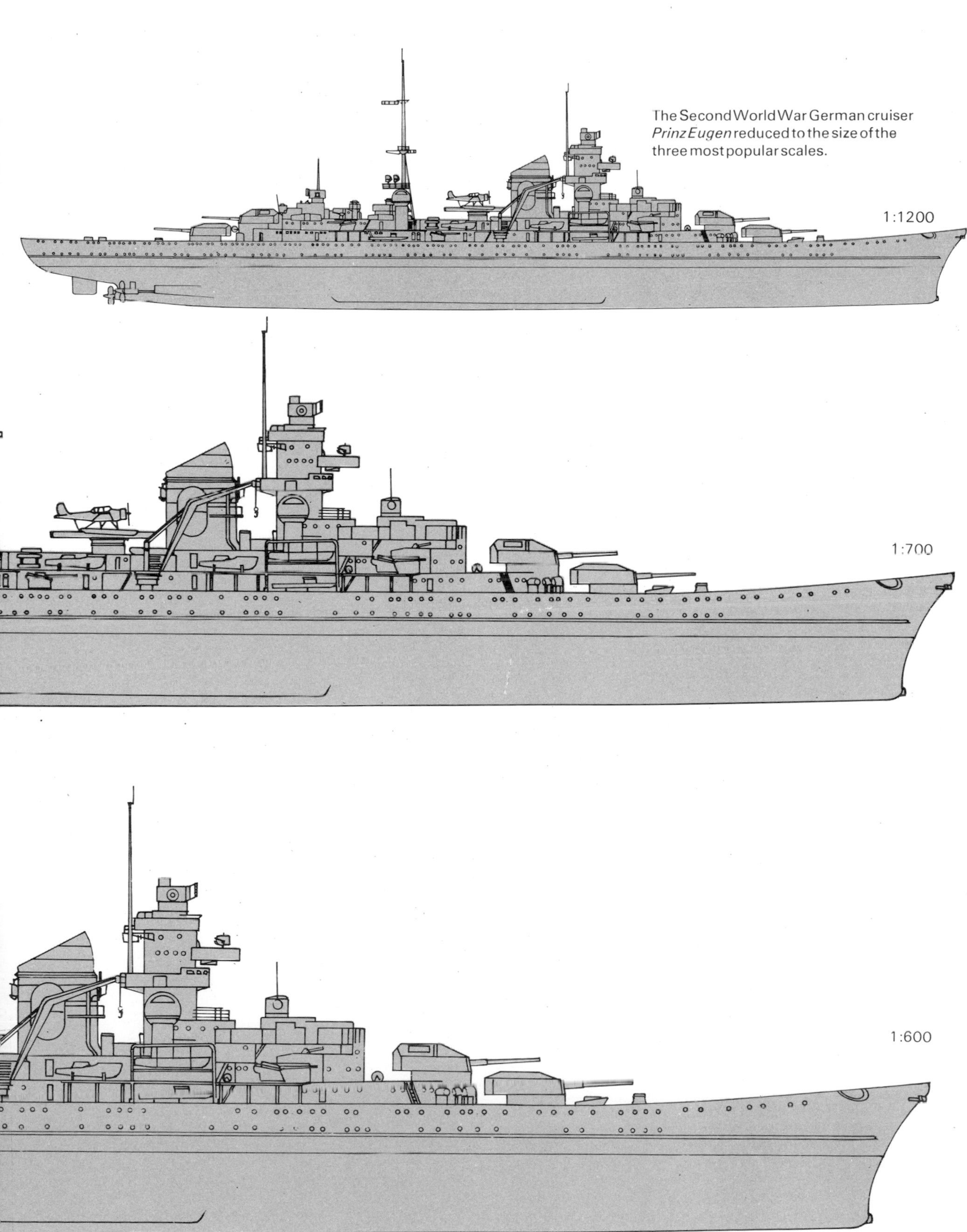

The Second World War German cruiser *Prinz Eugen* reduced to the size of the three most popular scales.

Military vehicle scales

German Sdk F2-251 half-track troop carrier reduced to the size of five popular scales.

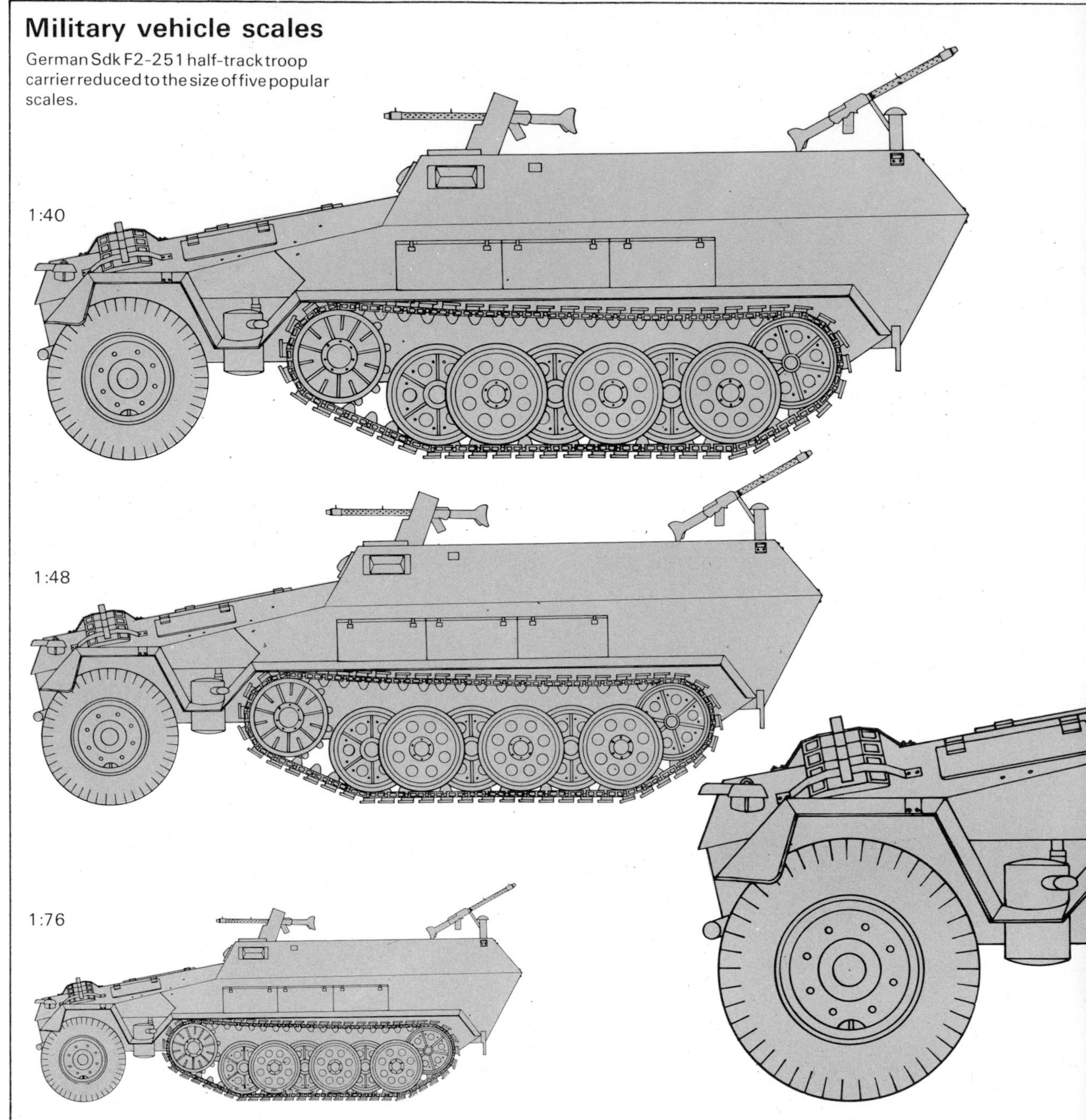

The following are the commonest scales in order of popularity and availability. If it is suggested that two scales are visually compatible this means that models of the two sizes are close enough together in scale to be acceptable when displayed together.

1:72 – 1 inch to 6 feet on original.
This is the commonest aircraft scale. Revell, Novo, Airfix, Kovozavody, Monogram, Tamiya and Hasegawa make a good selection of kits for modellers with average skill. Hasegawa also has an Armoured Fighting Vehicle range in this scale. Some Japanese kits may be 1:75, but they are visually compatible with 1:72.

1:48 – $\frac{1}{4}$ inch to 1 foot.
This can be termed $\frac{1}{4}$ scale and corresponds to O gauge model railway equipment in the USA. Monogram, Nichimo, Revell, Tamiya, Airfix and Hawk produce kits in this size. It is also a popular aircraft scale, though the range is more limited than 1:72. These larger, more detailed models give extra scope for meticulous finishing; however, blemishes on the kit itself will be more prominent than in smaller scale kits. Tamiya and UPC make 1:50 scale aircraft, Aurora and Bandai 1:50 car and tank kits, all are compatible with 1:48.

1:32 – 10 mm to 1 foot.
Corresponds to gauge 1 in model railways. This is standard slot racing size and many car kits are made to this scale. 'Collector' quality model soldier kits are also available in this scale, which is known as 'Standard' or '54mm' in the model soldier field. Revell and Hasegawa produce super detail aircraft in 1:32 and Monogram make tank kits in this size.

1:76 – 4mm to 1 foot.
Corresponds to British Standard OO gauge railway kits. This popular tank scale was pioneered by Airfix; the Fujimi AFV kits supplement the Airfix range. It is also a popular size for war gaming, and many sets of soldiers are available. As previously stated, 1:76 and 1:72 scales are visually compatible.

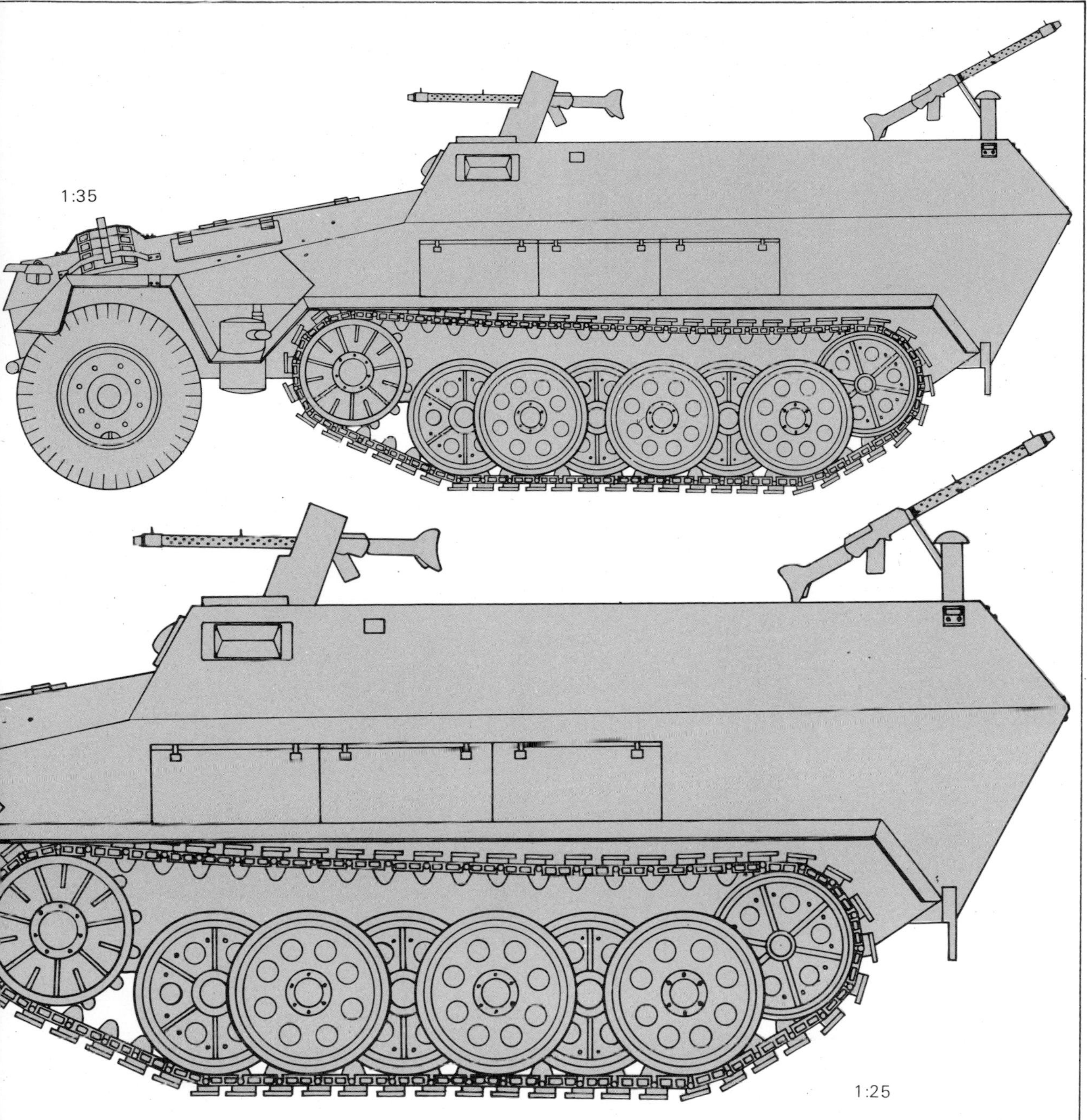

1:86–3·5 mm to 1 foot.
Continental model railway HO scale. Many railway accessory kits are made in this scale, as are AHM/Minitanks and Vikings trucks. Visually compatible with 1:90 scale, but not with 1:76.

1:40
Monogram, Revell, Midori and UPC make some AFV kits in this scale, which is not visually compatible with either 1:48 or 1:32 scales.

1:100–3 mm to 1 foot.
Faller and Tamiya produce aircraft in this scale. Some European makes of building kits, though labelled HO, will be made to 1:100 scale.

1:24 (1:25)–½ inch to 1 foot.
Monogram, MPC, Johan, AMT and Airfix make superdetailed car kits in this scale; Tamiya produce tanks, most of which have electric drive and internal detail, with remote control also available. Airfix also have a series of 1:24 scale aircraft.

1:35.
Most Tamiya AFV models and a few other Japanese-made kits are in this scale. The larger models are visually compatible with 1:32, but with smaller ones the difference is more marked.

1:43–7 mm to 1 foot.
Matches railway gauge O. Accepted scale for die-cast cars; compatible with 1:40.

1:12–1 inch to 1 foot.
Airfix and Aurora head this field, Aurora producing some excellent knights.

1:144–1 inch to 12 feet.
This is an ultra-small scale (half 1:72). Originally it was used for models of large jet liners; recently warplanes have appeared in it as well.

1:148/1:160–N scale.
These are British and European standard scales which match British and European/US N gauge trains respectively.

Other scales such as 1:8, 1:9 or 1:16 are in use, usually they are either for replica working models or 'showpiece' models.

Aircraft scales

A Hawker Hurricane reduced to the size of six popular scales.

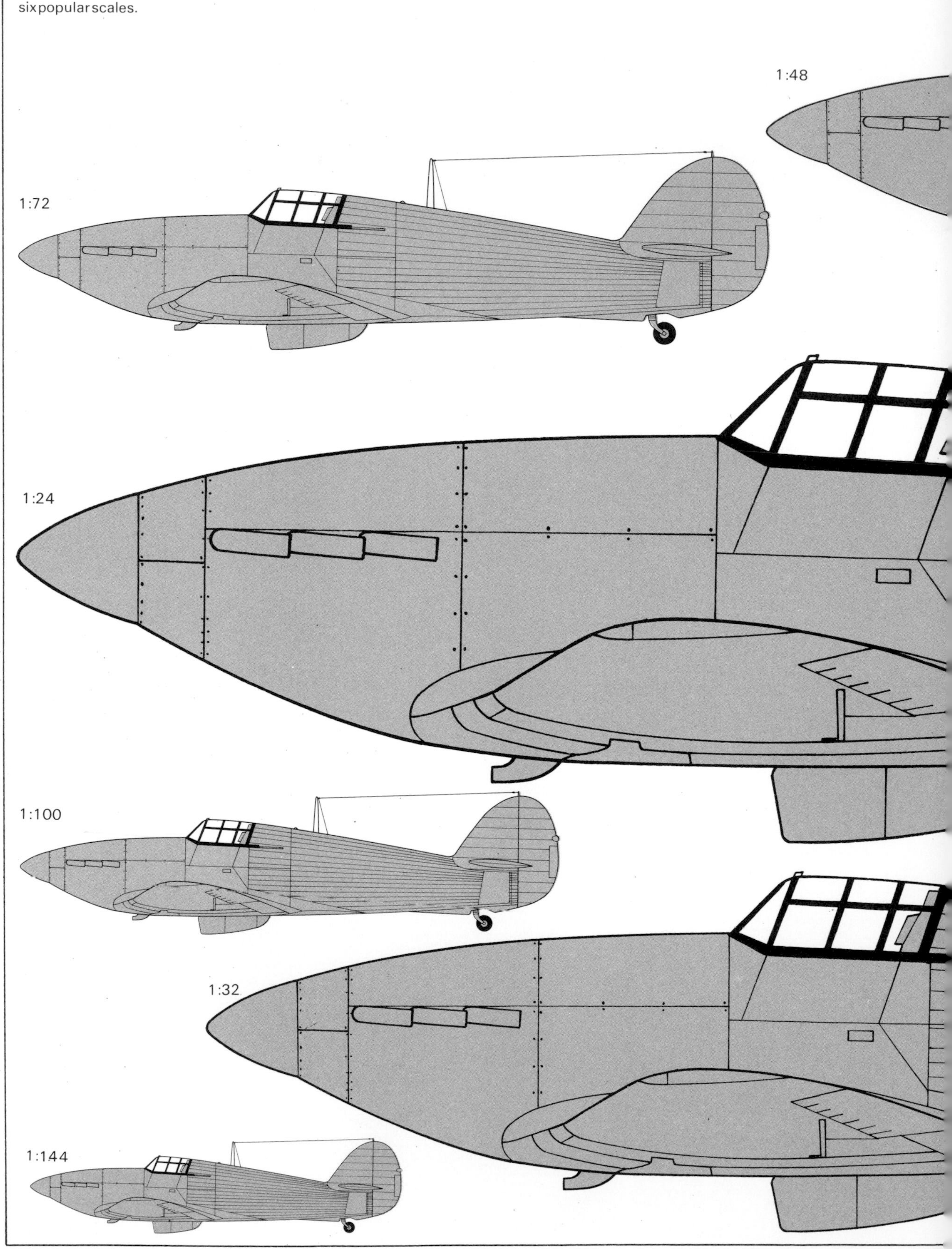

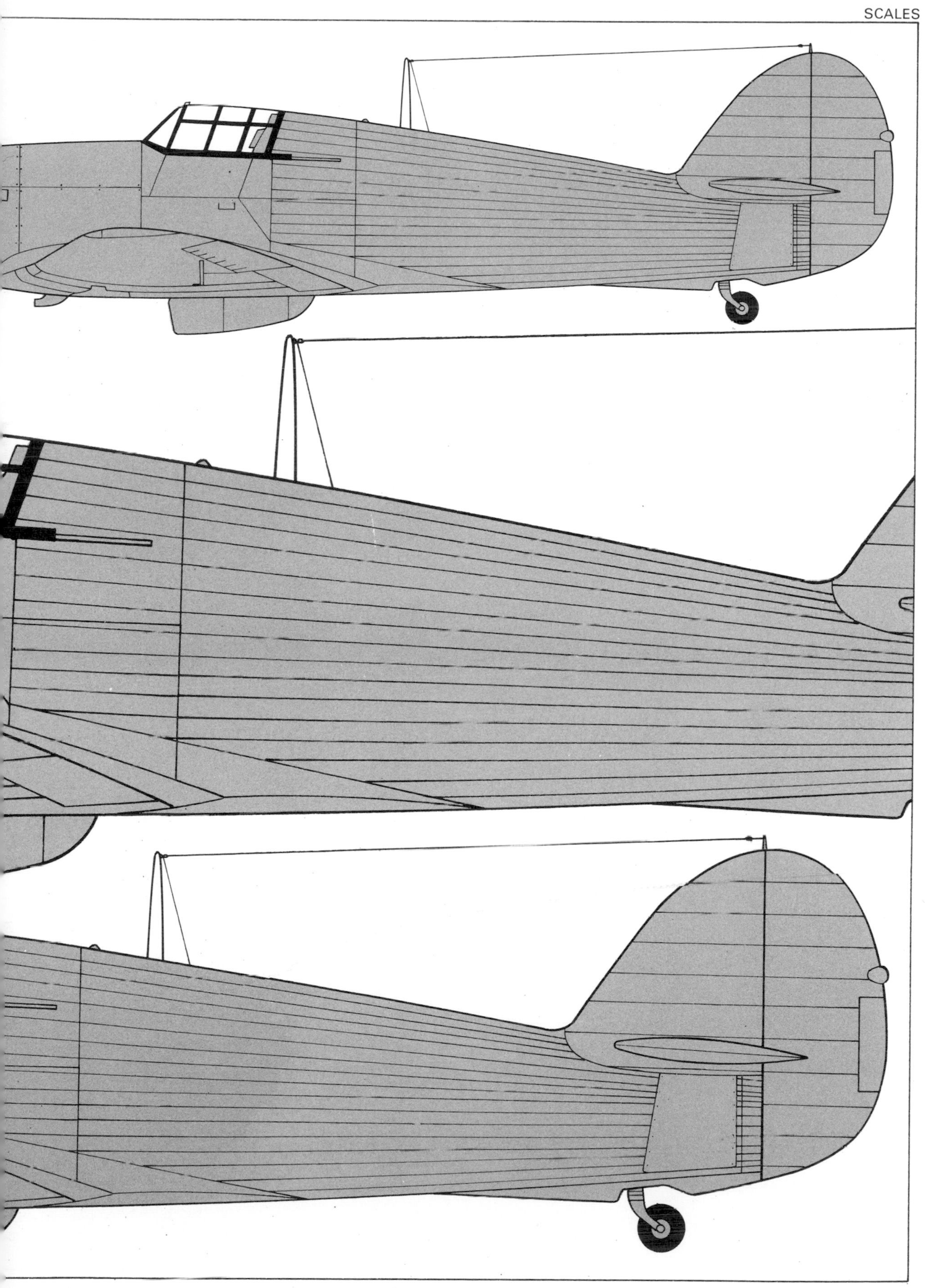

RESEARCHING THE SUBJECT

Strictly speaking, this chapter should be right at the beginning of the book, but it comes here because most novice modellers are much keener on assembling and finishing their latest kit than on reading how to go about it. With nearly every kit you will reach a point when queries will arise. What do the instructions mean? Which way up does this intake go? – the diagram is indistinct. What shade of yellow is 'trainer yellow'? . . . and so on. In short you will need to do a little research to supplement what even the most comprehensive kit instructions tell you.

This doesn't mean that you will need to invest a fortune in books and documents before you begin. It simply means – in the first instance – checking out all the detail you can find on each model subject as you come to it. Naturally, over the years you may well build up a big library of books and notes which will always be useful. But essentially research and background work is an adjunct to the actual model making which adds a fascinating extra dimension to the hobby. It also aids your general knowledge, for the idea behind many technical features only becomes fully apparent when you read about and assemble a model.

So where do you begin with background work or research? If you were interested in subjects such as aviation or cars or ships before you took up modelling, then you may well have quite a few useful books of your own already. If you haven't looked at them for years, look at them now. For a model, any visual reference – picture or diagram – is useful. Hence if you want to make a Spitfire or a Tiger tank, any book with descriptions or pictures of these is a good starting-point.

If you have no books on the subject you require, try your local library. And if your spending money runs to it, your local bookshops or larger hobby shops may have just the books you need. By looking at all the books you can

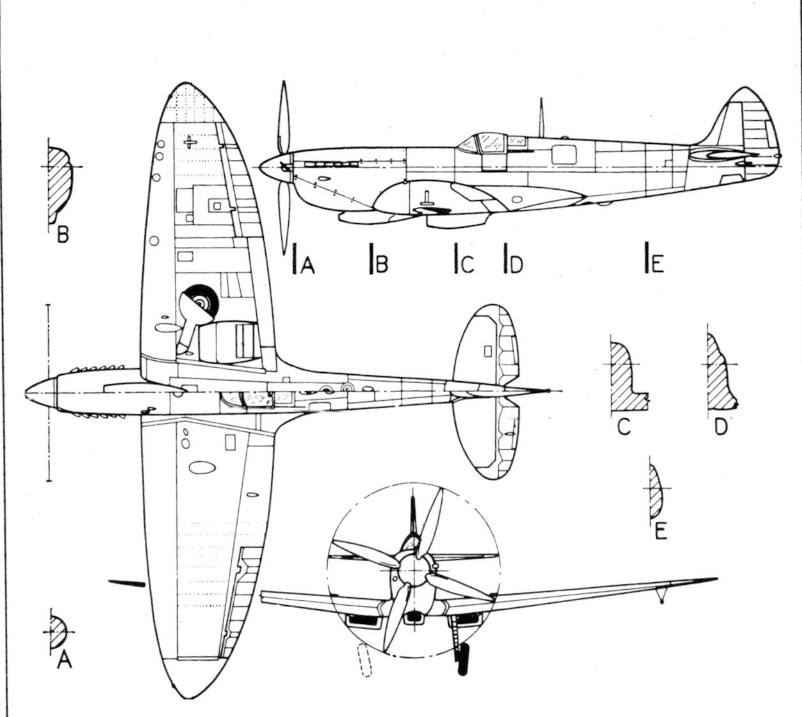

Magazines, books and technical journals can all provide the modeller with vital detailed information about his subject and with ideas for adapting his kit.
Above a multi-view plan from a magazine of the Mark XI photo-reconnaissance Spitfire.
Below a modeller's worktable complete with reference book.

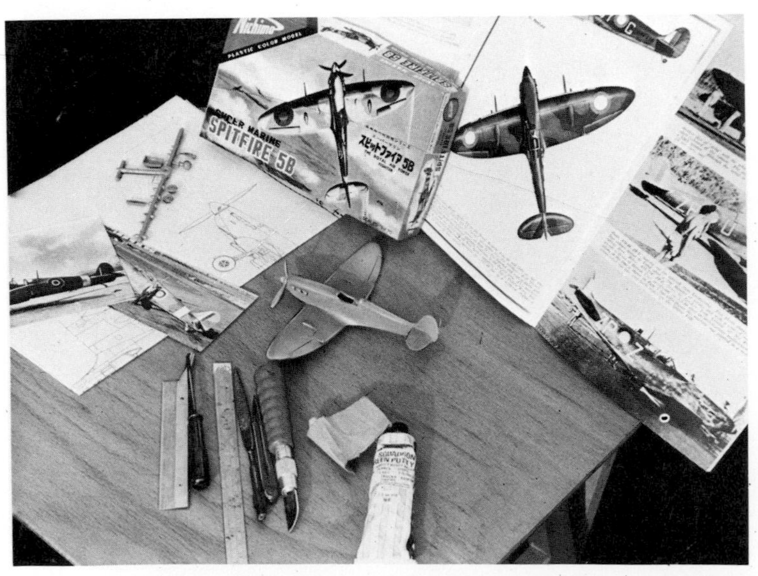

A multi-view plan of a harbour tug.

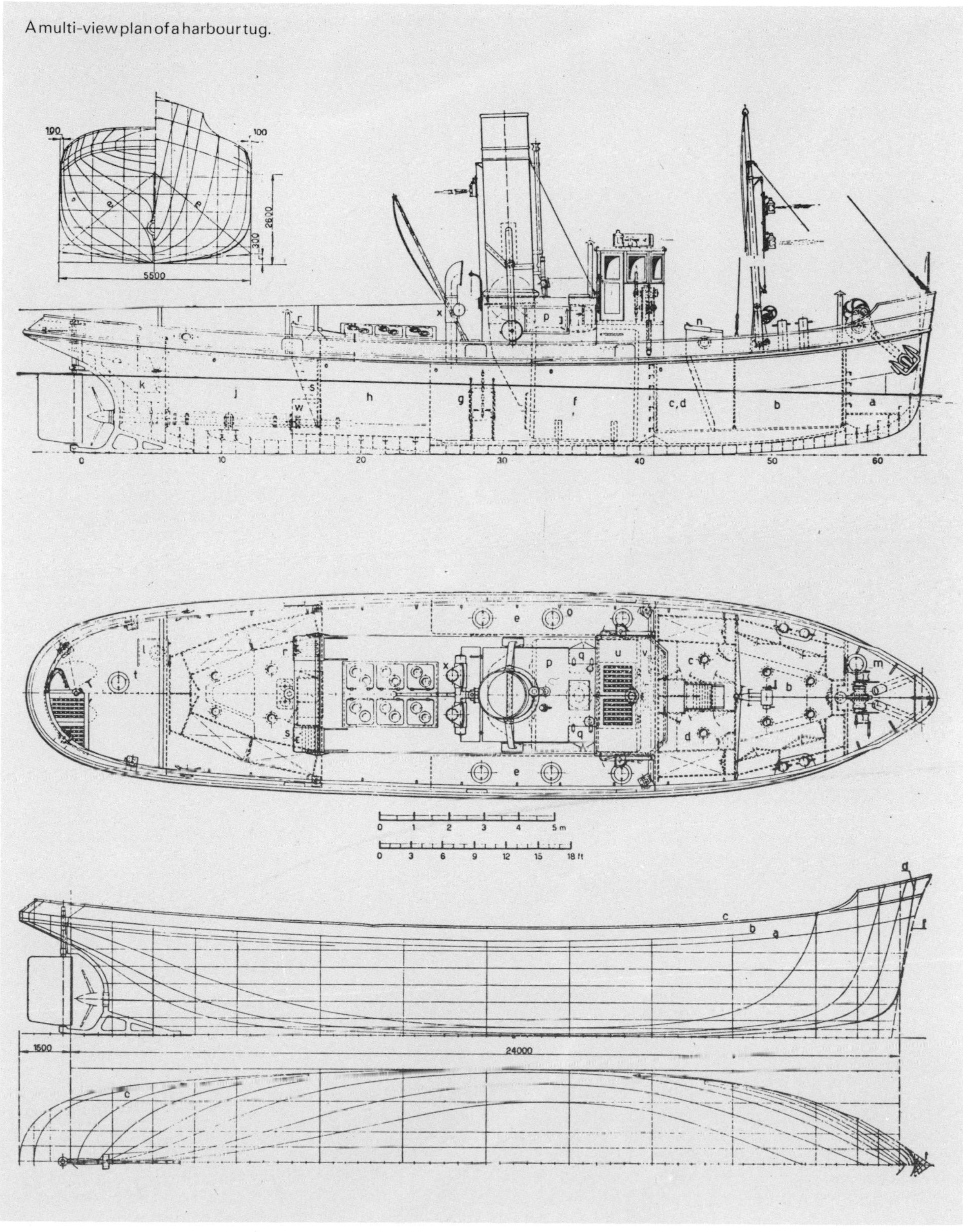

find on any given subject you will get really immersed in it and start to get a 'feel' for the finished model. You will be able to visualize how it should look when it is finished – and that is a major aid to successful modelling.

Start a notebook and take relevant notes and sketch details from any book you borrow or consult. Many books are published specifically with the modeller in mind, and these often include colour plates. Such series as Profiles, Men-at-Arms and Aero Pictorials are typical and almost self-explanatory.

The notebook can be used at all times, for, apart from reference books, there are many museums and displays where full-size originals of what you are modelling can be seen in close-up. Here you can make notes of actual colour schemes and details as you see them.

Supplementing reference books are the many specialist magazines on aviation, military equipment, motor cycles, cars and almost everything else you can think of. If you can afford to buy them, they are a good investment for the serious modeller, for over the years a huge collection of useful articles can be built up, to which you can refer when you get around to a particular model. Back numbers of specialist magazines can sometimes be had from the publishers or are on sale second hand. You may not have room to house a lot of magazines; if this is the case simply tear out and file any articles of importance (make sure the date is shown for future reference) and discard the rest of the magazine. The articles to keep, of course, are those dealing with particular items and containing pictures, scale drawings, cut-aways and the like.

Cuttings and notes can be kept in folders or a scrapbook (preferably of the loose-leaf type) and should be filed alphabetically for quick retrieval of information. Even newspapers yield useful pictures and articles from time to time. Some photo libraries also exist in museums and archives, where pictures can be examined and prints ordered, though they are sometimes expensive. Photographs distributed by manufacturers or official agencies, however, are frequently free of charge. In the case of motor-cycles, cars, trucks, and modern aircraft the manufacturer or selling agent will usually supply catalogues, leaflets or photographs if asked. The catalogues contain close-ups, diagrams, data and all manner of useful information which, if anything, is enhanced in value as the years go by. How useful it would be, for example, to have the original maker's catalogue when modelling a classic car or motorcycle.

A camera is also a most useful tool for research. If you visit a museum or see a full-size item elsewhere, you can take your own photographs and include details you might not find in general views. For instance, close-ups of wheel hubs, hatches, controls and other intricate parts are all of immense value to the modeller. In addition, you can photograph details of subjects you may wish to model in the future, even if that future is as much as ten years ahead. Bear in mind that many transport subjects have only a relatively short working life and that your own photographs will

Illustrations of the 'real-life' version of your model are useful, not only as reference, so that your version can be as accurate as you can make it, but also for overall comparison once you have completed the work. Shown here are model (top) and real life (bottom); opposite, a 1:21 German Mark III tank and, left, a Handley Page 0/400 bomber.

give you a permanent record long after the train, car, aircraft, ship or whatever has disappeared from service. You don't need an elaborate camera, any simple type will suffice. Modern 'pocket' cameras can be carried all the time, which is handy since you never know when picture opportunities may occur.

Next to a camera comes a pocket rule. This is sometimes useful for making measurements of dimensions such as wheel diameters, which will be needed if conversion or alteration work is necessary.

One golden rule to remember when visiting museums or displays is to check that photography is allowed. Very often you are not allowed to touch or climb on exhibits, but attendants may well give you permission to do so if you explain the reason first.

Consumer research is also important. Many popular subjects Spitfires, Mustangs, Tiger tanks etc are made in kit form by several different manufacturers. When these are first released, the specialist model magazines review the kits, giving a general opinion about their quality and sometimes pointing out special faults or features. Keeping track of these reviews could well save you time and money later, since you'll know which is the best kit available. Even if the reviews don't make any definite judgment, they will at least help you to form your own conclusions.

Last of all, it is very useful to join a club or society specializing in your own interests. For example there are model soldier, plastic modelling, car racing and armoured fighting vehicle societies, which often publish useful journals, hold meetings and exhibitions, and run club evenings where models are displayed and ideas exchanged. Among their members are experts who can give useful advice. Details of venues and club secretaries are normally included in the specialist magazines.

Colour reference

So much full-colour reference material is now available that there really is no excuse for not attempting detail work. Careful study of the Dewoitine D520 fighter, right, reveals not only colourful markings – those of Vichy France in 1942 – but also all the wear, weathering and chipped paintwork characteristic of a well-used combat aircraft. Below, close-up view of a Lancaster wheel-well, useful for ensuring accuracy of detail, and, opposite bottom, a Boeing P26 fighter.

4
DEWOITINE
D.520
N°248

TECHNIQUES

Since most modellers these days – and certainly beginners – start with plastic kits, and often remain there, the basic techniques for plastic models are discussed first in this book. In fact, many of the techniques used to work in plastic are equally applicable to wood, card or metal models.

The first task of all with any kit (in any material) before you spread out the parts and start building is to check the components: make sure they are all there and that there are no damaged or badly moulded parts. This may sound obvious, but it is often overlooked by beginners. All kits have a complaints, or inspection slip, and if any part is missing or damaged you can get it replaced free of charge. Read the instructions for more details. If the model is nearly complete before you discover the fault you may have difficulty getting the part, and your project will be held up anyway, just at its most interesting point. If in doubt, take the kit back to the retailer. Most complicated kits these days have a spares chart – a numbered guide to the parts – which makes checking quite easy.

At this early stage too, keep an eye open for any inaccuracies in the model which may need correcting later on. Most models these days are fairly accurate, but if you've done the preliminary research suggested in the last chapter before you begin, you may well either know of or discover some areas which need extra work – wing tips too sharp, propeller blades too long, mudguards too shallow for instance. At some time in the work you'll have to tackle these matters, sooner rather than later, and the instruction sheet won't mention any of them. Also, before you begin, decide on other refinements and extra details you can incorporate. For example, many model aircraft have wheel-well doors grossly over scale thickness since they are moulded with the other components. It is quite usual to replace these with thin new ones, cut from plastic card or card. Use the original-wheel well doors as templates. Obviously, it's too late if you decide to do this after you have firmly cemented the original doors from the kit in place.

When all these preliminaries are over, spread out the instruction sheet and read it through, identifying the parts as you go along. If any minor changes are necessary (replacing wheel-well doors for instance) you'll find the instruction sheet a convenient place to make notes. But above all read the instruction sheet and follow it as construction proceeds. A surprising number of beginners don't do this and are then disappointed when the model is spoilt or incorrectly assembled.

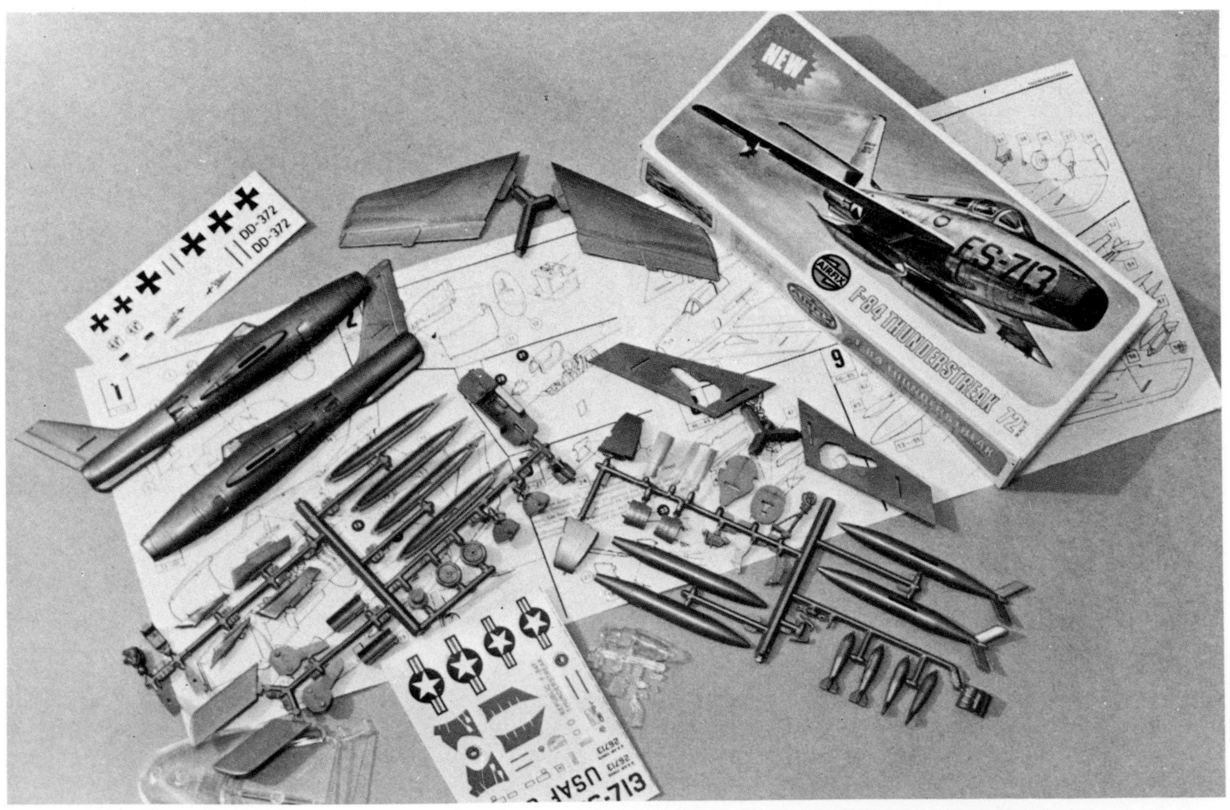

The components of a F-84 Thunderstreak kit; two sets of transfers are provided to enable the modeller to adapt his model.

Changing wheel-well doors

The wheel-well doors on many aircraft kits tend to be over scale thickness, so to keep your model as accurate as possible they should be replaced with the correct thickness of plastic card. Using the wheel-well doors supplied with the kit as a template, draw round them with a pencil onto 10 thou. plastic card and cut out with scissors. They are then cemented in position in the normal way.

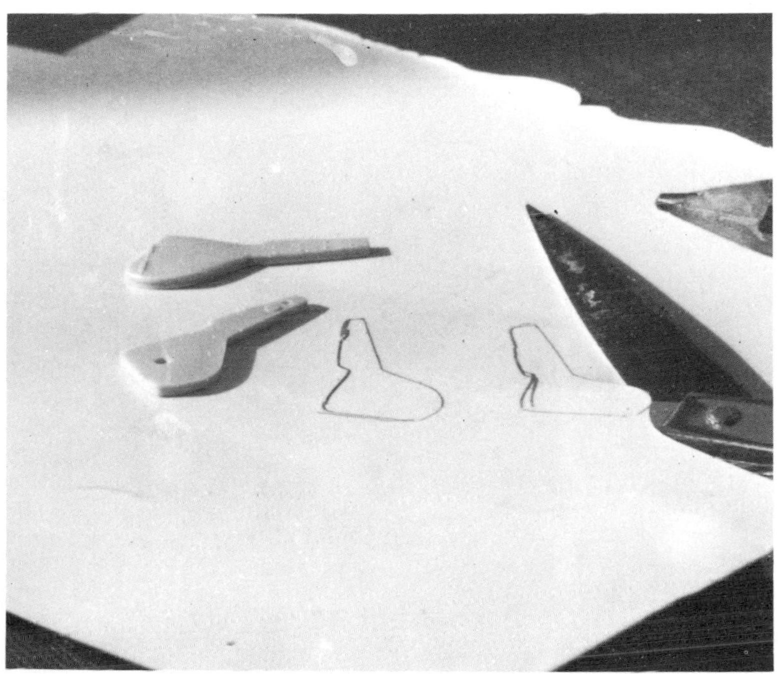

Basic model construction

The basic assembly process is the same for every kit. It is vital to study the instruction sheet and to follow the sequence it lays down, having first of all spread out the components and checked that none is damaged or missing. Decide, too, whether you need to modify any possible inaccuracies in the detailed parts of the kit and whether any other improvements can be made or extra refinements added.

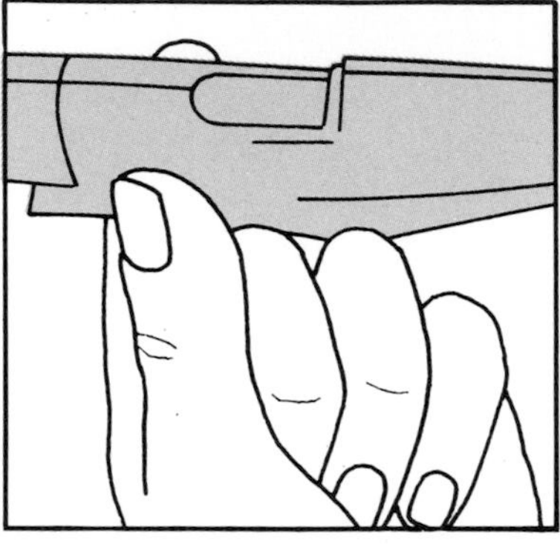

1 Follow the assembly sequence given in the instruction sheet. It is easy enough to skip too far ahead and then find out too late that premature addition of one component prevents another from fitting at all!

Do a 'dry run' with all the parts before you cement them. Often parts that should fit neatly together don't quite do so: a slight distortion may need to be corrected by careful bending, a little fiddling may be required to make locating pegs fit their corresponding slots, or they may need to be filed down or opened out to make a neat fit. Sometimes too you may need to establish which way up a part goes – the instructions don't always make it clear!

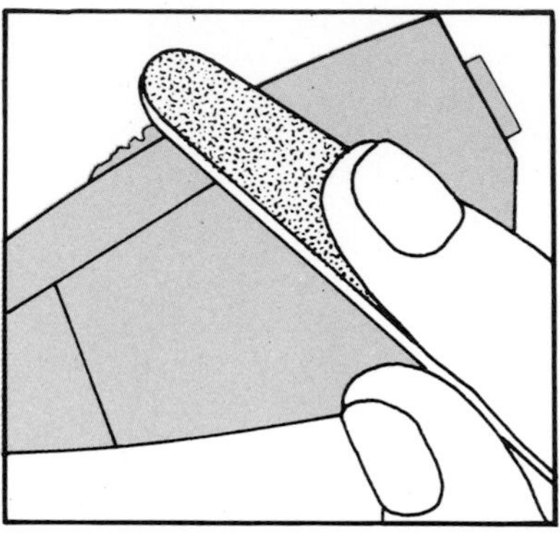

2 Remove any 'flash' at this stage. Flash is the (sometimes considerable) excess plastic left around the edge of a moulding during the manufacturing process; sometimes it forms a web between adjacent parts. Kit instructions and articles often tell you to file flash away before you begin. I find it worth leaving until the part comes to be cemented, as its presence can sometimes be a help if a gap or shrinkage has to be overcome. Recent kits, however, often have no flash at all.

Depending on its size, remove flash by filing or with an emery board or emery paper. Take great care not to scratch or damage any surface detail.

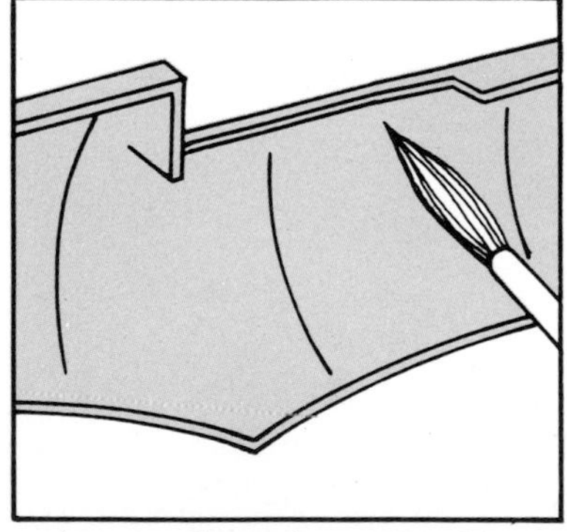

5 Paint as much as you can before assembly. Many parts are inaccessible, or at least awkward to paint, after assembly, and, obviously, interiors must be painted before roofs, windows or cockpit covers are cemented into place. Wheel wells, wheel covers, oleo legs, tyres, bogie wheels, chassis parts, mudguards, wheel hubs, seats are all parts which can be painted prior to assembly. You can always touch them up if necessary after the model is complete. Leave all parts on the sprue while you paint them, using the sprue as a handle. Wheels and tyres moulded in one piece are particularly easy to paint while on the sprue. Rotate the tyre round the brush, for example, rather than trying to paint straight lines by moving the brush. Painting of this sort can often be done while other parts are setting.

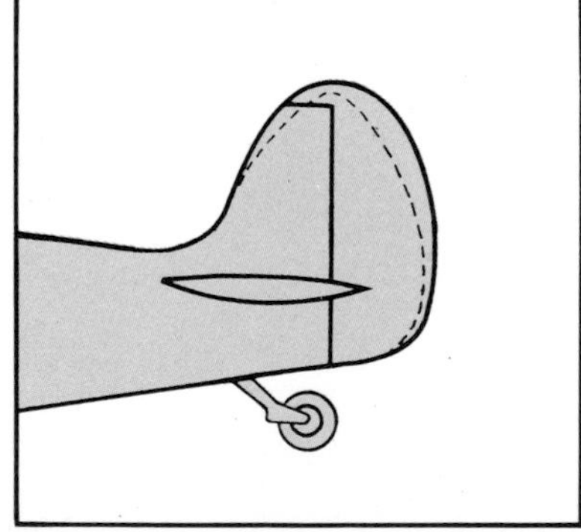

6 Carry out necessary conversion, detail or improvement work as you proceed. It's occasionally possible to modify a kit retrospectively, but it's rarely convenient to do so. Do your research and thinking ahead and you'll be able to plan any work of this sort before you begin to assemble the kit. On certain aircraft for instance, you may wish to change the shape of a tail or wing tips to depict another version.

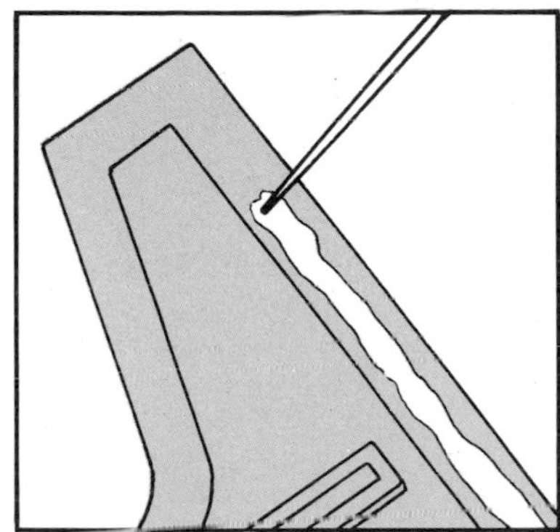

3 Apply cement carefully, using a pin or wooden cocktail stick as an applicator. Polystyrene cement is actually a solvent and melts the plastic to form a weld. Cement is no respecter of surfaces, and a careless blob or smear can eliminate surface detail and ruin the whole appearance of a model. It is therefore important to ensure that the cement is applied only to the surfaces to be joined. For liquid cement the technique is different: hold the parts together in this case and run a brush-full of liquid cement along the edges to be joined. Capillary action will do the rest.

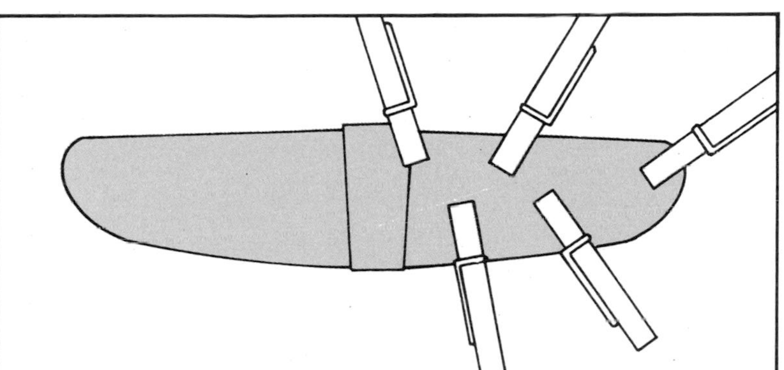

4 Be careful while the parts are setting. It is easy enough simply to cement two parts together and leave them to set with no further thought. The chances are that the parts, particularly if they are large, will bow outwards and the components will set out of alignment. It's too late to do much about it by the time you discover this. The best way I know of ensuring perfection while cement sets is to hold the two parts together for up to ten to fifteen minutes until the cement is well on the way to setting. This is not always practical, and large components, such as long fuselage halves may be too long for you to hold. In such cases, bands of masking tape carefully applied are probably the best answer, though it's no good, of course, using tape to hold parts together if you don't ensure that the parts remain aligned in the process. Clothes pegs or D clamps are sometimes handy for holding large parts together. Finally, leave all parts in a safe place while they set–propped across the corner of the box lid, for instance.

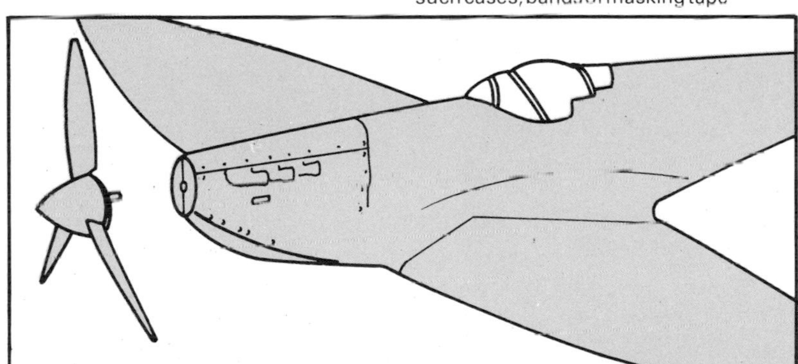

7 Leave small details until major assembly is complete. Don't put items such as radio aerials on fuselages before the basic model is finished. Tiny details are vulnerable while major assembly is in progress, but check (by dry runs) that such deviations from the instructions won't impede later work.

Many small parts are best left until all other painting is complete before they are cemented in place. Aircraft propellers and spinners can be counted in this category, incidentally, even though kit instructions generally tell you to fit them at an early stage. It is usually possible to omit the propeller and spinner, then paint and assemble them as a separate component and fit them without the retaining stud when the rest of the model is complete. Though this means that the prop will remain detachable, it does simplify painting, transportation and repairs. If a model is to reside untouched in a showcase, such a procedure is quite acceptable. For a model on open display or subject to much handling, it is not practical however; nor do some models (eg helicopters) lend themselves to detachable props. These remarks apply equally to vulnerable components on other sorts of model.

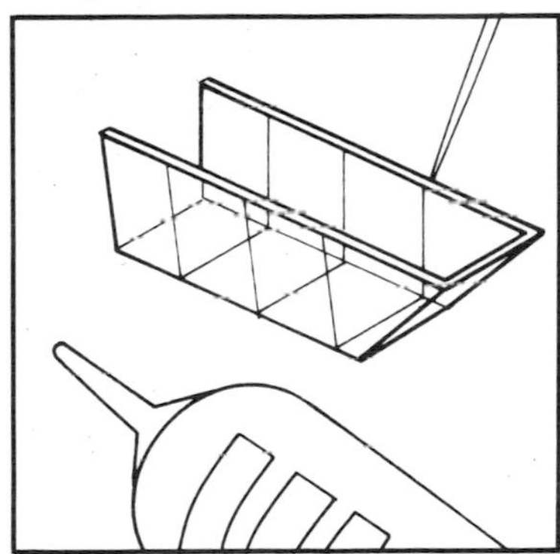

8 Add transparencies last of all wherever practical, and never use polystyrene cement to attach them. This applies to model cars, model aircraft, structures or any other models with clear parts.

Finishing

Even if you follow all the basic construction rules your model will only be as good as your assembly work. The biggest give-aways on plastic models are the join lines which show through the paint. Other models are ruined by cement smears or blobs which are also apparent through the paint.

So, once you have assembled the main structure of your model – the fuselage and wings of a plane, the hull of a ship or tank, the body of a car, the boiler and frames of a locomotive – your major task is to eliminate all traces of joins. And there are bound to be joins, because cement will have oozed out in the drying process and, however precise the mouldings, there will be a slight ridge along the line which has to be got rid of one way or other. If the join is neat and precise and smooth to the touch, gentle sanding with emery paper and/or 'wet and dry' may suffice.

Very small kit components such as axles, gun barrels, exhaust pipes and suspension arms can get snapped very easily. They can usually be repaired simply by cementing the two halves back together with rather more cement than you would normally apply for assembly purposes. The excess cement will form a 'collar' round the join. Allow the component to set really hard, leaving it overnight at least, and gently sand down the 'collar' afterwards to reduce the join to its correct diameter. This way you get an invisible repair. More serious breakages or fractures in components with cylindrical cross-sections can be repaired by binding the whole length of the component with masking tape.

Scale Rivets

One of the more controversial topics among enthusiasts, especially where aircraft models are concerned, is the desirability of rivet detail in the mouldings. Some people argue that since rivets on real aircraft are very tiny (and generally flush anyway) they will disappear completely when scaled down to 1:72 or 1:48; thus, they say, kit manufacturers are perpetrating a major blunder by peppering their products with tiny moulded rivets. However, it must be remembered that when a full-size object is reduced to a tiny replica our impression of the prototype does not reduce with it. Thus, if rivet and panel detail are noticeable on the full-size subject, they will be conspicuous by their absence on the model even if, by the laws of scale reduction, they should have all but disappeared in the reduction process. Normally, once the model has been painted, the rivets do virtually disappear, leaving just enough of an impression to capture the 'look' of the real thing.

Of course, there are exceptions. Kits made a few years ago very often suffered from overscale rivets. In such cases where rivets approach the size of scale saucers, they are best removed by emery paper. The best rule is to ask yourself whether the rivet detail will remain too prominent after painting. If you think it will, remove it.

Unwanted rivets can be sanded off as on this 1:72 scale Corsair.

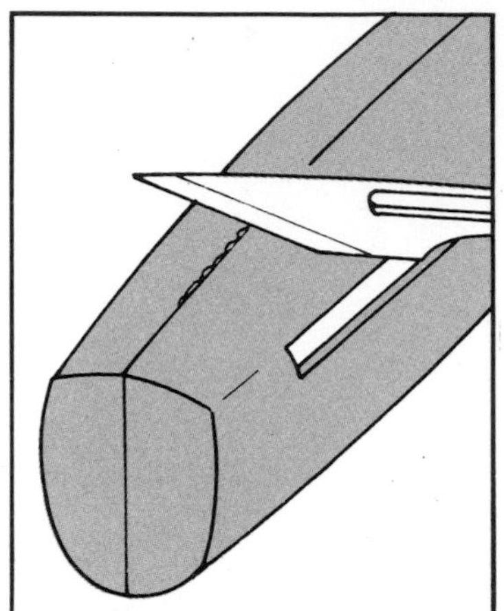

1 If large blobs or ridges of cement stand proud of the join, get rid of them by filing or scraping or by very carefully moving the blade of your knife back and forth like a plane so that the excess plastic shreds away from the ridge. Don't overdo it or you may well ruin the accurate outline of the model. The rule is little but often; after preliminary scraping to remove the worst of the ridge, check again and see if any excess cement remains. If it does repeat the process.

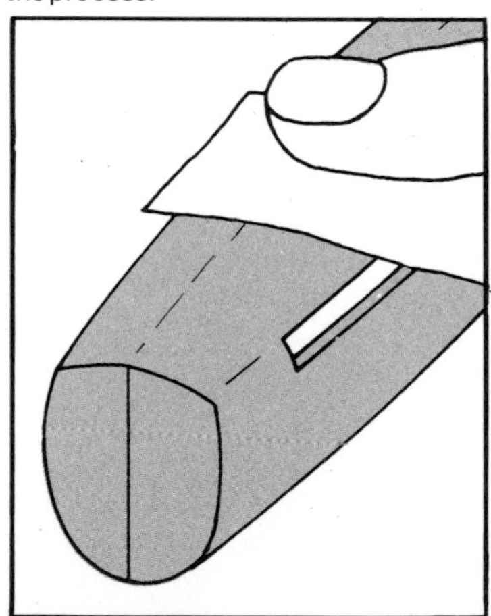

5 Allow the putty to set very hard (at least overnight) sand it down with fine glass paper, finishing it off with emery paper or 'wet and dry'.

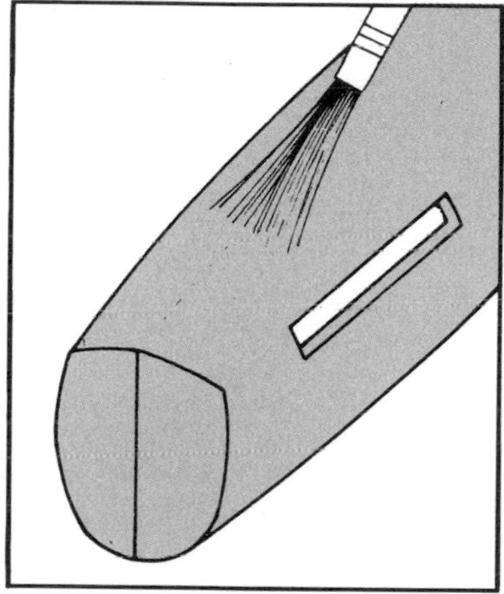

2 You can usually tell when you've eliminated the join line, often by just looking at it. To be certain, however, hold the structure in the direction of the window or room light and look along the join. If you've eliminated the ridge completely the join will disappear in the reflected light; if a ridge remains it will throw a shadow. When you're satisfied, give the join a rub over with 'wet and dry' paper and brush away any filings with a soft brush.

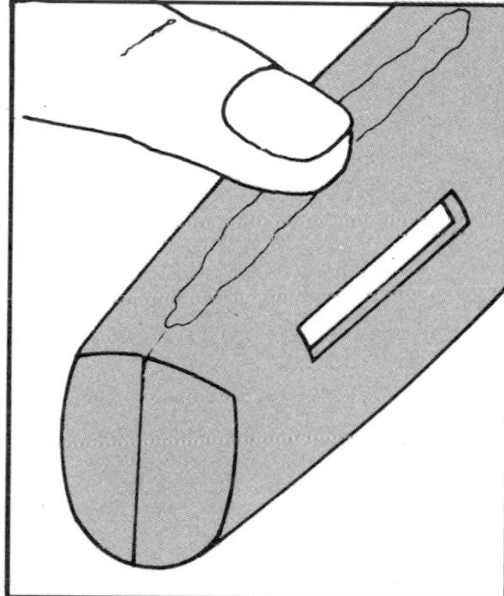

3 An effective way of dealing with a really prominent or obstinate join line is to rub hard with toothpaste and your finger.

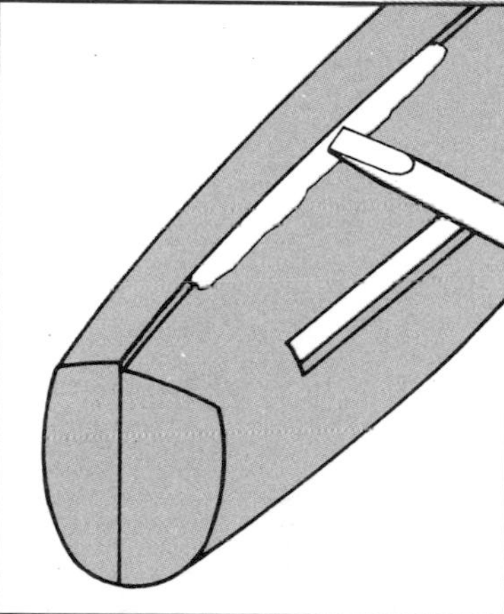

4 The limitations of the moulding process often give rise to unavoidable defects which may affect the components. Most commonly experienced is 'shrinkage'; two halves of a fuselage will not mate up exactly, for instance, which gives rise to a definite step along the join line. The easiest remedy for this is to cement the fuselage halves together and add plastic putty with the tip of a screwdriver, pressing it well into the step to build up the level.

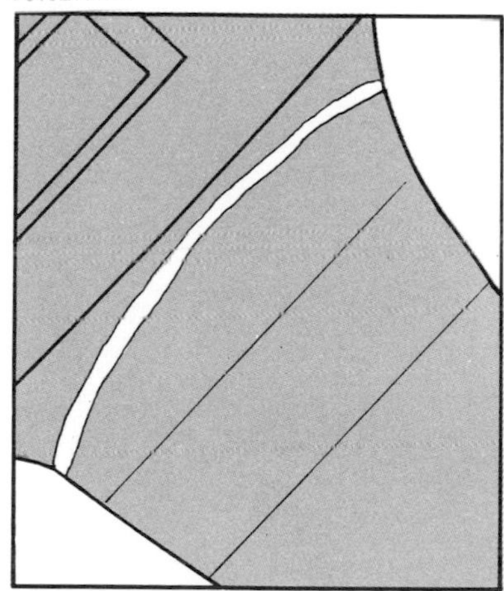

6 You may well experience similar trouble at the wing roots where the wing does not exactly match the fillet moulded on the fuselage. Treat this as you would shrinkage. Finally, you may get dimples, particularly when locating pins are moulded on the other side of a plastic surface. Once again the procedure is the same—fill up the dimple with putty, using a screwdriver tip as a spatula, leave to set and file down.

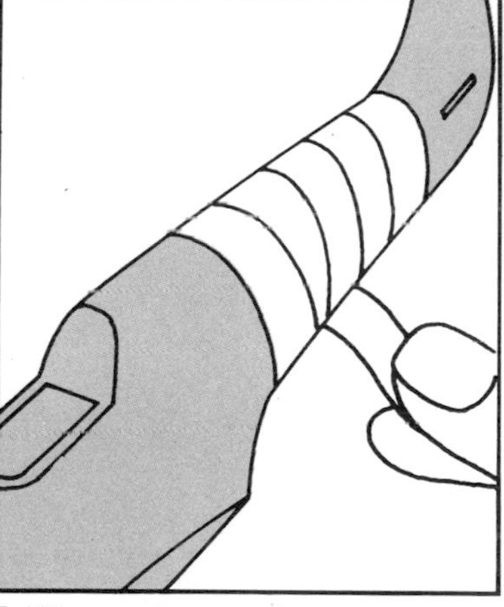

7 Where serious warping occurs you would be justified in sending for a replacement part, but the best remedy if say fuselage, wing or boiler halves are involved is to put rather more cement on the join than is normally advocated and bind the parts really hard with the widest adhesive tape you have handy.

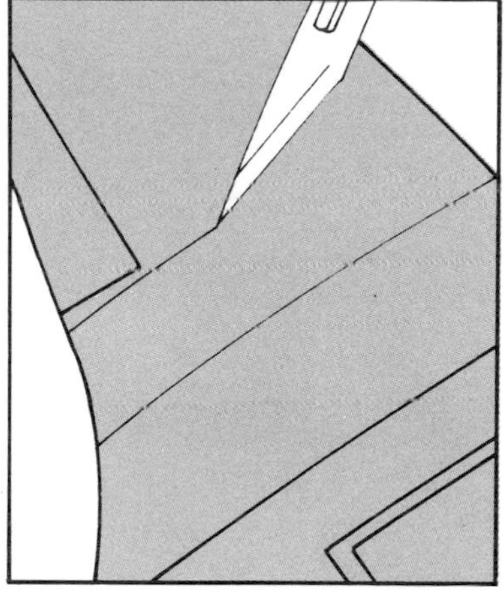

8 You may find that in eliminating the join lines you have also eliminated surface detail or panel lines that are sometimes moulded in the surface of a model. If so, the answer is to score them back carefully into position with your craft knife.

Plated Parts

Vacuum plated parts are often included in plastic kits to give a chrome or brass effect; all the better-quality large scale car kits, for instance, have plated 'chrome' bumpers, wheel hubs and radiator grilles. In addition, several aircraft kits are available in which all the components are plated to represent the shiny natural metal finish of the original.

The important point to remember with plated parts is that polystyrene cement will not act on the plastic through the plating. Thus to cement, say, a plated wheel hub in position it is necessary to scrape the plating away from the actual area of contact before applying the cement. This needs great care, for though it is a simple matter to scrape away the plating with a knife point it is only too easy to 'peel' off too much plating in the process.

However, it is possible to avoid this problem by using Uhu or a similar glue to attach the necessary components, for most 'chrome' parts such as grilles, wheel hubs and bumpers can be added last of all after the completed model has been painted. If you use a glue you not only avoid having to scrape away plating but also having to scrape away paint from adjacent parts. If you do accidentally remove plating where it shows, small patches of bare plastic can be touched in with the silver from the Humbrol Railway Enamel range, which gives just about the best 'chrome' finish of any silver paint available.

Below before cementing plated parts, scratch off plating with a knife and rub down on fine sandpaper.

Weighting

Something else you need to consider before proceeding too far is whether the completed model will depend on some sort of weight for stability. The classic case, of course, is the aircraft with tricycle undercarriage. Kit instructions rarely seem to point out the need for weighting, so it's something you must anticipate yourself. Generally, black plasticine suffices for the average small plane on a tricycle undercarriage. You simply stuff the nose full of it before the fuselage halves are assembled. Lead shot, bits of rolled up cement tube, small lead chunks etc. embedded in the plasticine can give extra weight if you think this will be necessary. Remember that it does no harm to have too much weight in the nose, so long as it doesn't make the undercarriage buckle. In models with big open areas in the nose you can't add much plasticine or other weighting, merely because the cockpit is sited right forward; in such cases add the weight in the front ends of the engine nacelles, forward of the oleo legs.

Other kits also need suitable weighting. For example, a bridge-laying tank will almost certainly need a large quantity of plasticine in the rear hull to prevent the vehicle nosing forward with the bridge at maximum height. And on locomotives the complete boiler almost always needs weighting above the main driving wheels if you want any sort of adhesion.

Conversions

A big attraction of the plastic modelling hobby is the range of possibilities it offers for altering, adapting or modifying the basic kit of parts to obtain a model which differs considerably – sometimes radically – from the one the manufacturer has set out to provide. All kits will benefit from as much extra detailing as the modeller cares to add – how much is entirely up to the individual and depends on the time and skill at his disposal.

Many kits have yet greater possibilities: they can be used as a basis for models almost totally different from the original kit subject. This art is known as 'converting'. Broadly it can be divided into conversions which depend mainly on the use of spares or components (major or minor) from other kits; and those in which only a part of the original kit is actually used and new structures or components are added from what amount to 'raw materials' (plastic card, wood, body putty and general bits and pieces). Both types of conversion are possible with all manner of plastic kits; aircraft, tanks, locomotives, cars and ships are especially suitable.

The art of conversion shows the fundamental difference in approach between the modeller who works with plastic kits and the modeller who builds either from scratch or from kits made in the basic materials such as wood or metal. In the days when model aircraft were made from wooden assembly kits, the modeller was so preoccupied with getting an acceptable model from the crude parts supplied that thoughts of altering it as well hardly ever came to mind. It was achievement enough to end up with a recognizable model after the toil of shaping wings and fuselage to correct cross-section and appearance! The plastic modeller has no such problems, as all the parts come fully shaped, sectioned and detailed, and ready for assembly. Since all the drudgery has been taken out of achieving

Plastic putty used to make a nose intake and reduce the chin intake on this Tornado converted from a Typhoon kit.

Plastic card sizes

Polystyrene Sheet
·125mm White
·25mm White
·375mm White
·5mm White
·5mm Black
·75mm White
·75mm Black
1mm White
1mm Black
1·5mm White
1·5mm Black
·25mm Clear
·5mm Clear

Assorted Colours
·5mm Red
·5mm Cream
·5mm Yellow
·5mm Green
·5mm Light Blue
·5mm Dark Blue

Polystyrene Strip
·125mm × 1, 1·5 & 2mm White
·25mm × 1, 1·5 & 2mm White
·5mm × 1, 1·5 & 2mm White
·5mm × ·5mm White
·5mm × ·75mm White
·5mm × 1·5mm White
·5mm × 2mm White

Assorted Colours
·5mm × ·5mm
·5mm × ·75mm
·5mm × 1mm
·5mm × 1·5mm
·5mm × 2mm

Polystyrene Building Sheet
(OO/HO 4mm scale)
Red Brick Grey Slate
Yellow Brick Road Signs

Polystyrene Rod
·75mm Diameter
1mm Diameter
1·25mm Diameter

basic realism, the more interesting prospect of altering or improving becomes the principal challenge – all of which means in the long run that you end up with a far more varied and interesting collection of models than you would ever have had time or skill for in the days of the wooden kit.

Given personal accomplishments such as skill and patience (which come with practice anyway), any potential kit converter's most important asset is a spare parts' box. It is absolutely essential to keep all spare parts left over from any kit you make. Very often a kit will give some degree of choice, so that you may have bombs, fuel tanks, aerials, wheels, doors, girder sections, spare track shoes, lifeboats, masts etc. which can either be included or omitted.

Some kits, especially the more recent ones, come with even more impressive options. Aircraft may have two noses which means that a choice of marks can be built from the one kit; some car kits can have raised or folded hoods, or even open or closed body work; and ships may come with billowing c furled sails. So make it a rule to keep everything left over in a special spares' box. Once you start converting you'll have even more spare parts left over, everything from complete aircraft fuselages, gun turrets, wheels and axles down to tiny unused locating pins. Even if you've made only a few models, you'll soon build up quite a collection of left-overs.

The best kind of spares' box is of transparent plastic. When your collection builds up, it's easy to see if you have what you need without having to sift through a cardboard box full of components. If you model several different types of kit, get a spares' box for each subject.

Very many spares can be used just as they come. Others need to be modified first. You may use some oddments merely as reinforcing patches under joins, however, so you'll find a use for everything you keep in the long run, even if it stays in your spares' box for years. Sometimes, too, kits contain duplicated parts because of packing errors; again, they may include items, display stands, for instance, you don't use.

Every plastic oddment you can lay your hands on should also go into your spares' box. Don't throw away your ball pen when it's empty – put it into the box; similarly, keep all plastic pen refills – they are useful for everything from chimneys, gate-posts, drainpipes, gun barrels and waste-pipes to axle sleeves and washers. Ball pen refills can be chopped into slices with a knife or scissors; plastic cocktail sticks are equally useful and adaptable. Any other items of varying diameter and of circular or oval cross-section should be hoarded – wooden skewers, wooden cocktail sticks, toothpicks, paper clips, pins, copper or steel wire, fuse wire, old pencils etc. Keep bubble packaging too, as bits of this often come in useful for cockpit canopies or fairings, saving you the trouble of having to mould them.

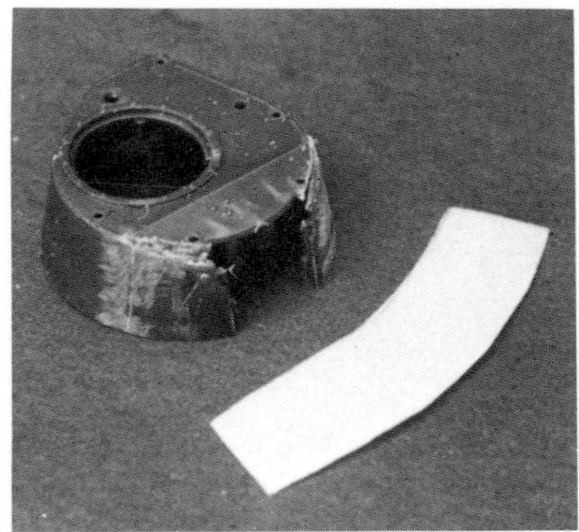

Basic materials, such as plastic card, are extremely useful for simple conversions. Here it is used to provide a new turret front for an unarmed command tank converted from a 1:35 Type 97 tank.

Above the completed conversion to a command tank, shown in progress opposite, painted and posed against a jungle background.
Right the Type 97 tank built according to the kit instructions.

Heat-stretching

Keep all the long, straight sprues to which the kit parts are attached except for those that are very twisted and short; straight sprues are as valuable to the conversion and detail fan as the rest of the kit. Normally they are either circular in cross-section or square. In their rough form, suitably sanded and trimmed, they can often serve almost as they come. Their greatest value, however, lies in the inherent ability of polystyrene to dissolve under heat.

Heat-stretching sprues is the most important technique in plastic modelling after kit-building itself. You can use stretched sprue for all parts which involve circular cross-sections of very small diameter. Hence con. rods, track rods, radio aerials, rigging wires, exhaust pipes, small gun barrels, ship's masts, brake levers, whip aerials and so on will all come within your province once you've mastered the art of sprue-stretching.

You need a selection of sprues, a candle and some courage to get started.

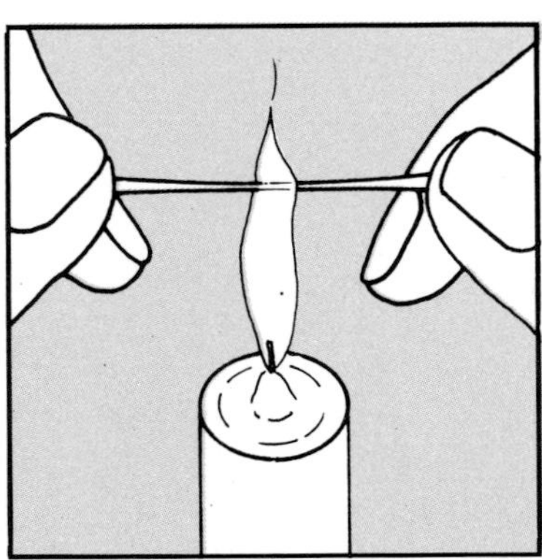

1 Rotate the sprue very slowly about an inch above the candle flame until the area over the flame starts to wilt and turn floppy.

2 Lift the sprue clear at this precise moment, at the same time steadily pulling the ends apart so that the melted section starts to attenuate as you pull. Once you learn the knack you'll get thin lengths of perfectly-rounded narrow-section plastic. Judgement is the key, but to ensure success you must hold the ends when the desired diameter is reached until the plastic has set hard. Failure to do this will simply cause it to sag or break. Don't be discouraged if your first few attempts end in broken sprues – it happens to everyone. Using thick sprue you can get filaments of very finely stretched sprue the full span of your arms and no thicker than a human hair; these are ideal for aerials and rigging wire.

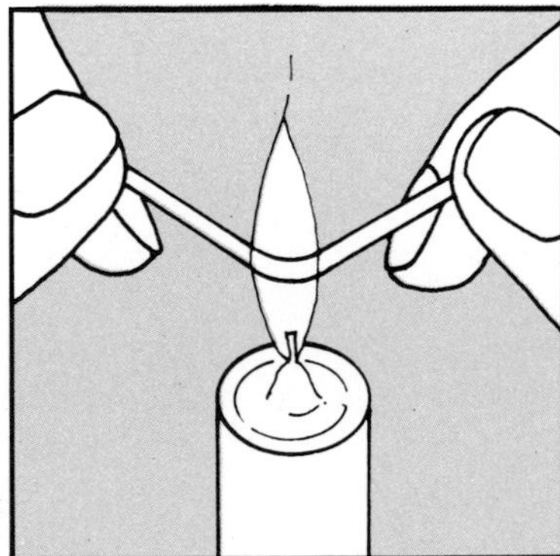

3 With a little practice, you can mould corners on thicker bits exactly where you need them. Simply hold the part near the flame for an instant and bend it gently. With suitable trimming any sort of exhaust pipe can be fashioned inside five minutes.

A Sopwith Snipe with heat-stretched rigging.

Rigging

This leads us straight on to the most important and vital technique encountered by anyone who makes any sort of biplane model – building the interplane rigging so characteristic of old aircraft. With one or two exceptions, mainly the larger scale kits, all model biplanes come complete with the interplane struts but lack the material for the rigging or even any mention of them in the instructions.

Biplanes without rigging look very stark and unrealistic, and there's absolutely no reason for ignoring it. It need hold no terror if you use heat-stretched sprue pulled out to filament length. In this style it's just like a hair in appearance, rather thicker in fact, and surprisingly strong. Once you've mastered making this filament, the actual task of fitting the rigging is so absurdly easy that you won't believe it until you try.

The kit box lid normally shows the real aircraft and will act as a guide to the rigging wire positions if you do not have a suitable picture for reference. Normally cross wires are rigged diagonally from strut to strut, so the basic scheme is a series of criss-cross patterns. There may also be rigging wires in the undercarriage assembly and external control wires on outriggers just clear of the fuselage. Sometimes there are also straight up-and-down interplane wires as well. On a 1:48 scale biplane you can add every wire, but on a 1:72 scale model you may need to simplify a little – perhaps substituting a single wire for double wires on the prototype machine. It won't be noticeable, because the filament is a little over-scale anyway in 1:72 scale, and effect is the most important thing in this size of model.

Leave all the rigging until you have completed and painted the model. You can even put the transfers on if you like; this should certainly be done if any of the attachment points are on top of a roundel or serial.

Polystyrene filament can be used for many other purposes: it makes excellent whip aerials in small scale warships, tank aerials, aerial wires on any aircraft models, rigging for sailing ships, or even clothes lines in miniature gardens! In each case the method of attaching is exactly the same as that described for biplane rigging.

Use silver sprues as the basis of rigging wires, although some modellers favour using clear sprue for rigging wires. For tank aerials use dark green sprues. Choose other colours according to your needs.

There are other methods of rigging, using fine thread or fuse wire, for instance, but they are fiddling and, quite honestly, the sprue method does seem superior.

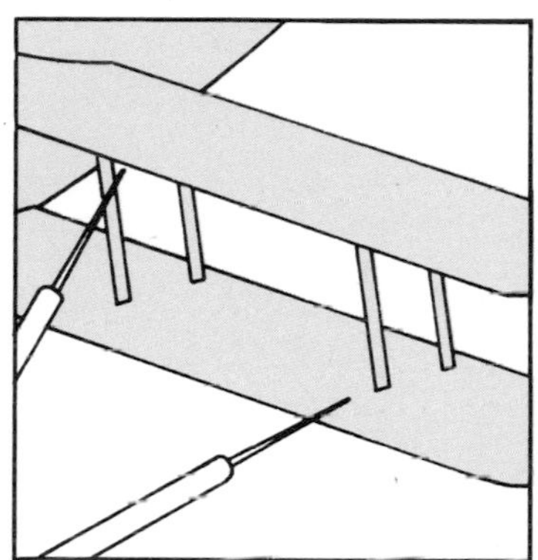

1 Start with the principal wires, say the diagonal cross wires. Place the model in a convenient but firm position, supporting it across the corner of a box lid if necessary, and use a pair of cheap school dividers to measure the precise length of your first length of wire from locating point to locating point.

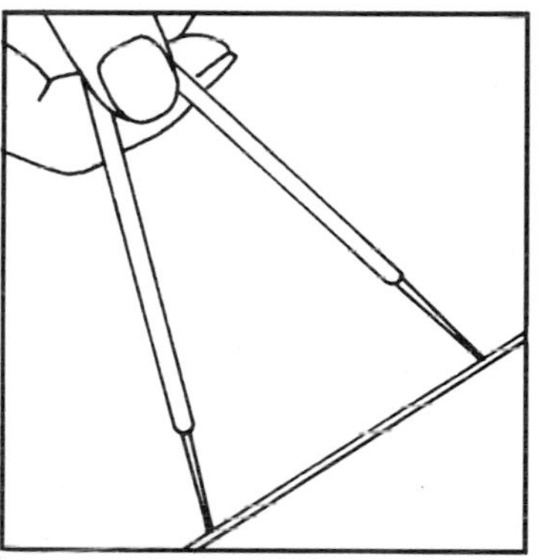

2 Without moving the points in any way, transfer the dividers to the filament, which should be stretched out straight on your working surface. Place the points against the filament and snick off the appropriate length with your craft knife.

3 Take a pin and place just the tiniest drop of polystyrene cement on each of the two locating points. Pick up the length of filament with your tweezers and pop it into place. The cement will hold the filament perfectly.

4 Follow the same procedure with all the other wires, though my advice is to cement wires in place on alternate wings as you go along, as this gives time for the cement to set before the next cross wire is added. With a little practice you can really move fast using this method. The cement will hold through the paint sufficiently to make a permanent job of the wire, but if you are uncertain scratch the paint away at the locating point with a pin. It is essential for neatness that the cement be used very sparingly. If you do accidentally apply too large a blob, leave it to set, scrape it off and try again – it costs nothing except time. Any scratches or blemishes which remain round the attachment points after you've finished can be touched in with paint.

Details

Heat-stretched sprue also comes in useful for adding small details not provided in the kit because of moulding limitations or economics. The older kits still available are often particularly sparse on details and you can do much to improve them. Pictures, drawings or even the illustration on the kit box lid generally show details that you'll search for in vain in the kit – pitot tubes, VHF aerials, foot steps, exhaust pipes and gun sights for instance. Similarly, conversions will almost always involve adding details somewhere along the line.

There are other fittings, however, which, by virtue of their nature or physical form, cannot be made up from stretched sprue. This is where all those bits you collect come in so useful. For example, a loop aerial would be difficult to fashion from even the finest stretched sprue; but it's a very simple matter to make it from fuse wire looped round a suitably sized knitting needle to give the necessary diameter. Twist the ends to lock them, snip the loop off, and cement the finished aerial in a hole drilled in the appropriate location. Stirrup-type steps can also be formed from fuse wire or thicker wire, while wire staples come in handy for many purposes, in particular for grab rails on tanks or locomotives or foot rungs on ships' bulkheads. I find the 'Bambi' type handiest, but there are larger sizes too. A further use for staples is to join the ends of tank tracks as supplied in Airfix and other kits. They make a very strong and almost invisible join, particularly if the join is arranged under a wheel or track cover. It's also a much quicker and safer process than the heat welding system sometimes advocated.

Cocktail sticks or ball pen tubes can often simply be trimmed to length for gun barrels, transmission shafts, stump masts, drain pipes and so on, while matchsticks make good timber baulks or wooden shores and convincing lorry or wagon loads. I've used soft copper wire – which bends very easily and

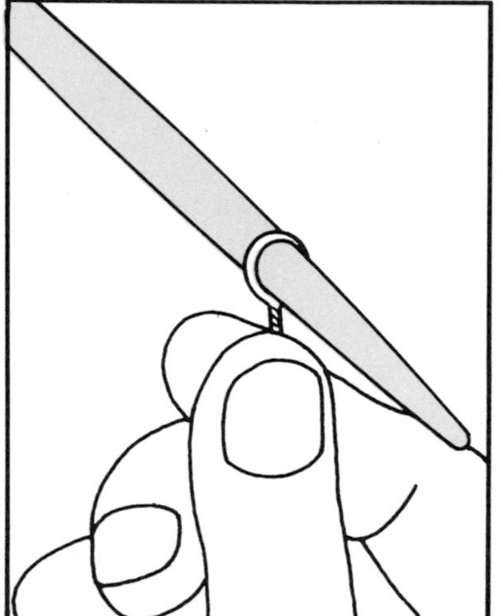

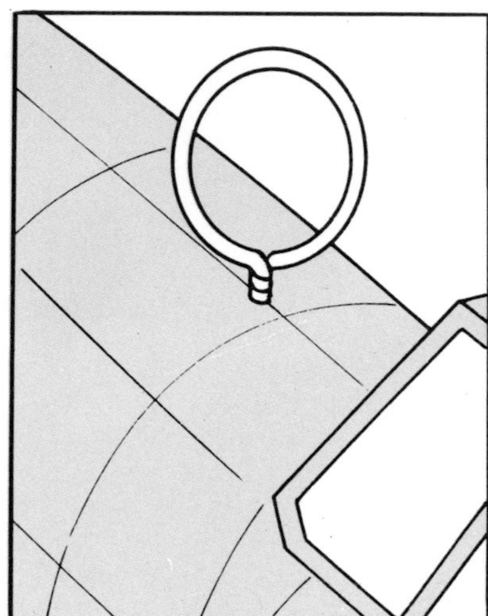

Making a loop aerial from fuse wire wound round a knitting needle.

smoothly – for piping on hydraulic systems, steam pipes on ships or locomotives and exhaust pipes. Thick thread or tinsel, salvaged from Christmas parcels, makes excellent rope or (when painted) wire rope in the smaller scales, useful for representing the tow ropes of small scale tanks or a bosun's gear just lying around on sailing ship models.

Such items are rarely included in the kit; when they are, they are often just surface mouldings best removed and replaced by the real thing. Old nylon stocking material cut and rolled as necessary makes ideal camouflage netting in OO/HO scales (similarly, muslin serves in larger scales), and green and brown paint 'blobbed' on to the complete roll at random makes a good representation of the 'garnishing' found on full-size nets. Tissue paper cut, rolled or folded, or alternatively coarse-grained paper, is excellent for canvas tarpaulins associated with almost any kind of model from tanks to sailing ships.

You'll also find that items and materials intended for other types of modelling are equally useful on plastic models. Model railway signal chain, for instance, has scores of applications, such as towing chains on tanks, anchor cables on ships, rigging chains on old-time artillery and so on. You can also buy larger-size chain from model shops which specialize in ship models and a huge range of cast metal fittings, from steering wheels and binnacles to lifebuoys and fairleads, which are invaluable on plastic model sailing ships. Model railway shops stock and supply cast metal fittings for locomotives which include tiny hurricane lamps, shovels, etc., as well as boiler fittings. They also sell flanged wheels which can sometimes be skimmed down as wheels for other models (eg horse-drawn wagons); most important of all, they sell signal laddering which has scores of uses – including scaling ladders for OO size model soldiers, entry ladders for aircraft and so on.

This does not exhaust the possibilities of the odds and ends in your spares' box, but it does show what a vast amount of detailing can be done by improvisation. Even old cement tubes can be cut up and fashioned into flags, rolls of canvas or cloaks and other items of clothing for the larger scale of soldiers. So, before dismissing a project as impossible because of a lack of components or materials, take a hard look at what you have around in the way of scraps and oddments.

Part of the large range of plastic fittings from Plastruct.

Minor alterations

There's nothing to stop you building all your models just as they come in the kit, but it's infinitely more interesting to aim to alter every model you make in at least some small way so as to give it your own individual stamp.

In many cases these are often improvements as well. This is the case with the older aircraft kits still available; these were often supplied with 'solid' instead of hollow cockpits with the pilot's head moulded as a little bump on top. This is far below modern standards; today's kits include at least a pilot's seat in the kit, sometimes full cockpit detail as well. With these old kits you need to cut out the plastic which fills in the cockpit aperture and make up interior fittings from plastic card. This is where your razor saw and craft knife really come into their own.

Some older aircraft kits still on sale have no wheel well for a retracting undercarriage or at best simply have its outline moulded into the underside of the wing. Since the wing usually comes in two halves, it is not difficult to cut out the wheel well shape in the lower half, using the mould lines as a guide. After cleaning up the edges you'll get a perfect hollow wheel well, once the wings are assembled.

The same procedure applies to any other model in which an area of plastic needs to be removed from the centre of a larger component – cutting out the opening for a turret cage in a tank conversion or a spare wheel aperture, for instance.

Aircraft control surfaces can be treated in a similar way. In some kits the ailerons at least, and sometimes the elevators and rudder too, come as separate mouldings, often pivoted, which means that they can be set at appropriate angles characteristic of an aircraft on the ground or in flight. Other kits merely have all these control surfaces moulded integrally with the rest of the wing or the tail. In these cases you can choose between leaving them just as they come or trying to cut them out and re-set

Cutting a hollow cockpit

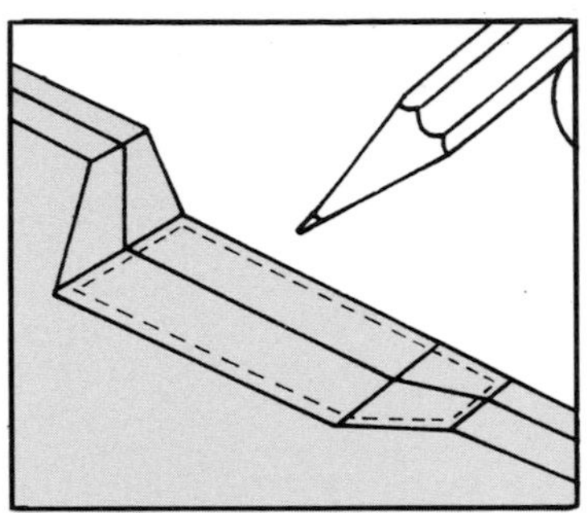
1 Hold the two fuselage halves together and lightly pencil in the area to be cut away for the cockpit. Check, however, with the transparency that you don't mark out too large an area.

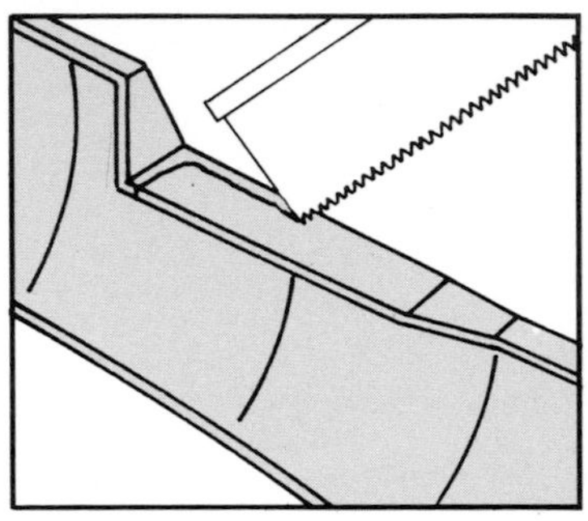
2 Saw out the marked section with a razor saw.

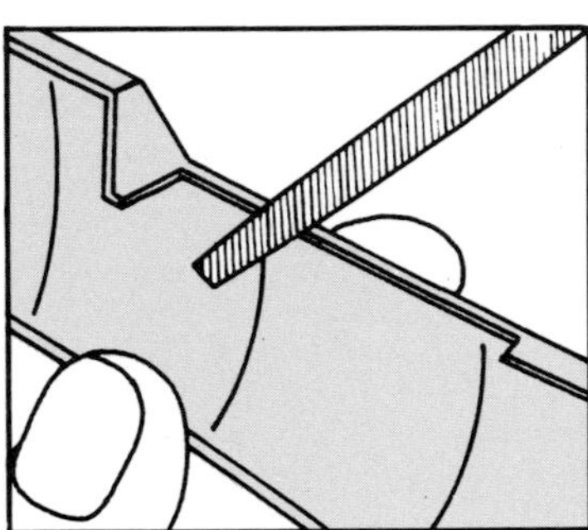
3 Square and clean up the edges with a file.

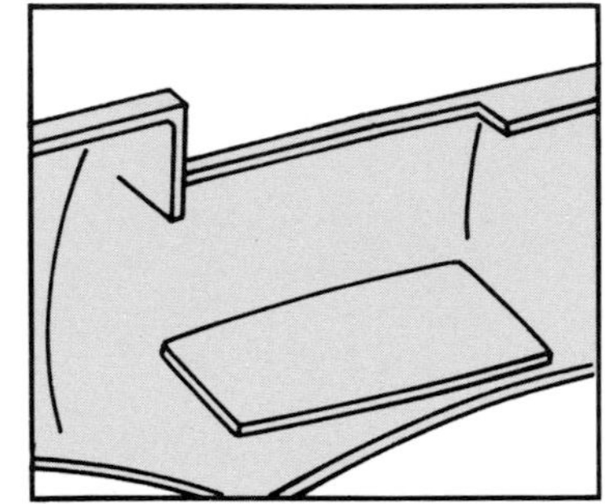
4 With a deep fuselage you may need to add a cockpit floor from plastic sheet.

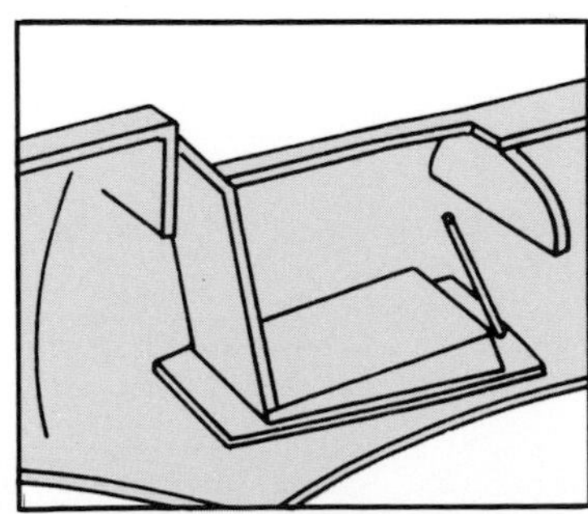
5 Cut out plastic sheet to make a seat, dashboard and bulkhead and use stretched sprue, wire or a pin for the control column.

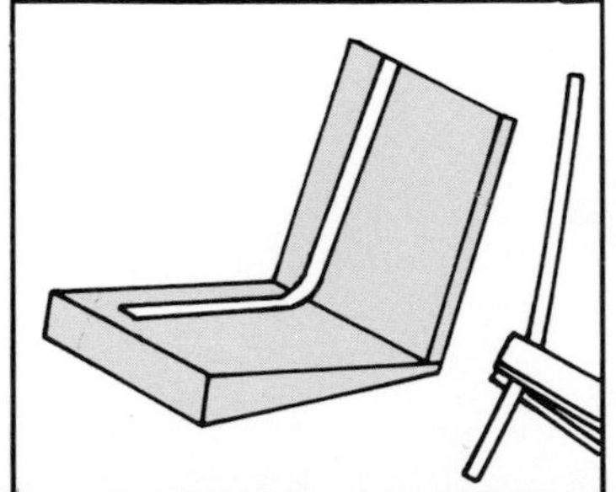
6 Having painted the cockpit, you will certainly want to add seat straps from thin strips of brown paper or parcel tape.

Cutting out wheel-wells

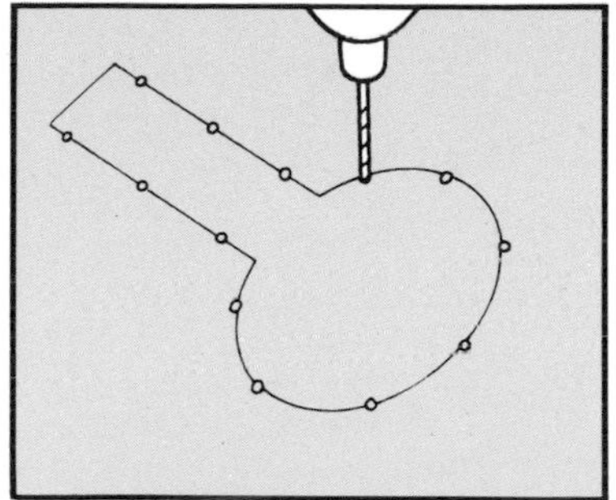

1 Drill a series of holes (using a fine drill, according to the space involved) round the inside of the area to be removed.

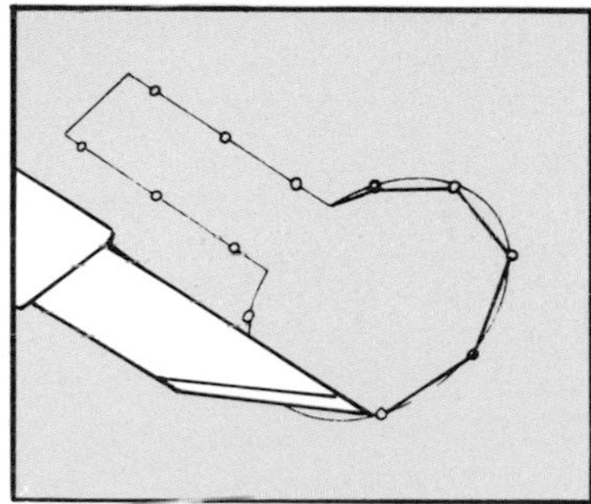

2 Cut from hole to hole using a pointed blade in your craft knife.

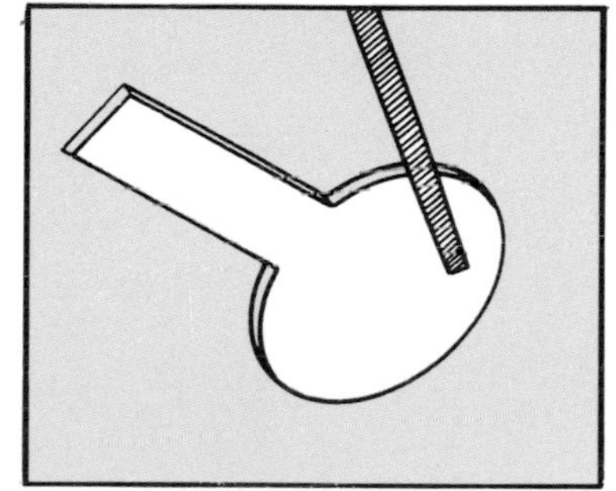

3 Once you have roughly removed the plastic it is a simple matter to clean up the inside edges with a craft knife and rat-tail file.

Cutting out a separate rudder

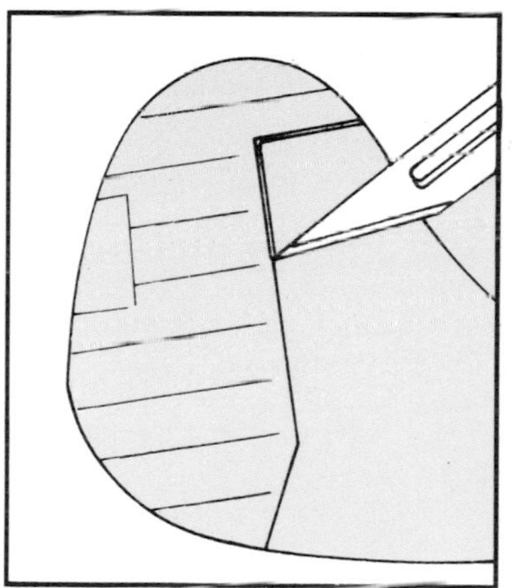

1 Remove rudder with a knife or razor saw, using the panel lines as a guide.

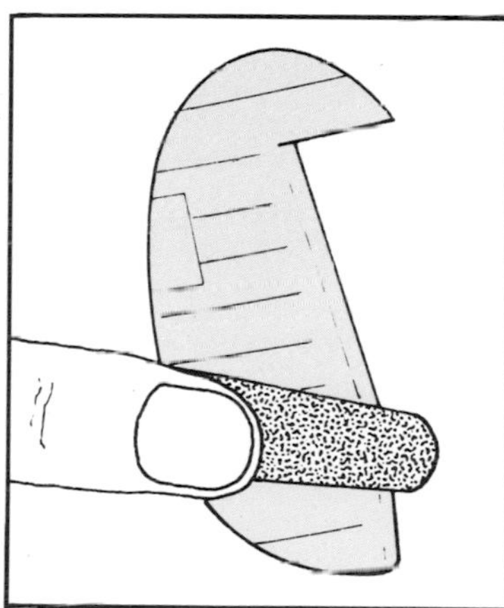

2 Clean up the cut edges with an emery board, shaping to an aerofoil section.

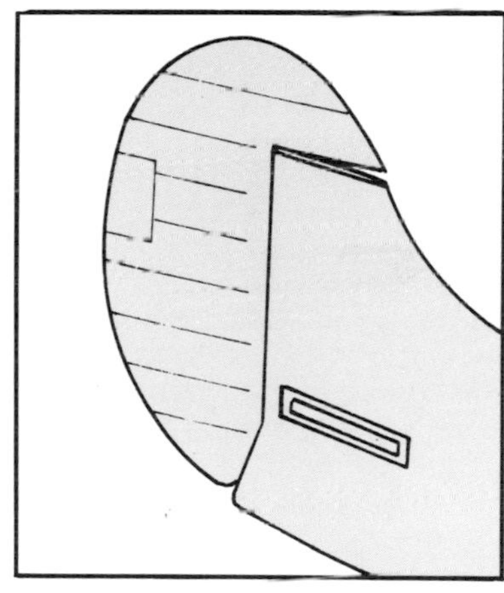

3 Cement rudder back in position at the desired angle.

them at angles to break up the outline. For ailerons, just cut along the moulded hinge line, separate the part from the wing, clean up the edges with emery paper and cement the aileron back in place with a slight droop. If you think this is a risky job (it isn't very difficult, in fact), the next best thing is to nick the join lines at the trailing edges of wing or tail so that the control surfaces are at least visibly separated from the surrounding areas.

Rudders are generally much easier to cut away completely as they are more accessible than the other moving surfaces. Better still, however, is to cut out the flaps from the lower wing trailing edge; this is a very simple task when the wing comes in two halves. Before assembly saw the flaps away from the lower wing half and cement them back in place (drooping) after assembly. This is even easier than altering ailerons and elevators.

Like everything else, all this is a matter of choice. Some model aircraft can be made up straight from the kit, and you can leave all control surfaces just as they come. In others you cut out and re-cement every single flap.

The same principles apply to many other types of model – doors in buildings, doors in ships' bulkheads, car doors, turret hatches in tanks and so on – in which the existing component is moulded integrally with the surrounding area. Simply saw it out and re-cement it at a new angle.

'Glazing'

Glass or other transparent areas in kits are full of pitfalls for the modeller. They are generally moulded in clear plastic which scratches or smudges easily if clumsily handled. For that reason it is best to use Uhu or another transparent cement for positioning canopies, since any excess adhesive is virtually invisible. Also, don't handle clear mouldings until you really need to. Similarly, if you are cutting or sawing cockpit canopies or windows, take great care to avoid any slip which could deface the entire moulding. The really safe way of cutting transparencies is to mask off the entire area with strips of masking tape, leaving just a tiny uncovered strip along the line of the cut. This not only provides a guide for sawing but also protects the rest of the surface if the saw slips. Once cutting is completed, just strip off all the tape. Incidentally, always use a razor saw for major cutting work with transparencies. A knife can be very dangerous since it not only stands a chance of slipping off the (usually) curved surface into your finger but any undue force can crack and ruin the canopy completely. Once you've sawn through a canopy, though, you are left with rather rough and opaque edges, and a knife then is the tool to pare off the roughness and clean up the edges.

Clean up transparencies which are accidentally scratched or discoloured with toothpaste; simply rub it in well with your fingers. It is possible to reduce a curve in a canopy by sanding down with emery paper even though this contradicts all the handling rules outlined above. This will give a modified shape but also an opaque canopy; toothpaste will restore the shine.

The major problem facing every aircraft modeller at the start is how to represent the canopy frame lines. Generally the canopy framing is either lightly etched or moulded in the surface of kit transparencies. The kit instructions rarely give much guidance on how to colour them but leave you with the assumption that they have to be painted in. Well, you can do this, but you must have care and a steady hand or you are likely to ruin the canopy if your paint brush slips. In recent kits the frame lines are very cleanly etched and seem to guide the brush quite effectively, which makes painting in the frame a more feasible proposition.

Undoubtedly the simplest way of making framing is to use tape cut into strips. Adhesive tape comes in a range of colours, and it is sometimes possible to find a precise match. You can also buy 'chrome' tape, which is perfect for silver aircraft. More often you will have to pre-paint clear tape to match the colour of your model.

Once again, this method is equally applicable on other models, especially for house frames, car windows and locomotive windows. You can also use tape strips for boiler bands and for strapping on other parts of models. The procedure is precisely the same.

Flat windscreens, portholes, or canopies made up of flat panes can be fashioned from polyglaze (transparent plastic sheet), acetate or acetone. Polyglaze is easier to buy and to cut. Flat polyglaze panels will butt together very well if you apply Uhu with a pin. If you make any canopies from individual faces, assemble them straight on to the model after painting. It's almost impossible to make up a canopy from scratch without some datum point to work on; this is logically the cockpit edge. You can also combine polyglaze panels with an existing transparency moulding.

Brewster Buffalo in 1:72 scale, using painted adhesive tape strips to make the cockpit framing.

Cockpit canopy framing

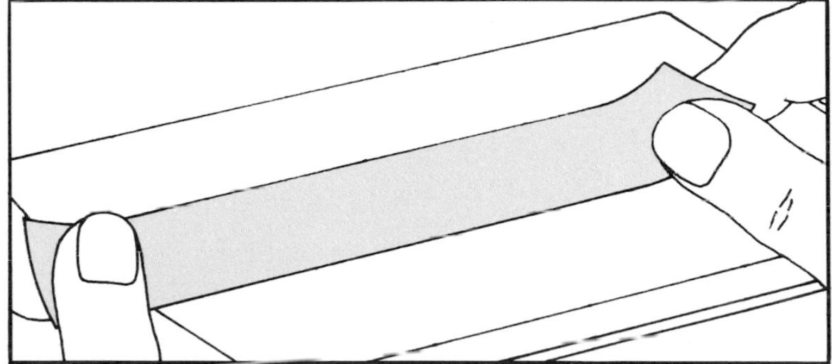

1 Take a suitable strong metal cutting surface such as a tin box used for school instruments.

Peel off about 4 inches of clear tape from a roll and press it gently, without wrinkling it, along the centre of the box lid. Make sure no big dust particles are trapped underneath.

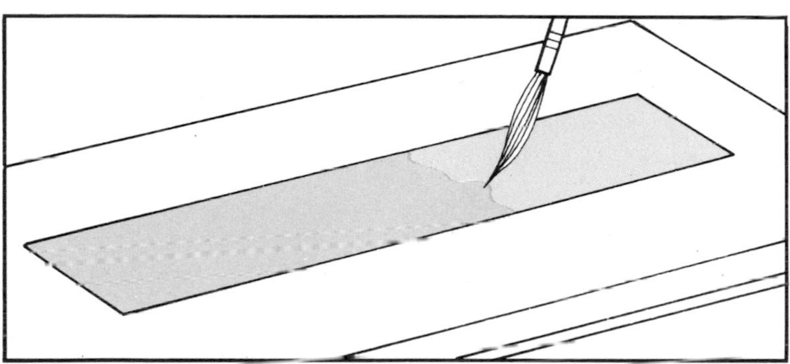

2 Paint the tape the desired colour to match the model and leave it to set hard. (If you are using coloured or chrome tape, this is of course unnecessary.)

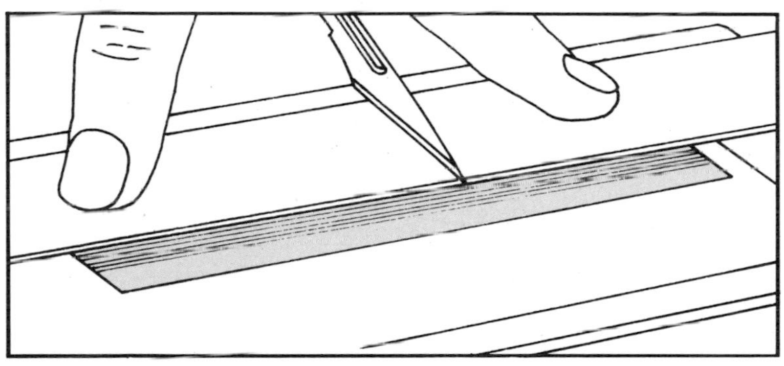

3 Place your steel ruler along the centre of the tape strip and make a long stroke the full length of the tape with a sharp craft knife.
Continue to make parallel cuts at the intervals necessary for the scale of your model. You must judge these by eye. The simple way is to sit so that the room light comes over your shoulder at such an angle as to throw a shadow from the edge of the ruler; then make each cut with the outer edge of the shadow along the line of the previous cut.

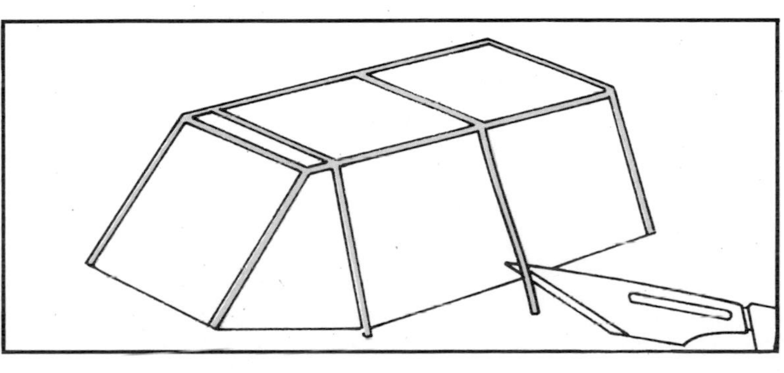

4 Once you have prepared enough strips, simply remove them from the cutting surface a strip at a time with your knife tip or tweezers. I always cut strips much longer than required, place them over the canopies to follow the etched frame lines and cut off the surplus with the knife or nail scissors. With the normal sort of canopy always leave a slight excess (say 0·5 mm) at each end of each frame strip and tuck it under the edge of the transparency when it is finally cemented in place.

AIRCRAFT

Miniature scale aircraft are easily the most popular type of model. In particular, by far the greatest numbers of new plastic kits are model aircraft, and there must be more model aircraft enthusiasts than any others. Real aircraft cross international boundaries, and most types are known to everyone. Airline liveries are colourful, and the aircraft they use are constantly changing, thanks to the rapid advance of aviation technology. Thus model aircraft have much to offer to the modeller seeking maximum variety allied with good availability and ease of construction.

The fact that many types of aircraft are available in model form to constant scales also appeals to the collecting instinct, and the romance of the history of aviation can be captured in a collection which need be limited only by time and space available. In nearly three decades of modern plastic kit production hundreds if not thousands of different aircraft types have appeared. Early kits now withdrawn from the market have themselves become rare collectors' pieces, and some hobbyists prefer to collect and barter the kits themselves rather than make the models!

For most of us, however, making the models is the main objective, and the local hobby or toy store is the main source of supply of currently available kits – and new ones appear nearly every month. Kits vary in scale, complexity and price; they come from the USA, Great Britain, Germany, Italy, France, Japan, and Czechoslovakia. Among the biggest manufacturers are Airfix, Revell, Heller, Italaeri, Hasegawa and Tamiya (most of whom make other types of kit as well as aircraft). If you are a complete newcomer to model making, then miniature aircraft models are probably the easiest way to get started. Try a simple monoplane from any of the familiar kitmakers – the price will be low and you will be paying only 'pocket money' prices for the experience.

Most kits of recent years are accurate and fit and assemble well, though many kits still on sale were designed ten or more years ago. Some of these are cruder in detail and less delicate in surface finish. If

The number of different aircraft available in miniature scale form is practically countless, and the modeller can build up a collection on one, or more, of many different themes. Shown here are, left, a group of German Second World War aircraft and, below, a range of British Aircraft Corporation planes. All these have been built on the 1:72 scale, the commonest aircraft scale.

A 1:48 scale Zero, fighter typical of modern, highly detailed kits. This model has a sliding cockpit and much fine detail.

you carry out a survey of the subject before beginning, as suggested in the chapter on research, you should have a fair idea of what to expect when you buy the kit. Pitfalls in assembling a modern kit are few. The major rule is to think ahead; don't just cement everything together straight from the box. Every kit these days has a good instruction sheet showing a recommended sequence of assembly; in general you cannot go far wrong if you follow this. But on thinking ahead you may find that you wish to vary or modify the recommended sequence; this applies more to model aircraft than to almost any other type of model made from kits.

Construction points

1 Paint interior parts. Cockpits and wheel wells for example. It may be too late or too difficult once the model is assembled, so paint as many small parts as possible before assembly and, indeed, before you remove them from the moulding stalks. Also, paint any visible interior areas of fuselages and wings before they are glued together.

2 Check for technical accuracy. Some kits have minor errors which published reviews or your prior research may have revealed. You may wish to make minor changes (eg reshaping wing tips) before assembly.

3 Weighting the model. Most aircraft nosewheel undercarriages need to be weighted in the nose to balance them; otherwise they drop tail down.

4 Leave details until last. The instruction sheet will often suggest that fragile parts such as aerials be added as assembly proceeds. These parts are all too easily knocked off later, particularly if you have to clean up join lines. Similarly, transparent canopies are best added after painting.

5 Improving on details. Most small scale model aircraft can be greatly improved if parts such as wheel covers and flaps are replaced by new parts cut from plastic card, since the kit plastic is usually of overscale thickness. While you are doing this, check the undercarriage. On the ground the oleo legs compress under the aircraft's weight. If your model is to depict a machine on the ground, then the oleo legs may need to be shortened to give a realistic appearance.

Two kits, now long out of production, that have become collectors' pieces.
Above Convair 990, built to 1:100 scale.
Left Avro 504k, built to 1:48 scale.

Vac-form

Much rarer than the normal polystyrene kits are vac-form models. These are generally produced by small companies who model the rarer types which the big kit manufacturers don't consider popular enough to sell in huge numbers. Vac-form kits are made by vacuum-forming (as the term implies) a sheet of plastic card over component patterns. The resulting sheet has to be cut into its component parts and assembled by the modeller. Careful cutting, trimming and fitting are all necessary. Techniques differ from those used with ordinary kits because there are none of the locating pins and slots which make ordinary kit construction so straightforward.

In general, vac-form kits are made only in limited numbers (sometimes 500 or less) and become true collectors' pieces because of their rarity. Vac-form kits are not really suitable for absolute beginners, but they can be safely tackled by anyone with some experience. Because the vac-form process does not reproduce fine details such as struts, oleo legs and airscrews with the precision of injection moulding, these are always the crudest and least satisfactory parts of this type of kit. Usually, one can cannibalize a conventional plastic kit to provide these parts, making sure, of course, that parts of the correct size and pattern are selected. Long-timc modellers often have a fair stock of spare parts salvaged from discarded models or left over from kit conversions, so this may not actually be a very expensive process.

Vac-form kits are sold only in larger model shops or by mail order.

Right above 1:72 scale Dewoitine 52 of the French Air Force, a typical vac-form kit model.

Right 1939 Devastator torpedo bomber. Carefully made vac-form kits can produce highly realistic models, as here. Both of these models have been finished with paper backed self-adhesive metal foil. See page 125 for details.

Vac-form construction

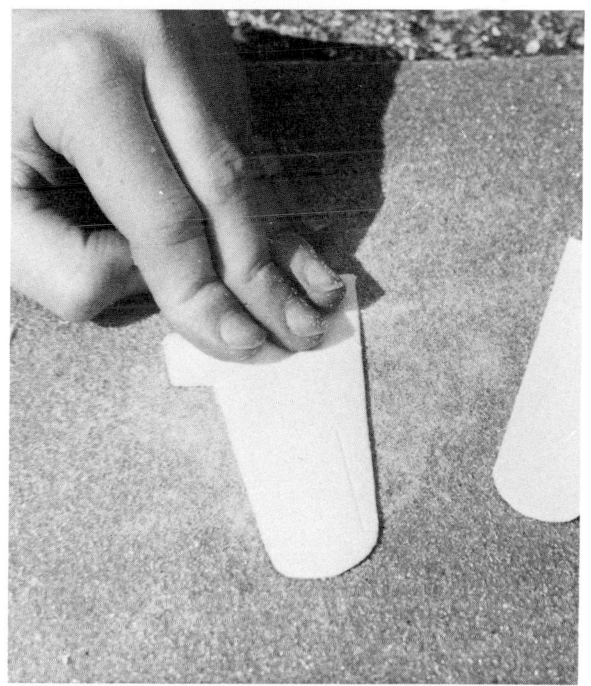

Rub down edges on glass paper to get an exact fit.

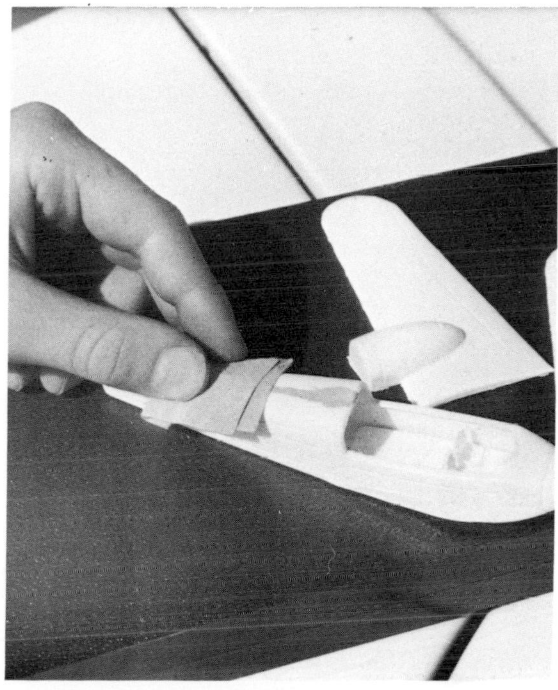

Make joins good with plastic putty and then rub them down.

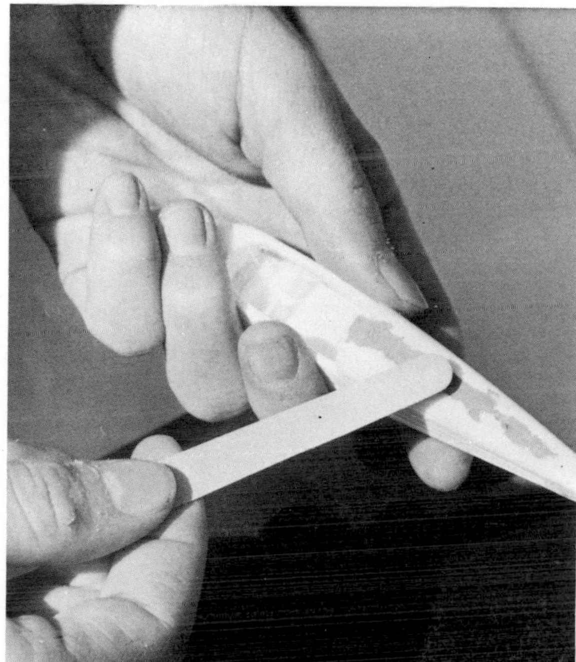

An emery board is sometimes a good substitute for a file.

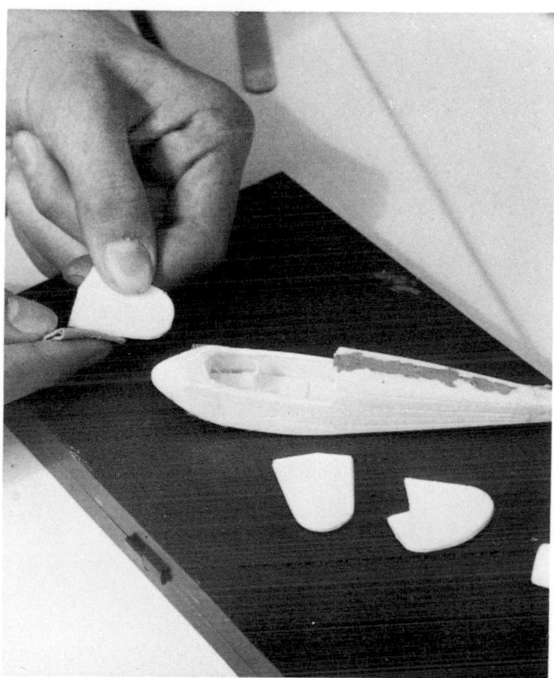

Tail assembly on a vac-form Bobcat.

GRP kits

Some kits are produced in GRP (glass reinforced plastic, otherwise glass fibre). Again they are on sale only in specialist outlets. They are more expensive than conventional plastic kits (as indeed are vac-form kits) but come in only a few parts – fuselage, wings, tail, propeller are typical. They are nicely detailed on the surface. Assembly is simple, but on some the modeller has to add extra details (undercarriages, aerials etc); once again cannibalizing ordinary plastic kits provides the answer.

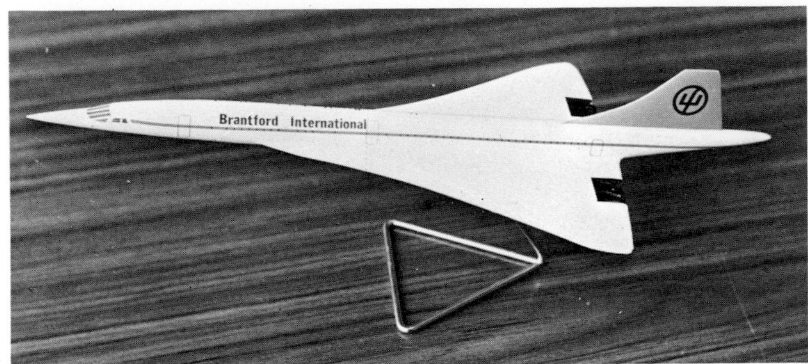

GRP kit of Concorde: this type is often seen in travel agents' windows.

Model aircraft scales

Though a few kits can be found in non-standard scales, most are made to constant internationally accepted scales, so enabling the modeller to build up a collection of models all to the same scale. The scale is always clearly marked on the kit packaging and in manufacturers' leaflets and catalogues.

You may well wish to try out models in all scales, but most modellers weigh up availability (by far the majority of kits are in 1:72 and 1:48), price, size and conversion or detail potential and then concentrate on one scale. In the 1:72 and 1:48 scales, some modellers concentrate in particular on a specific period or types (eg fighters, civil airliners, World War One and Two, the inter-war period) in order to keep the collection to a reasonable size. This is a matter for personal choice.

These are the main scales:

1:72 scale – 1 inch to 6 feet.
By far the commonest scale; the ideal compromise between size and detail potential.

1:48 scale – 1 inch to 4 feet
(sometimes called $\frac{1}{4}$ inch scale). A very nice size for fine detail without producing too big a model. Big bombers in this scale are rare, however, and those that are available make big models.

1:32 scale – 3/8 inch to 1 foot.
This is also a popular scale, producing models which are big and finely detailed.

1:24 scale – $\frac{1}{2}$ inch to 1 foot.
Only a few models are produced to this scale. They are intricately detailed and most spectacular. Airfix is the major manufacturer in this size.

1:100 scale – 3 mm to 1 foot in linear scale.
This is a handy, compact size for those short of space, though relatively few kits are available.

1:144 scale – 1 inch to 12 feet.
Exactly half the linear scale of 1:72, the models take up only a quarter of the volume. This is a popular size for airliners, and some warplanes are also modelled to this scale. It is a great space saver – twelve single-seat fighters take up the area of a shoe box.

A few models are made to slightly odd scales such as 1:50, 1:75 and 1:96, but these are very close to 1:48, 1:76 and 1:100 and in visual terms they all fit happily together.

Scratch building

Beyond kit building lies scratch building – that is, making a model aircraft entirely from raw materials. These days this usually means sheet plastic card, though hardwood or balsa can also be used. Accurate scale plans including cross-sections are absolutely essential. Though experts with years of experience can make the whole idea of scratch-building seem easy, in reality great skill is required for perfect results. Articles on specific projects appear from time to time in the model press. Techniques vary with the subject: an old-time biplane may be built up with a box structure fuselage and frames and stringers very like the real thing, while the fuselage of a modern jet fighter may be moulded by forcing heated plastic card over a wood pattern to give two fuselage halves, rather like a home-made vac-form kit. Because of its complexity scratch-building model aircraft is a subject in its own right; several books have been published concerned solely with this specialized aspect of the hobby.

Scale modelling on the grand scale: below, this scratch built 1:12 Lockheed Hercules is powered by four 6·5 engines, flies at 70 knots and can drop 48 parachutists; above, the modeller (left) and the radio control 'pilot'.

Conversions

For most of us, the best way to build up a distinctive collection of models is to use the ordinary plastic kit as a basis for variations on a theme. These days kit conversion is not as common as it once was because of many variants of the most popular aircraft types are available in kit form. In essence kit conversion entails making either minor or major changes to produce a model different from the one intended by the kit manufacturer. A typical example is a change of mark number, involving either detail or structural changes. Adding a second cockpit might convert a fighter into its training version; removing turrets might make a transport version of a bomber; changing armament and fittings might make a later version of the type supplied in the kit. In every case you end up with something a little different – a model which incorporates your own imaginative touches and stands apart from a similar model assembled unaltered from the kit components.

Sometimes major changes will produce a spectacular model which loods very different from the basic kit. A classic example is a twin-engine Manchester bomber made from a Lancaster kit; the kit's wings are shortened in span and the four Merlin engines are replaced by two Vulture engines (which have to be fashioned from scrap plastic or wood), while small detail changes have to be made to the fuselage. The colour scheme and markings also change.

One pleasing trend is that these days the manufacturers help things along by supplying alternative parts and markings. Alternative markings and colour scheme details in a kit are now quite common, but you can still choose some other colour scheme appropriate to the model and use the marking sets sold separately in the major model shops.

Model Westland Whirlwind with detail modifications and a new colour scheme and markings.

P

Converting a Focke Wolf 190

This 1:72 conversion of a Fw 190 to a two-seater trainer is an ideal project for a beginner. Use Airfix, Matchbox or Hasagawa kits for 1:72 scale or Monogram or Otaki in 1:48, increasing the sizes by half.

Use a razor saw to cut the windscreen from the rest of the canopy. Make the rear canopy from clear plastic material, and cut the rear fairing from thin plastic card. The photograph, right, shows the extent of the conversion.

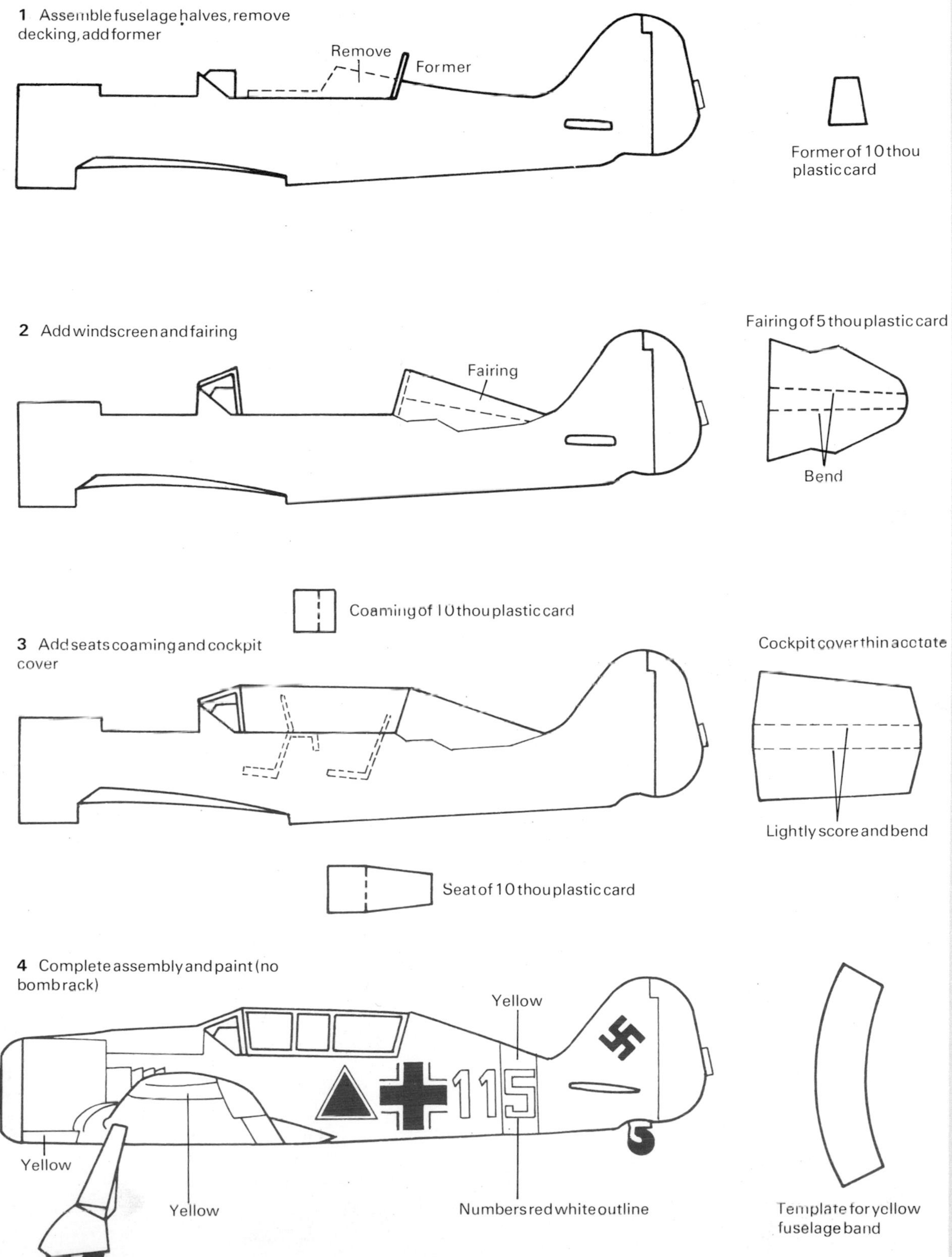
Actual Size
1 Assemble fuselage halves, remove decking, add former
Remove
Former
Former of 10 thou plastic card
2 Add windscreen and fairing
Fairing
Fairing of 5 thou plastic card
Bend
Coaming of 10 thou plastic card
3 Add seats coaming and cockpit cover
Cockpit cover thin acetate
Lightly score and bend
Seat of 10 thou plastic card
4 Complete assembly and paint (no bomb rack)
Yellow
115
Yellow
Yellow
Numbers red white outline
Template for yellow fuselage band

TANKS AND MILITARY VEHICLES

The hardware of modern war – especially tanks and artillery, but also transport vehicles and other types of mechanized weapon – has a very large following. Those who make or collect model soldiers often make the equipment to go with them: an excellent scenic diorama can be made up using, say, infantry riding on a tank or a complete gun crew and gun in action. This gives interesting variety; if you get a little weary after painting or making six model soldiers, you can always turn to a tank for your next project before going back to making more soldiers.

Though some cast metal kits of AFVs (armoured fighting vehicles) are on sale, most AFVs are available in plastic kit form; the very best are truly excellent replicas. Prices match those of model aircraft kits of comparable size. If you don't fancy kit building there is also the excellent 1:87 scale Roco-Minitanks range; made in plastic, it is sold ready made and only needs painting. These models are to scale with HO model railways and 20 mm figures. Slightly bigger at 1:76 scale (equal in scale to OO model railways and 25 mm figures) comes a great selection of kits; the most popular and economical of all are made by Airfix and Fujimi; with these you can alter basic model vehicles into all sorts of variants, such as recovery tanks, engineer tanks and so on. The 1:48 scale (roughly equal to O gauge model trains and 40 mm figures) is rather more detailed; Aurora and Bandai offer a good selection. The 1:35 scale is the most popular after 1:76, however. It is roughly equal to 54 mm scale soldiers. Tamiya, Italaeri, and Nichimo have between

Very slightly bigger in proportion are 1:32 scale kits, most of which are made by Airfix. Bigger yet are 1:24 and 1:16 (plus a few items to odd scales). The selection in the larger scales is small, and the models are invariably fully motorized.

Even a complete novice can usually turn out a good job with one of these kits in the more popular scales – and because most tanks are fairly dirty and 'battle worn' when in action you don't necessarily have to be a very good painter to finish up with a realistic enough model.

In the model AFV field, radio-control is also very popular. In the smaller scales, a great deal of scratch-building is carried out by the more experienced workers in 1:76, 1:48 and 1:35 scales.
them produced dozens of fine kits in this scale, some motorized, some unmotorized.

Opposite page 1:35 scale, M24 Chaffee light tank
Below 1:76 giant German railway gun Leopold, built with cut-away section.

Conversions

Firms such as Matchbox, Airfix, Fujimi, Edai, Hasegawa and Esci produce many inexpensive kits in 1:76 scale and the very close 1:72. All sorts of associated accessories are available too, such as soldiers in the OO/HO sizes and railway scenic items and buildings, so that the military modeller in this scale is never at a real loss for material.

By conversion, the range of 1:76 scale AFVs can be extended almost indefinitely to cover every sort of variant of the basic vehicle supplied in kit form. It is possible, for instance, to build over 100 different versions from a Sherman tank kit. Some conversions are quite difficult, but an equal number of very simple projects are well within the ability even of the novice.

In this simple 1:76 project, an M3 half-track vehicle is converted to a White scout car. The rear track units are replaced by a spare wheel and axle set; the chassis and body are shortened and the body sides are filled in with plastic card (shown white).

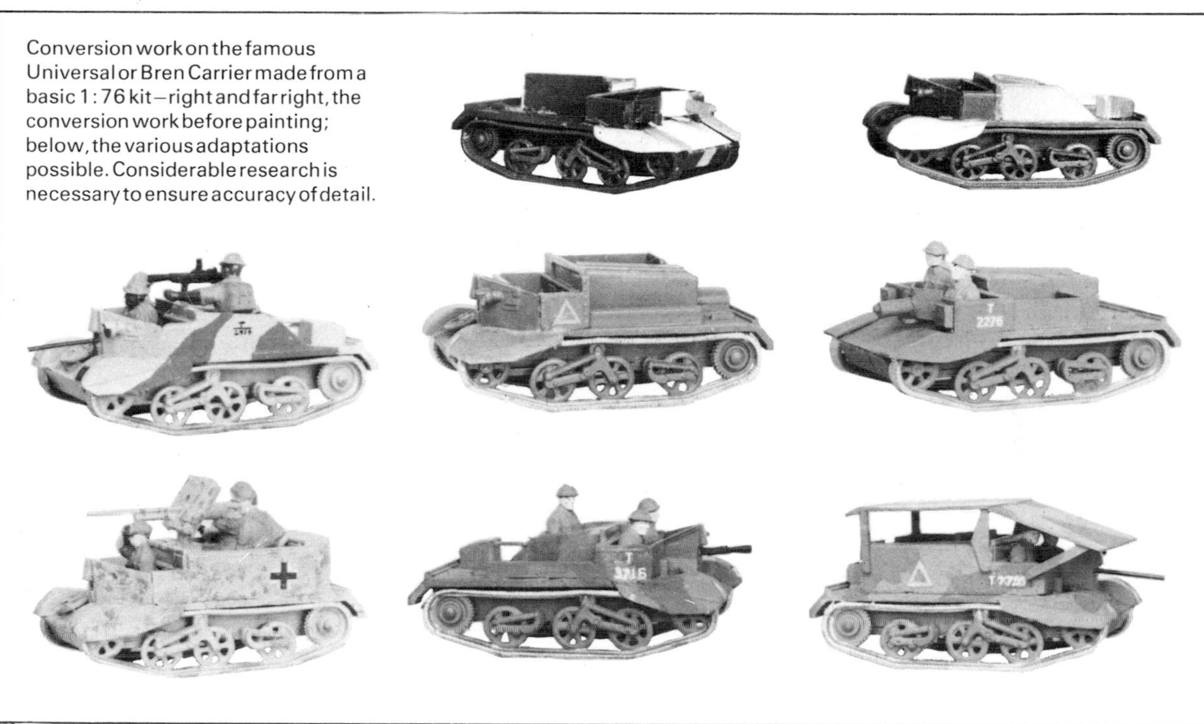

Conversion work on the famous Universal or Bren Carrier made from a basic 1 : 76 kit – right and far right, the conversion work before painting; below, the various adaptations possible. Considerable research is necessary to ensure accuracy of detail.

Three adaptations to 1 : 76 AFV models. Left, the Stu GIII with its early shot gun and an earlier type of superstructure. Below left, painted model of the first modified Stu GIII and, right, a model with side skirts added and painted.

Converting an M16 half track

The M16 Multiple Gun Motor Carriage half-track kit as made by Matchbox and converted it to the earlier M13 variant which had two guns instead of four. It's a pleasant little project, not much more than a good evening's work for the basic unpainted model. You may think it a fairly minor task as conversions go, and so it is, but when the M13 is placed alongside the standard M16 model made straight from the kit the difference in appearance and character is surprising. The conversion can also be done with 1:35 scale version of the M16 by Tamiya, though rather more small details are involved in the bigger model.

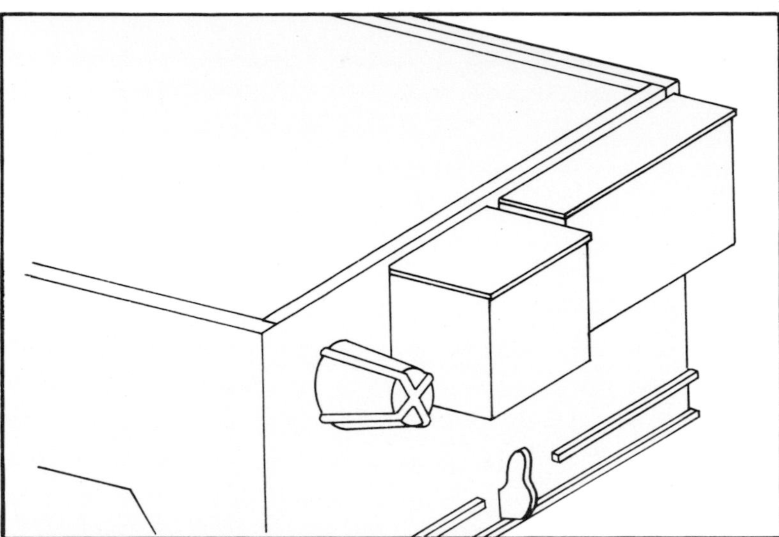

1 Starting with the M16 kit, build the chassis and superstructure exactly as instructed in the kit leaflet with the sole exception of the rear superstructure. Here use a sharp knife to slice off the two lower locating pips for the stowage lockers. Then cement the lockers in place slightly higher, almost flush with the top edge of the superstructure. Locate the locker top about the thickness of a postcard below the actual edge. With fine emery paper or an emery board smooth away the plastic where the locating pips have been removed.

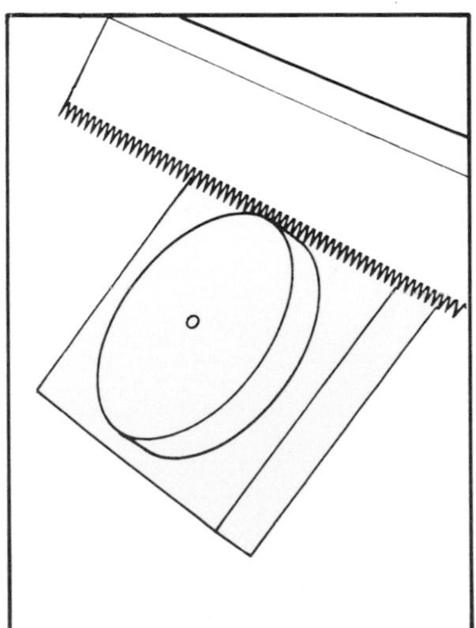

4 Now take the gun mount base, and using an X-acto razor saw cut off the square plinth to leave only the circular portion. This is the trickiest part of the whole conversion, though it is quite easy if you own a razor saw, a key tool for all conversion work.

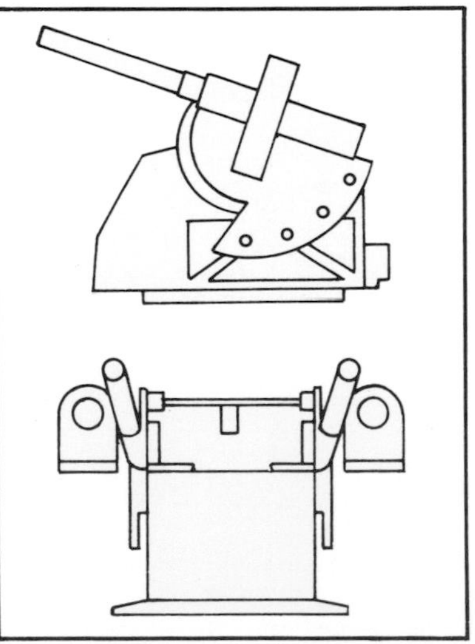

5 Assemble the rest of the gun mount following the kit instructions, though omit the lower pair of guns, leaving just the two upper guns on the mount.

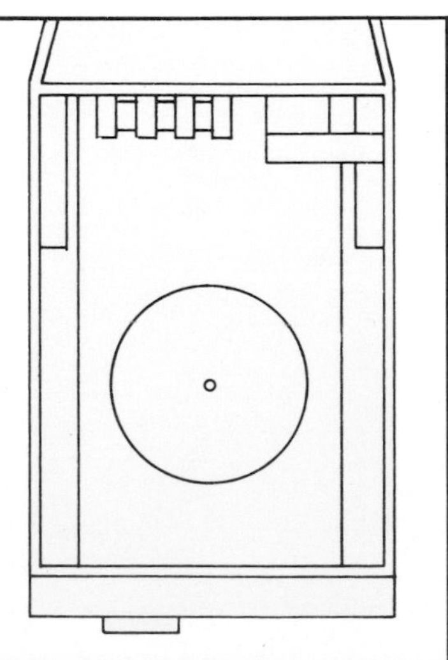

6 When the assembly is dry, cement the circular base on to the vehicle floor, siting it exactly between the locating holes which were provided for the original square base. Interior stowage for ammunition is as for the M16.

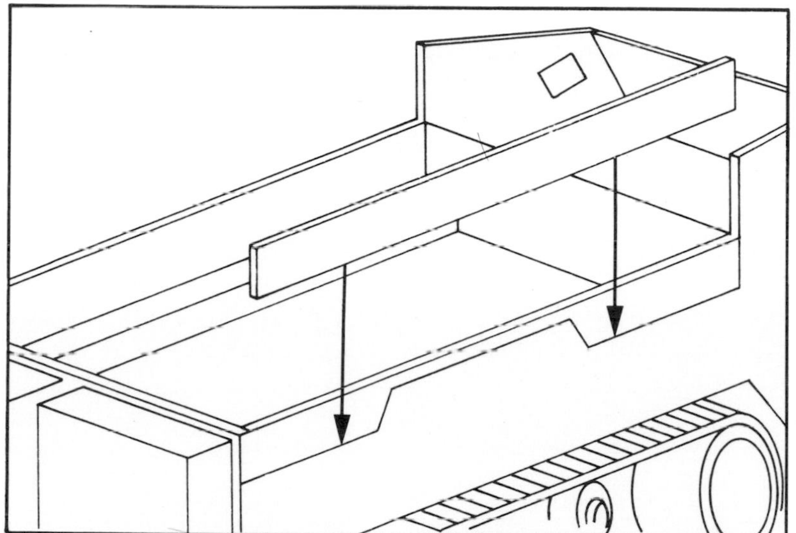

2 Now look at the side flaps (the top sections of the superstructure sides) which in the real vehicle folded down and outwards to give clearance to the gun mount when it traversed. Matchbox have moulded these in the folded position, the least convincing part of the model in my view. Taking measurements from the moulded flaps, mark depth and length on a piece of post card or a 10 or 20 thou plastic card. Cut out the resulting rectangular strips and cement them along each side, on top of the original moulded flaps. Note that, though the M16 had slight cut-aways in the middle of these flaps, The M13 had plain straight flaps. Incidentally, if you are simply making the M16 straight from the kit, you'll find its appearance improved considerably if you cut new plastic card side flaps and cement them over the moulded flaps.)

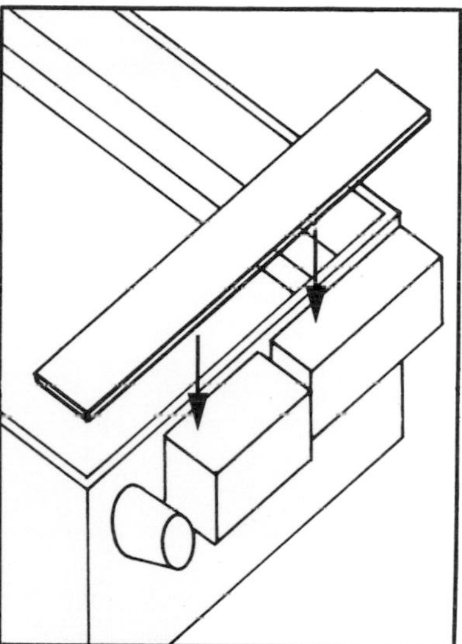

3 You can use the rear flap, which is a separate piece in the kit, as supplied, but as it is over scale thickness I suggest you use it as a template to make a new flap from card or plastic card to match the side flaps. On some M13s the rear flap was straight edged, but in later vehicles there was a cut-away in the middle, as on the kit piece. This rear flap folded horizontally on to the top of the rear lockers.

SHIPS

If you want to make the most impressive ship models of all, the wood kits produced by European specialist firms such as Billing and Graupner are for you. They are not suitable for beginners, however, and their many parts, all cut and machined in wood, have to be finished by the maker. Some of these kits are built up rather like a real ship with frames and planking, others follow the 'sandwich' principle, deck upon deck. The finished models are imposing; many of them can be motorized and are suitable for pond running with or without radio control. Among the subjects offered are tugs, fishing boats, yachts and lifeboats. The prices of these models tend to be high in comparison with plastic kits, simply because production runs are lower, the material is best quality wood, and much hand packing and preparation is involved.

The plastic ship kits are in a different class altogether. They come in widely contrasting categories and appeal to all interests.

First, there is the modern warship. Most of those date from World War Two or subsequent periods; very few models from World War One or the pre-Dreadnought age of steel ships are available.

In general plastic warship kit manufacturers have not adopted common scales, so there is a great diversity of sizes among the different ranges. The biggest selection to date is in 1:700 scale (about 1 inch to 60 feet). The 'Waterline Series', produced by a consortium of Japanese firms, is probably the biggest single series of all constant scale warship models. Their first range covered most of the Imperial Japanese Navy of World War Two. It set new standards of fine moulding and engraving. Almost all the models had a metal weight which could be built into the hull; the boot-topping was a separate moulding, so avoiding the need to paint this tricky area, and provision

Some of the most challenging ship kits to build are working models, whether motorized or fully rigged vessels.
Opposite top a scratch-built wood Thames sailing barge afloat.
Opposite bottom detail view of a large scale working model of HMS *Hood*
Right 1:32 scale model of a harbour tug made from wood, using model farmyard figures as crewmen.
Above the *Lesro-Sportsman*, a power boat made from a wood kit. It can be motorized by any suitable system, such as an electric or small petrol motor. Access to the engines is available by removing the cabin top.

was made in the designs for all ships in a given class to be made.

Because these kits are moulded with great precision in a shade of grey accurately matched with Japanese colours, you can go against the general rule and not paint them overall, unless you want to change to a camouflage scheme. Details such as top masts and cable decks should be painted; then pennant numbers can be added and the entire model is painted with clear matt varnish.

After they completed the Japanese warship series, the 'Waterline' consortium moved on to British, US and German ships of World War Two with equal success. Since then the British company Matchbox has introduced 1:700 scale waterline models which match the Japanese kits, while Revell has long had a small 1:720 scale series (virtually the same scale in this small size). The collector who wants a large but compact display of model warships could do worse than opt for these.

Many other plastic warship kits are available in larger scales – 1:600, 1:500, 1:400, 1:300 and 1:250. For very precise detail and fine moulding quality the 1:400 scale models produced by Heller, the French company, are worth considering. Nearly all their warship models are French, but some German World War Two vessels are included.

All the models, except those in the 'Waterline' series, are full hull.

Cutting models down to waterline level.

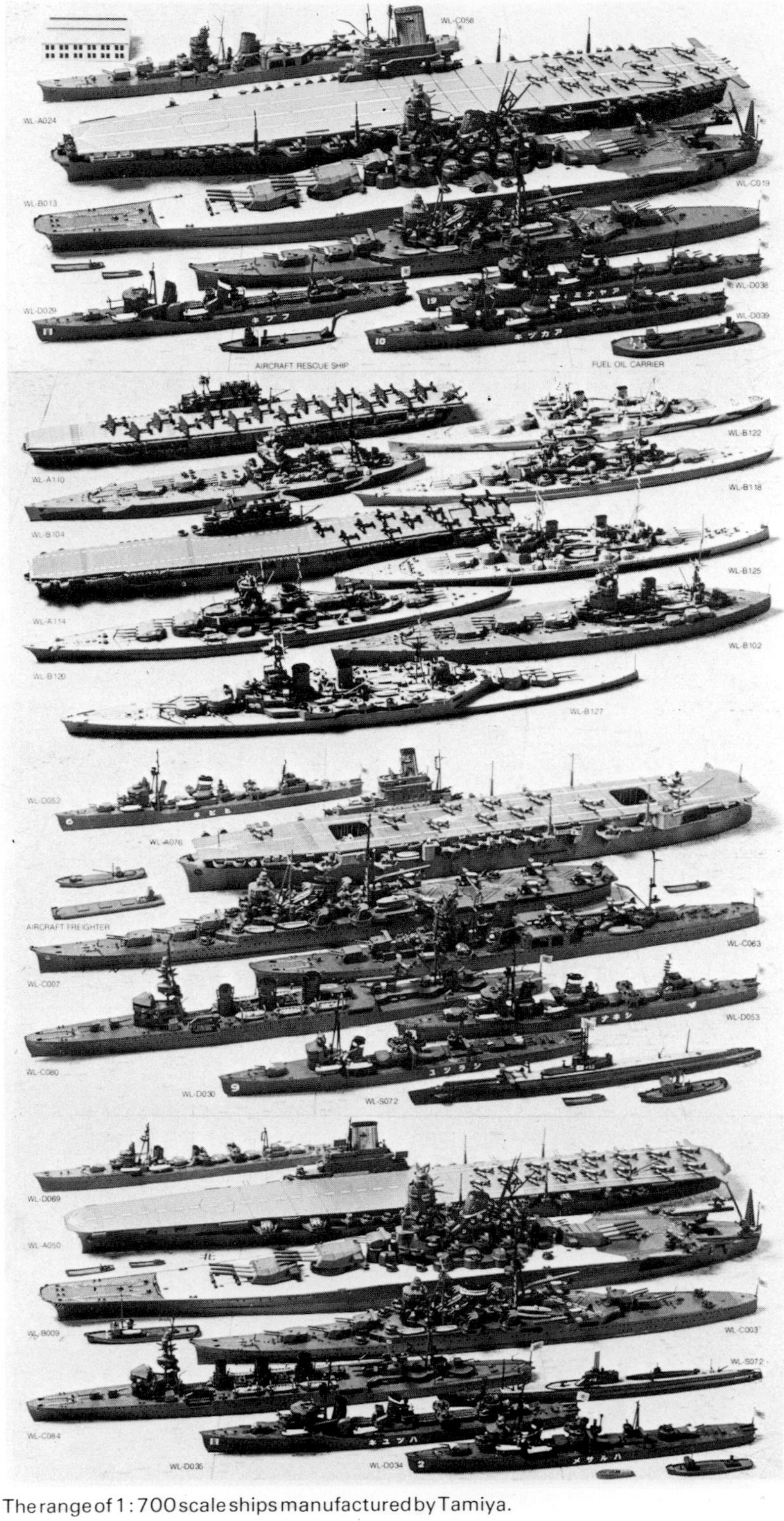

The range of 1:700 scale ships manufactured by Tamiya.

This offers you the extra challenge, if you want to take it up, of cutting models down to waterline level. This can be tricky but, using strips of masking tape as a guide, a neat cutting job can be done with a razor saw. Some recent kits have a 'blind' score line moulded at waterline level on the inside of the hull moulding to facilitate the cutting.

The key to success with model warships in these small scales is knowing what detail to leave out, for items such as guardrails or small AA guns can look very crude if incorporated in an overscale fashion. Some kits can be improved by removing crudely moulded guardrails, bulwarks or other detail. One reason why the 1:700 scale 'Waterline' models look good is that the designers wisely omit items such as guardrails which they cannot possibly mould finely enough.

Warship kit models lend themselves to almost endless and fascinating conversion projects for the simple reason that the armaments and fittings (and very often the superstructures) of the full-size originals were constantly altered. There are many differences of detail and appearance in large classes of warship, not to mention camouflage schemes in wartime and changes made at different periods of the ships' careers. A kit for a four-stacker US destroyer of World War Two as made by Revell (1:250 scale) and Airfix (1:600 scale) could be converted in a hundred or more different ways representing a wide selection of the many ships of the standard four-stacker type.

Most of the conversion work can be done with plastic card, Microstrip, Microrod or heat-stretched sprue. You must rely on your own research for the details.

Another interesting field is the miniature 'table top' scale of 1:1200 (1 inch to 100 feet); here a small selection of plastic kits of waterline type is available, backed up by a huge selection of cast metal models made by some smaller manufacturers. In Europe manufacturers prefer the very similar 1:1250 scale. Because these models are so small, conversions are simpler (there is less small detail to incorporate), and it therefore becomes possible to take a kit such as the Airfix 'County' class three-funnel cruiser of World War Two and convert it quite simply to about twenty different sister ships – in fact to the whole class if you like.

As well as these popular warship ranges, many miscellaneous modern vessels such as tugs, trawlers, freighters and ocean liners are on sale in a wide range of different scales. They are suitable for use in harbour scenes with model railways or for 'amphibious operation' dioramas with model tanks. Often they lend themselves to much extra detailing. For example, the well-known Revell Harbour Tug (a replica of a standard US wartime type) is greatly enhanced by adding crew figures from OO/HO figure sets.

1:72 scale model of an early type German E boat comes with every possible detail.

Tugboat by Revell, enhanced by the addition of crewmen.

Sailing ships

Sailing ship kits are virtually a specialism in themselves. Manufacturers such as Revell, Airfix and Heller make beautiful plastic kits of exquisite quality. Some recent ones are so highly detailed that there is not much left for the builder to do other than assemble and paint them carefully. Many, however, can be enhanced by adding detail such as blocks and a convincing amount of running and standing rigging in place of the simplified rigging invariably suggested by the manufacturer. This is all quite straightforward if intricate work, but it demands immense research on the part of the builder. In the case of very famous ships (the *Cutty Sark* and *Victory* for instance), complete books are available both on modelling and on all other aspects of the vessel. A beginner would do well to choose one of these well-known ships simply because the information is so much easier to come by. And, obviously the experience gained in making a well-known clipper ship such as the *Cutty Sark* will be valuable when it comes to the next model.

Above a fine brigantine model which lends itself to extra detailing.
Left the *Cutty Sark*, one of the largest and most elaborate plastic sailing ship kits.

Motorized and sailing conversions

One final branch of plastic ship models offers a good deal of fun – the motorized ship kit: 'instant' packages are available which include a motor, a model of between 1:400 and 1:200 scale and all the necessary parts; these can actually be floated on a pond and will run realistically through the water. Such kits cost rather more than non-motorized kits, of course, but they make an interesting project. If you are not skilled enough to build a motorized ship model from scratch, this sort of kit is the next best thing.

Much the same goes for the idea of sailing conversions (for calm weather only!) of plastic sailing ship kits. The simpler sail plans and hull forms are best – a Viking ship, the *Santa Maria* and so on. All you need to do is glue, a plastic card keel beneath the hull, make the yards pivot with hooks and wire loops, and replace the sails with new sails cut from fine cloth or old handkerchiefs.

Right motorized version of HMS *Discovery* using a cheap electric motor and batteries. A section of deck is removable to give access to the motor.

Above and left the *Royal Sovereign* converted to a sailing model. Plastic sails were replaced with fine cloth cut to the same pattern; the rigging was arranged to furl and hoist the sails, and a false keel of tinplate brought stability.

CARS, TRUCKS AND MOTORCYCLES

Anyone who wants to build up an impressive collection with the minimum of problems will find plastic kits of road transport subjects offer rich possibilities. In the most common scales, 1:48 or bigger, plastic moulding is just right for depicting delicate looking parts to precise scale thicknesses, so that a well-made top-quality model in, say, 1:24 scale can have a real museum 'look' about it. And even a bare chassis and engine will stand as an interesting model in its own right even before you add the body shell.

The majority of road transport kits available today have plated parts to depict the bright areas of a real car – grille, bumpers, door handles and so on. These are sometimes too bright on a model, but a careful coating of clear varnish will tone them down nicely. As plated plastic will not glue at all to other plastic, you will have to scrape or sand the plating carefully away from any surfaces which have to be cemented. Alternatively, use a Uhu type 'universal' cement or Five Minute Epoxy for the joins; in this case the plating need not be removed.

In very many kits the parts are moulded in their basic colours. For example, seats and interior may be black, bodywork in a conventional bright colour and brightwork plated. The same applies to motor-cycles. This is one reason why modelling cars or motor-cycles can attract anyone who doesn't like painting or is not too skilled at it.

Unless you are planning any conversion work, follow the sequence given in the instruction sheets when assembling model cars, trucks or motor-cycles. Paint small details as you go along, or in advance of assembly: this is very important and can make or mar a road model. Even if the complete interior of a model car is moulded in a realistic matt black, there is still a little painting to do – the dashboard dial lettering must be picked out in white and various switches and warning lights, the gear shift knob and many other

Above 1:24 scale Datsun 240Z with the body shell removed.
Below the same model complete.

small details, none of them difficult, must all be attended to. Just look inside a real car of similar type and note the subtle colourings if you think I'm exaggerating. The white sidewalls of tyres may need to be painted in too. Always check moulded tyres, for there is often a slight ridge of flash around the centre line of the circumference. You can easily remove this by sanding gently with emery paper before you fit tyres to the hubs. There are many books on cars and it is generally quite easy to do background research on the model you are making.

Modern plastic kits are so good that there is surprisingly little you need to do to improve them. Study the model carefully as you go along, for even the kit which the manufacturer claims is 'fully detailed' may prove to have missing parts. For example some motor cycle kits look good and well detailed, but a moment's study of the finished model will reveal the complete absence of brake cables: the moulded brake handles are there but nothing leads from them. Black plastic covered bell wire solves the problem in a moment; Just cut it to length, curve it and glue it in place. The fuel lines and wiring of the engine are commonly missing, even from the most complex kits; the model's appearance will be greatly improved if you add them yourself. Similarly, you can greatly enhance a car's interior by covering the plastic moulded upholstery with textured wall covering material (such as Fablon) of an appropriate colour.

Because of the very large and ever growing choice of car, truck and motor cycle kits available, specialized collections become vital, both for financial and space reasons. Depending on your interest you might, for example, collect racing cars, GT cars or production cars or trucks, perhaps

Left highly detailed and realistic 1:6 Honda CB70 police motorcycle.
Below 1:12 Tyrrell-Ford. The possibilities of detailing are great.

Converting a Model T Ford

If the idea of converting a plastic kit is new to you, model car converting is quite an easy way to start. Veteran cars were often converted in real life into light commercial vehicles by alteration of the original bodywork to provide space for a pick-up platform or covered panel van. The Ford Model T was widely converted in this way, but so were most other popular types. Our conversion here is typical of many possibilities.

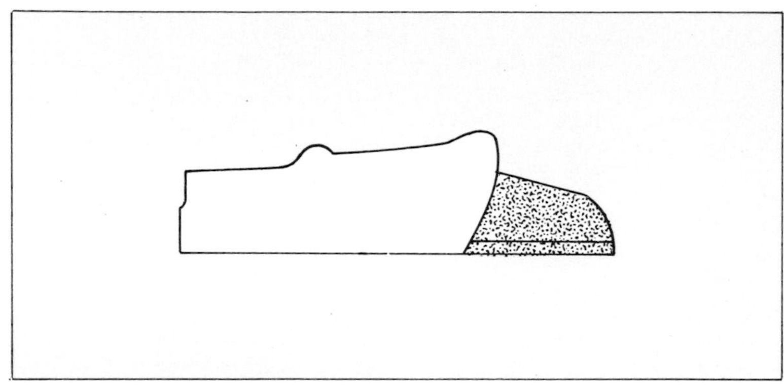

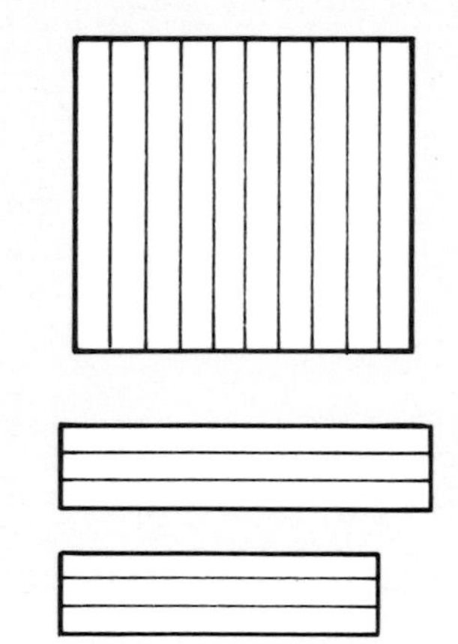

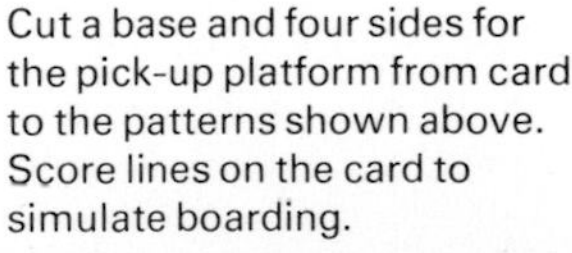

Cut a base and four sides for the pick-up platform from card to the patterns shown above. Score lines on the card to simulate boarding.

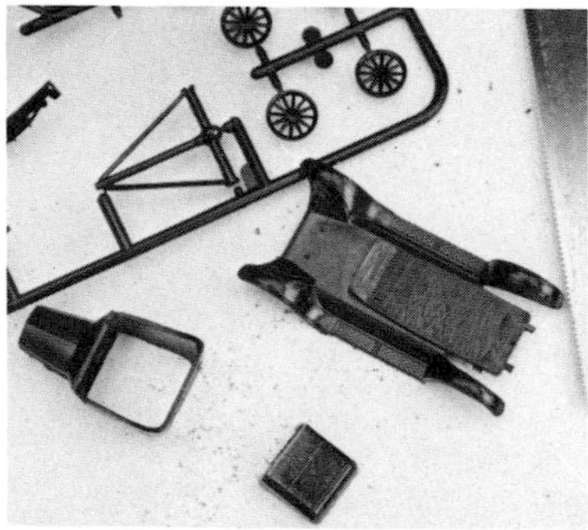

Above remove the back section of the bodywork with a razor saw as indicated.
Left the back section removed.

Above the pick-up platform ready to be glued in position on two $\frac{1}{8}$ inch square bearers.
Left the completed conversion.

Six conversions all built from a standard Airfix B type bus in 1:32 scale.

motor cycles or public service vehicles – the choice is enormous. The top of the price range has very elaborate and costly kits for large scale cars and motor cycles so complex that you will only have time to build two or three a year. At the other end of the range are the very cheap but good vintage car kits, in 1:32 scale. The moulding on these will be one colour, so they may need more painting and work than the more expensive kits.

Though some kits need extensive painting, it is often possible to eliminate paint work almost completely from model vehicles. The colour and finish of most kit body shells is so good that it seems a pity to cover them with paint (and brushmarks). Polishing the unpainted moulding can be more effective and rather simpler than painting. For a very smooth finish, use a piece of Duraglit or similar pad; this will buff up the plastic beautifully to give what looks like a proper enamelled metal finish.

'Custom cars' – heavily modified vehicles for show and/or competition purposes – were a craze which started in the USA and then spread elsewhere. A typical example is a modified Ford Model T fitted with a modern Chevy V-8 engine and new modern wheels and tyres. Numerous 'custom car' kits offering many assembly variations are now available. In addition existing 'stock' car models can be customized.

Conversions of car and truck kits are not as common as in other categories of model, but there is scope for commercial vehicle conversions since there are so many body variations and styles in real life. Pick-up bodies, panel van bodies and so on can be fitted to basic car chassis to give interesting new versions of the basic vehicle. Other favourites are competition versions of 'stock' cars; for example, rally cars with wide tyres and extended wheel covers are quite simple if you use a little imagination.

At the extreme end of the vehicle model scale is the ultra-small HO size. An extensive range of high-quality plastic scale miniatures is made by Viking, and other firms in Spain, the USA and Austria also produce models in this scale. There are also some plastic assembly kits in this small size. Though supplied ready assembled, the Viking models (which are excellent) still have scope for a little improvement, such as painting the tyres and some lights. A collection of these excellent small scale vehicles takes up very little room and the models are so good that they almost certainly are an investment.

Construction steps of a Datsun pick-up truck

Generally speaking, model cars and trucks built from plastic kits are straightforward exercises in careful assembly. Here is a 1:25 scale Datsun pick-up truck under construction to show the typical work involved.

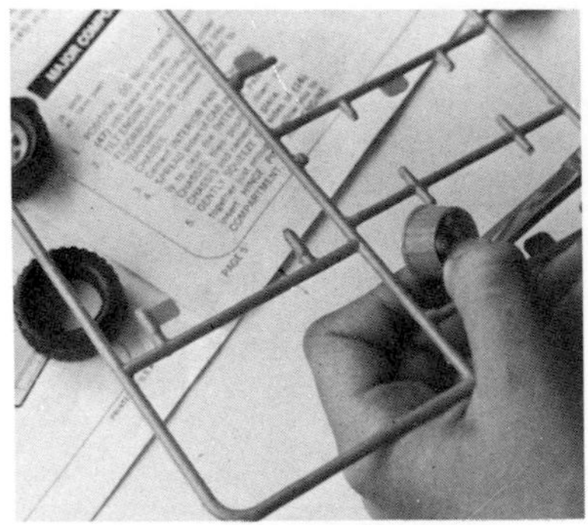

1 Detach parts with small scissors.

2 Test the fit of parts before cementing.

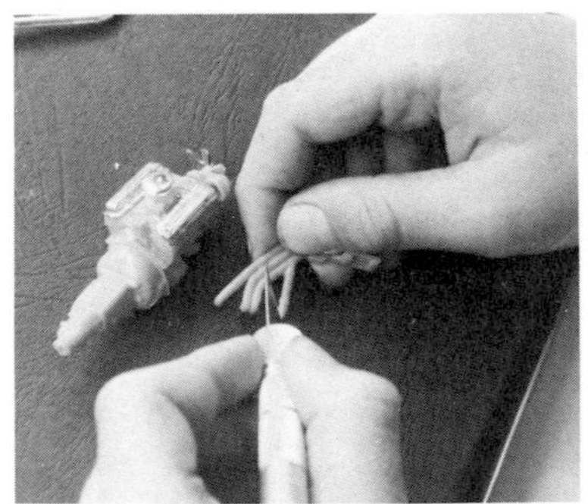

3 Clean off flash and moulding marks.

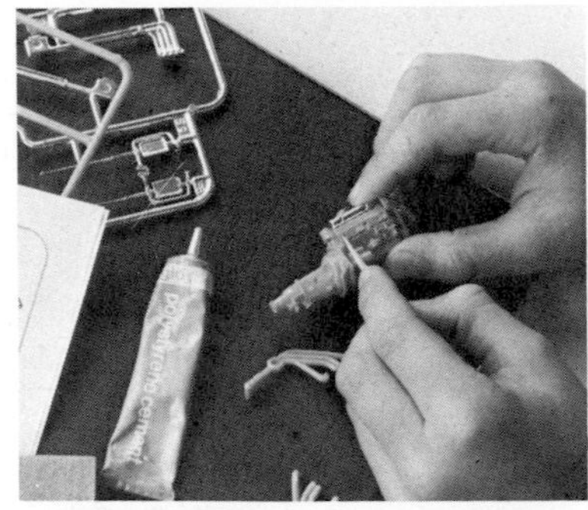

4 Use a small stick to cement small parts.

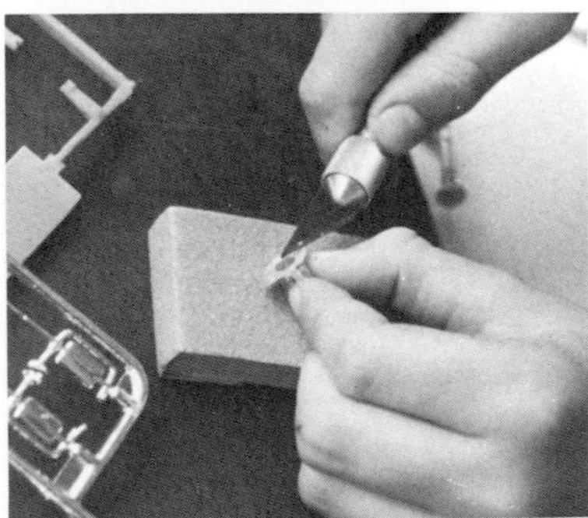

5 Sand plated parts before cementing.

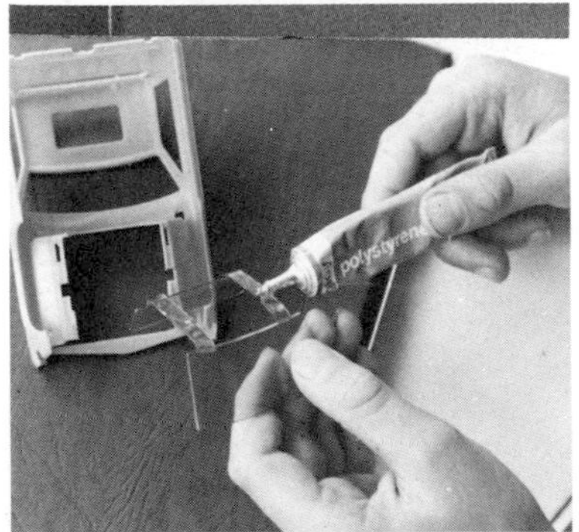

6 Avoid cement on windshield.

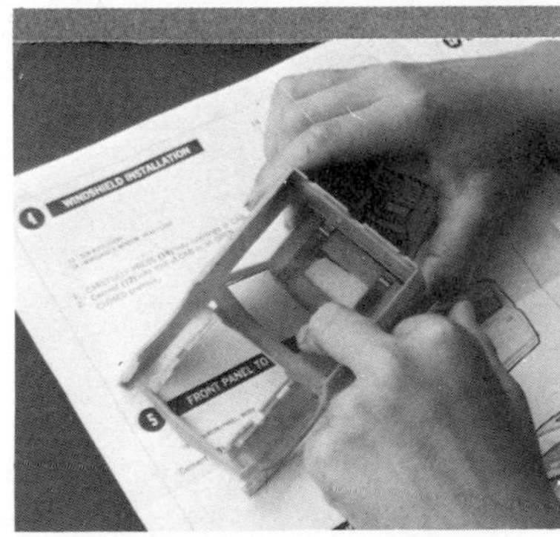

7 Positioning windshield in cab.

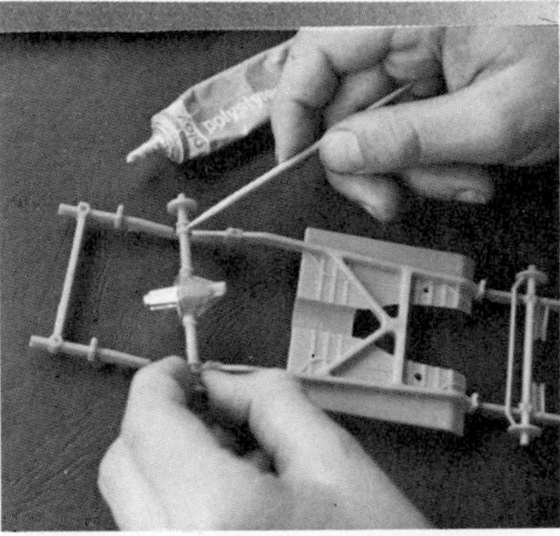

8 Back axle being cemented to chassis.

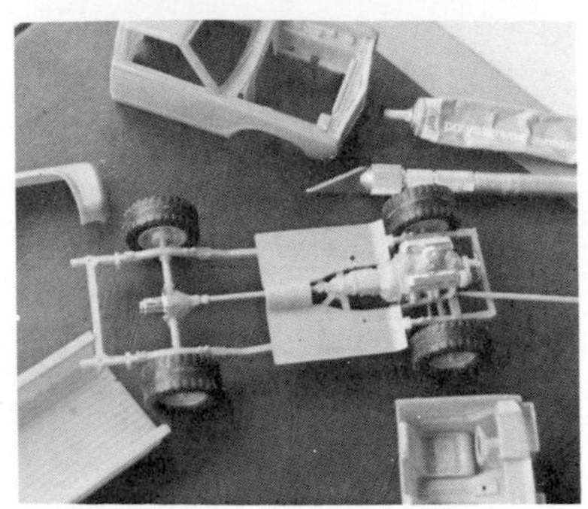

9 Completed chassis ready for body.

10 Painting cab interior before fixing.

11 Painting engine parts.

12 Parts ready for final assembly.

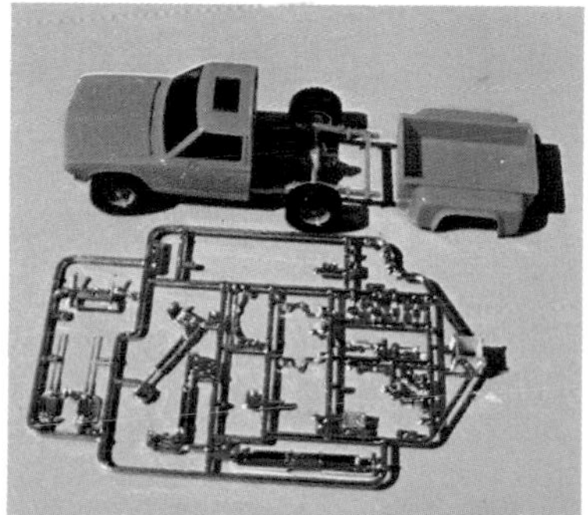

13 Plated customizing options.

14 Wear and weathering being added.

METAL MODELS

With the exception of some miniature handgun and artillery replicas, most modern die-cast models are of cars or trucks. The emphasis is generally much more on kit-built and ready-made models than on hand-made models. Though a few car kits were available before the days of plastic kits, it is only comparatively recently that the car construction kit has become commonplace. Model cars have since before World War Two been dominated by die-cast scale model cars. Famous names in the toy world such as Dinky Toys (Great Britain), Tootsietoys (USA) and Marklin (Germany), plus other fairly big concerns, were all making die-cast model cars in the 1930s and were probably instrumental in starting off what soon became a model car collecting 'craze'. Replicas of contemporary cars and trucks were turned out almost monthly at little more than pocket

Above pre-Second World War Schuco Studio model racing car.
Below modern 1:43 Dinky Toys British Striker anti-tank vehicle with firing missiles.
Opposite boxed set of model aircraft made by Dinky Toys between 1936 and 1939.

DINKY TOYS
Manufactured by
MECCANO LTD
LIVERPOOL
No. 60

DINKY TOYS No. 60.
200 VARIETIES
Manufactu[...] England by
MECCANO [...]., LIVERPOOL
200 VARIETIES
IMPERIAL
AIRWAYS
LOW WING MONOPLANE
D.H. "LEOPARD MOTH"
"GENERAL" MONOSPAR
CIERVA "AUTOGIRO"
PERCIVAL "GULL"

1910 lithographed London bus, complete with the original plaster driver, conductor and passengers.

money prices. They were aimed, of course, at the juvenile market and were primarily thought of as toys; none the less they were also virtual scale models of the real thing and were instrumental (along with the toy soldiers and toy trains of the time) in spanning the gap between playthings and scale models.

Since World War Two, the die-cast model car has gone from strength to strength, and almost every country in the world now seems to have at least one manufacturer. Names such as Matchbox, Solido, Schuco, Corgi and Politoys are almost household words. The favourite size is 1:43 scale (or thereabouts); some makers go for smaller sizes and others for bigger models such as 1:24 or 1:32. While aimed at children and produced literally in millions, these die-cast model cars are also collected by a growing adult fraternity of enthusiasts, and old out-of-production models are much sought after and like stamps sometimes change hands at high prices. Models are restored (if second-hand), converted, detailed and improved, though some enthusiasts prefer to keep them in original condition. Recently, some more expensive finely detailed die-cast model cars have been produced in more limited runs for the collectors' market. An allied field is collecting old tinplate 'toy' cars, though these are scarce now. Recently assembly kits and models made entirely in plastic have been released in 1:43, notably in France and Italy.

Occasionally, Dinky and a few other manufacturers release some of their models as sets of castings for home assembly. This is a simple screw-together or plug job, but you can spend time giving a superior finish to the model. The tools required are no more than a screwdriver and a file.

Soft cast metal models

Despite the dominance of the plastic kit, there is still a place for metal kits; indeed, this material continues to flourish, perhaps more than ever before. Because the big plastic kit manufacturers have to sell kits by the million they tend to play safe and make the most popular model subjects. So, if you want something more exotic, the chances are that you will turn to cast metal kit manufacturers. Subjects produced in cast metal include small scale AFVs, model soldiers, and ships, and a few model aircraft; however, road or racing vehicles and locomotives and rolling stock predominate.

It was locomotives and rolling stock that set off the present growth of the metal market. Railway modellers wanted a good selection of locomotives; one way of satisfying the small market was to produce bodies which would replace the mass manufactured plastic bodies on existing chassis. Soon, firms such as Wells and Ks were producing small runs of cast kits of the popular locomotive types. The cast metal (or white metal) used is an alloy of lead and antimony. The metal can be made softer or harder by varying the proportions. The casting is done in rubber centrifugal moulds; both the hand-made masters and the rubber moulds are very much cheaper than the steel moulds used in injection moulding, so very small manufacturers with limited capital can get started. Hence the very rich variety of metal railway kits, which now include not only 'body line' locomotives but complete kits with mechanisms and wheels, rolling stock and hundreds of station and scenic items.

Rare and exotic model cars also started on the same principle in the 1960s; now an extensive selection of road vehicles is available as cast kits. Most cast kits are simpler than

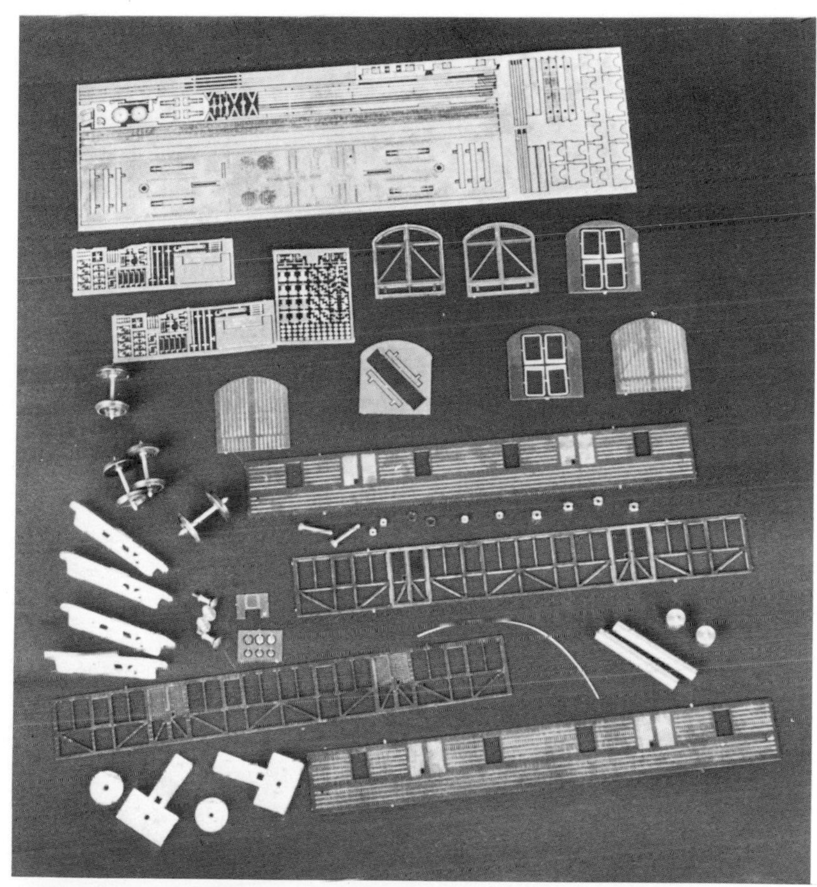

Right a 00 scale railway carriage in metal, shown unassembled (top). Note fine texture and detail in close-up view (bottom).

their plastic kit equivalents and have fewer parts (though some large scale motor-cycle kits are more complex in metal). Nearly all car kits are 1:43 scale, the popular collecting scale, but buses and trucks tend to be 1:76 scale. Only a few kits are to larger or smaller scales.

Ships, in both kit and ready-made form, are the other big category of cast kits. Most are in the popular 1:1200 scale (in which only a few plastic kits are produced); some even smaller scales for wargamers, such as 1:3000. are becoming popular. Fleetline is one of the top names in this field, but German firms such as Navis and Viking also produce hand-painted models for collectors which come ready assembled.

Another recent growth area is rail and scenic accessories. Signals, station equipment, bicycles, canal barges, lock gates and horse-drawn carts are among an ever growing selection of useful little models available.

As there are generally fewer

Right and below assembly of a 17th century cannon from a kit; the parts are shown laid out, being cleaned up with a file and assembled with 'Five Minute Epoxy' cement.

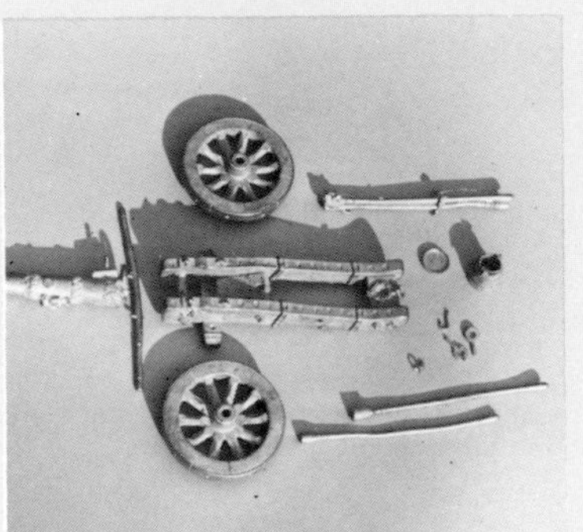

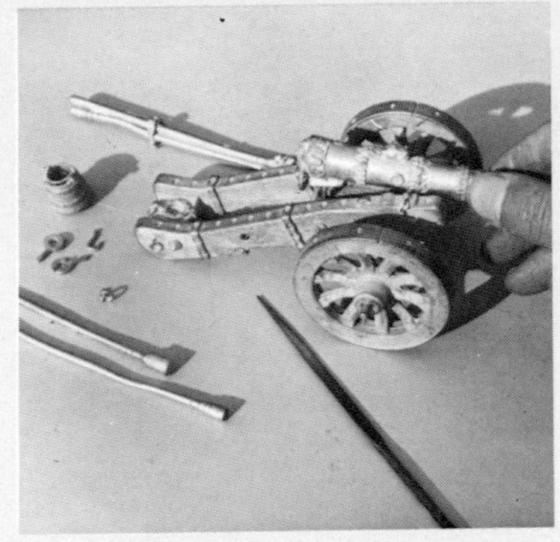

1:76 Daimler Scout car made from a cast metal kit.

parts, cast metal kits are usually quite simple to assemble. Great care must be taken none the less, for it is easy enough for the soft metal to be distorted, and even easier for parts to be assembled out of square.

Low-melting-point solder, which allows metal kit parts to be assembled and joined by soldering, is now available. Remember that cast metal cannot be soldered at normal soldering temperatures, or with normal solder, for the heat will just melt the metal. If you want to play really safe use a universal adhesive such as Uhu or Five Minute Epoxy. Cast metal is of course very much easier to file, so there is no problem when it comes to the important task of cleaning up mould lines or flash. Similarly, it can be drilled easily, so 'super-detailing', (additional handrails for instance) can be undertaken. The metal is soft enough for a fine drill, even a hand-held one.

Getting the assembly square is most important. Great care is essential because the locating lugs are generally cruder than those in plastic kits. Use a set square and work on a perfectly flat level surface, leaving everything to set hard before proceeding to the major stages of assembly.

Item for item, cast metal kits are very much more expensive than their plastic kit equivalents, but they have 'heft' and character and greater investment value. Many collectors in the car and ship hobby actually prefer metal models to plastic.

$2\frac{1}{2}$ inch gauge live steam coal-fired locomotive, the *Lady Iris*; this model is sadly no longer available.

METAL FIGURES

The origins of scale metal figures, still so popular today despite the dominance of the super detail plastic kit figures, were in the tin soldier of the nineteenth century. Initially sold as a toy, it soon became a serious hobby after being taken up by modellers and adults – as well as children. Foremost in promoting model soldiers as a hobby was the British Model Soldier Society and, by the 1920s and the 1930s, enthusiasts in several countries had begun to meet. At that time, they were a small select band, but out of their interest arose a new sort of model soldier – the true scale replica, cast in lead or a lead alloy and much more detailed and finely finished than the 'toy' type. Produced in small runs (unlike toy soldiers, which were cast in millions), these soon achieved their own rarity value.

The lead scale replica soldier is still produced by many specialists, of whom the most famous include Stadden, Erickson, Rose, Series 77, Hinchliffe, Lasset, Old Guard and Phoenix. Some figures are produced in runs of as little as a hundred, and there is a great variety in poses and animation. The only way to keep track of this highly specialist and constantly changing output is to read the hobby magazine advertisements. You can expect to pay a good deal of money, even for a single unpainted figure.

For the 'antique' collector, there is the charm and nostalgia of the toy figures of yesterday. The old toy soldier now fetches, at showroom sales, prices which quite frequently run to three or even four figures. Their popularity has increased as the range has gradually disappeared. Indeed, their manufacturers – including Britain's (the major producer) and Johilco in the UK, and Heyde in Germany – would have been amazed had they been able to foresee the value their metal 'toy' soldiers have now acquired. That value is evidence enough that we should not neglect metal scale modelling in an era now dominated by the super-detailed plastic kits.

Left battle scene made in the mid-19th century by Heinrichsen and Hilpert of Nuremberg.
Below display box of Roman soldiers, with two tents in the corners, made in about 1890 by Heyde of Dresden.
Opposite top American military band made during the 1930s by William Britain and Co. of London, mainly for export to the USA.
Opposite bottom early 20th-century set of 9th Royal Lancers with their original box, made by William Britain.

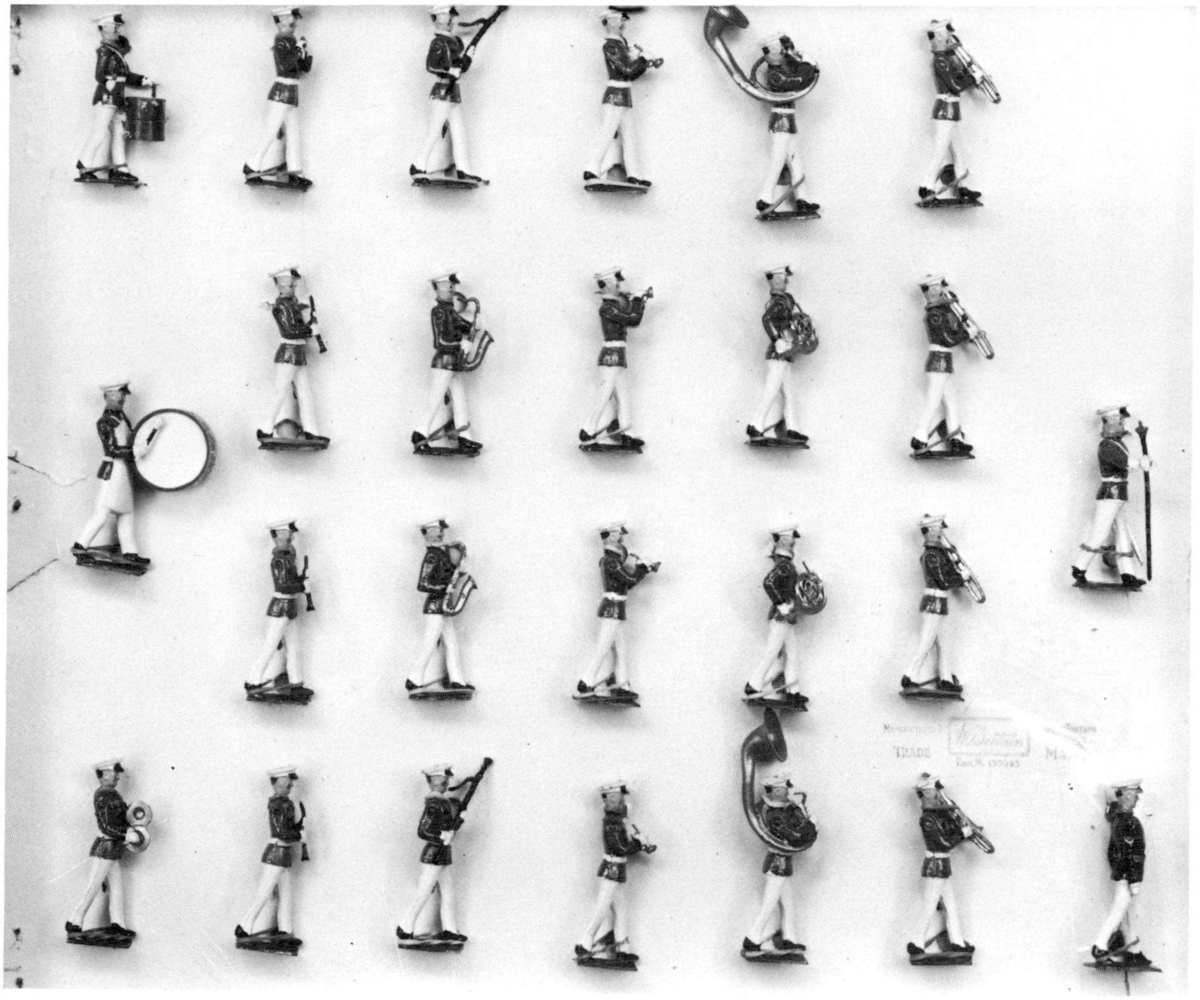

BRITISH SOLDIERS.
Copyright Models by
William Britain, Jun.
"PENINSULA"
"SOBRAON."
"PUNNIAR."
"PUNJAUB"
"CHILLIANWALLAH"
"GOOJERAT"
"DELHI"
"Lucknow."
"Charasiah."
"KABUL 1879."
"KANDAHAR 1880"
"AFGHANISTAN 1878-80"
9th

In the last few years a number of firms, have been producing 'new' toy soldiers. These are not direct replicas of any previous figures, though some are remarkably similar and might at first glance be taken as 1900 period models. Naturally the regiments and uniforms are the same in any case, but the most inventive manufacturers have come up with figures and poses never before attempted.

Certainly the best of the bunch is the new 'Soldiers' range made by Soldiers. These are to 54 mm scale and match Britain's exactly in style and proportions.

Soldiers have carried the original Britain's idea of many variations on one figure to its ultimate point. Add in the options of great coat and gaiters, NCOs with either swagger stick or notebook and the possibilities for the collector or diorama maker are almost limitless.

German troops from a 1:24 series. The bodies are cast metal, and the accessories and display plinths plastic.

1:24 scale RAF pilot, produced to accompany model aircraft.

British officers of 1890, with contemporary mess furniture. These models are typical of the high standard of realism achieved by recent releases.

Figure scales

The most common scale is 54 mm, which is equivalent to about 1:32 or 1:30 scale in proportional terms. The measurement refers to a figure's height (naturally, there is some variation, since real people are not the same height!); 54 mm is the common 'toy soldier' size too. A slightly bigger size is available at 77 mm and 90 mm; smaller sizes are 40 mm (quite rare), 35 mm, 30 mm, 25 mm and 20 mm. Prices change roughly in proportion to size. In the smaller scales, 20 mm and 25 mm, both plastic (Airfix) and metal cast figures are on sale; the price per figure is minute. Smaller scale figures are quite challenging to paint and detail; they tend to be preferred by those who wish to make dioramas – scenic set-ups depicting a battle and including many figures – and by wargamers.

Don't think that 54 mm scale (or the larger 77 mm and 90 mm scales) are the end of the matter, however. The scales smaller than 54 mm are often referred to as 'wargaming' scales: wargaming is a specialized aspect of the model soldier hobby and is outside the scope of this book; pieces are usually purchased, painted and deployed *en masse*. Most of the very small scale soldiers available – 20 mm (HO), 25 mm (OO), 30 mm, 35 mm and 40 mm (O) – are sculpted or moulded with a degree of detail equal to the best of 54 mm.

Above military models made to a variety of scales.
Below the same figure as it appears in the commonest scales used for figures.

Those, however, who want the very best, certainly in investment terms, should turn to the products of the connoisseur or 'collector quality' manufacturers including Hinchliffe, Rose, Stadden, Old Guard, Lasset, Greenwood and Bull, Hinton Hunt and many others. They are noted for precise anatomical accuracy as well as for historical precision in uniform and equipment details. The majority of these figures come ready assembled and animated; generally they are cast in a 'spreadeagle' position and then animated by the manufacturer. This means that no two figures are quite the same. Often the manufacturer will animate to order: if you want a man marching with slung rifle, you can have him. Runs are low and sometimes models are replaced in ranges, so you can end up with some unique pieces. Some firms, among them Hinchliffe and Rose, produce their figures in simple kit form, often with no more than four pieces. They are simple to glue together after the castings have been cleaned up, and there is a slight chance of conversion work in the process. Hinchliffe and Rose are among the firms who sell parts such as heads and weapons separately, a most valuable service for the conversion enthusiast. They also make accessories such as guns and carts in cast metal to go with the soldiers. These make fine showpieces in their own right and are in fact in some ways easier to make than the soldiers, since painting an artillery piece is rather easier than painting a soldier!

Above and above right a British grenadier dating from 1810, as purchased and as converted into a private of the 55th Regiment of foot.
Far right top a ballerina figure as purchased.
Far right bottom the same figure reshaped to a different position.
Right metal figures are usually cast in the 'splayed' position and then animated as desired.

Home casting

A recent 'toy soldier' development is in Germany, where 'tin figures' (*Zinnfiguren*) have returned in some force. Several companies are making sets and moulds for home casting figures in the traditional German toy soldier style, and very charming they are too. The big German toy firm of Schildkrot is a major manufacturer; their range is sold under the name Zinnbrigade (tin brigade). Their casting set consists of crucible, tin ingots, mould, solid fuel pellets, paints, etc ; the hard rubber moulds can be bought separately.

The Zinnbrigade range is 40 mm in size (known as the Nuremburg Scale) and concentrates on the Imperial German Army of 1900–14, with Prussian and Bavarian infantry and cavalry. Officers and men and bandsmen are included in both parade and field day orders. Instructions for painting in full colour are given with each mould.

The German armies of Frederick the Great, Waterloo and the Franco-Prussian War, plus American Civil War figures, are all included in the extensive list of moulds from Scad; artillery pieces, half-round figures of great delicacy and charm, are also featured. Prinz August by Kittler is another nice range which includes eighteenth-century artillery as well as cowboys, indians and animals. They provide a spirit fired burner for the crucible. Nurnberger Meisterzinn are in 50 mm size, half-round, and cover the army of Frederick the Great, with grenadiers, musketeers and cavalry.

If you want to economize you need only buy the moulds, so long as you have a suitable source of tin alloy and a crucible (or old saucepan) and a heat source (or a cooking ring and the necessary domestic approval to use it!).

These interesting 'toy' category figures of various types offer a hobby of their own which has great charm as well as a lot of historic interest.

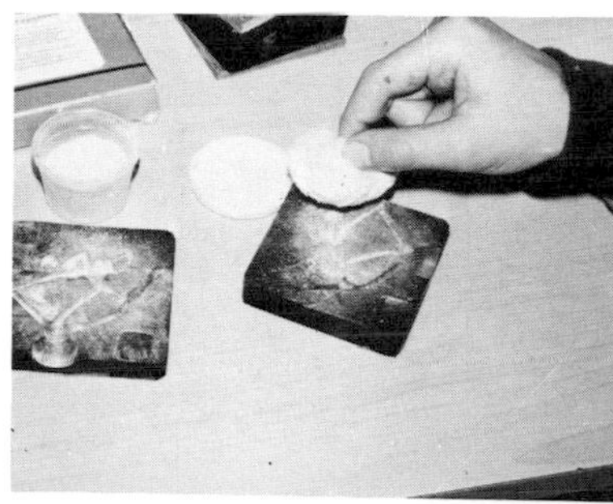

1 The rubber mould comes in two halves with protective board covers. Separate the two halves and dust talcum powder into the recesses of the mould.

2 The metal ingots are melted over a heat source in the ladle provided. Many sets provide a spirit heater, but a domestic gas cooker is more effective. The mould halves are clamped together and the molten metal poured smoothly in. Note the use of gloves to hold the mould.

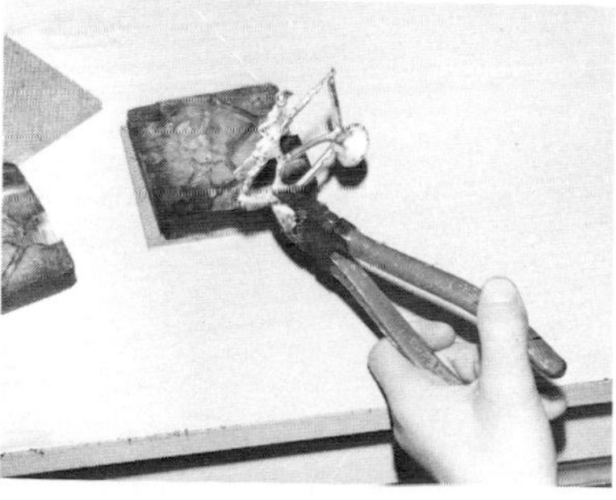

3 Leave the mould to stand for ten to fifteen seconds, then separate the halves and gently lift out the figure with pliers. If there are any imperfections, melt the figure down and try again.

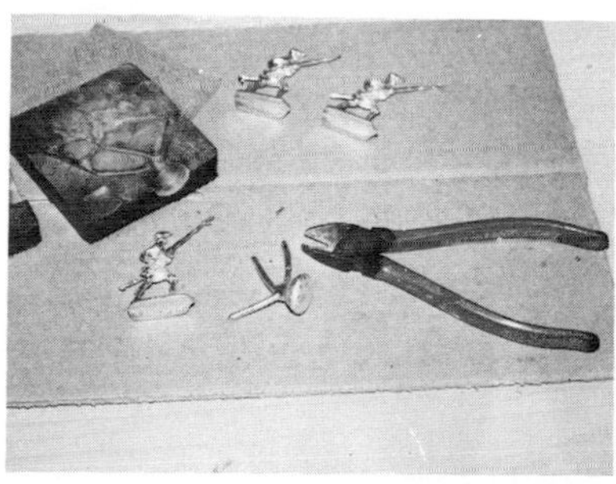

4 Snip off the runners with pliers and return them to the ladle for re-melting.

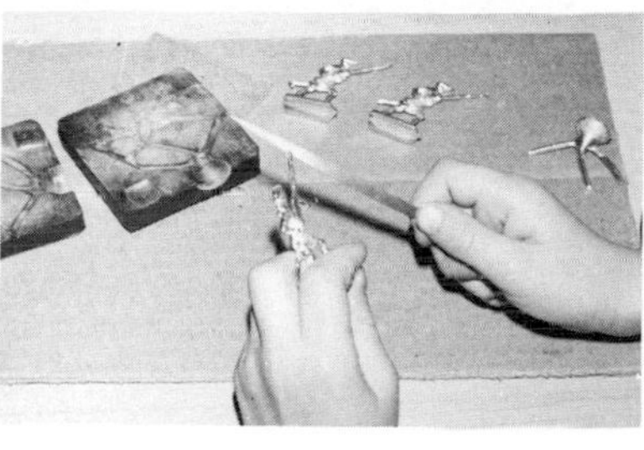

5 Clean up the figure with a file removing any flash and rough edges. The figure is now ready for painting.

PLASTIC FIGURES

While toy soldiers, toy guns and toy army vehicles have long been popular playthings for children, it is only in the last twenty years or so that military miniatures of all sorts have come to interest serious modelling enthusiasts on a large scale. Nowadays the output of new military kits and models matches, perhaps even outstrips, model aircraft kit production.

Military modelling actually covers a multitude of quite varied interests, and the appeal of this particular hobby probably lies partly in the fact that there is something for every degree of skill and preference. If you are a skilled painter you can turn out exquisitely finished model soldiers in colourful full dress; on the other hand, if you have good financial resources you can build up an impressive collection simply by purchasing finished figures of the highest standard, even if you are a complete duffer at model making and painting. The other part of the appeal of military modelling lies in its intrinsic historical interest; this in turn fires the imagination and inspires the modeller to build up an interesting collection. Most important of all, these days, is the fact that the cost of military modelling can be as varied as its scope.

Let us take a brief look at the different aspects of the hobby. This may help you to decide what might interest you most.

Cheapest of all are the modern 'toy' figures, usually made in polythene or PVC as one-piece mouldings by firms such as Britains and Airfix. You can buy an anatomically accurate Britains' 'Deetail' figure, alter it slightly, repaint it and end up with a collector's piece which can stand happily alongside expensive metal cast figures. Many modellers work almost exclusively in these cheap but accurate models, altering, converting and painting to very high standards. Their expenditure per figure is trifling.

Model figures sold as a plastic assembly kit are not much more expensive. Airfix again have a fine range, mainly in 54 mm scale but with a few kits in 1:12 scale. These kits cost the same as the smaller plastic model aircraft kits. Moulded in polystyrene, they can be assembled, worked and painted just like any other plastic kit and have almost unlimited potential for alteration and conversion. Further up the price range, but in similar style, come the French-made Historex models; these pioneered the plastic figure assembly kit in the late 1960s. The Historex range mostly centres on the very colourful Napoleonic era; the detailing of the parts is most exquisite. In many kits even the badges and buttons come as separate mouldings, sometimes smaller than a pinhead! The price per kit is a little less than that of the expensive metal cast figures. Complete gun teams and even a mobile forge are included in the vast Historex plastic kit range.

Selecting a scale is no great problem. The 54 mm scale is an excellent proposition for those who like kit assembly or conversion work, plus a fair degree of intricate painting. The choice of subjects is very wide, and virtually every period of military history is depicted. There are plenty of ready-made models which need only minor preparation and painting before they are ready for display, so the collector pure and simple is catered for as well as the practical model maker. Plastic models, many in kit form, are increasingly common in 54 mm scale. Plastic is an excellent modelling medium even for a relative newcomer and has really opened up the hobby to everyone; many model soldier constructors now work entirely in it. When kits and models of soldiers were only available in metal, conversion or assembly needed rather more technical skill.

Above and right figure of Anne Boleyn, in 1:12 and a conversion to a WRAF (Women's Royal Airforce).
Opposite page finely detailed 54mm French Hussar. This series sets high standards and has much fine detail.

OO/HO Scale

Airfix and Matchbox offer plastic sets in the OO/HO sizes at ridiculously low prices for the number of figures in the set. Because these figures are so small, very intricate painting can often be omitted; for instance, in 20 or 25 mm scales a Highlander's kilt will look acceptable painted dark green, whereas in 54 mm scale you have to paint in the tartan pattern as well. Effect in the small scales is rather more important than absolute precision. The smaller scale figures lend themselves to realistic diorama work, a gun and its crew in action, an infantry company forming square, a regimental headquarters and so on. A base of wood only 6 inches square is quite a big area for OO/HO size figures; for the scenic work all the usual model railway scenic aids and techniques are used. Some collectors have carried out quite spectacular work: for instance a large diorama depicting the epic defence of Rorke's Drift by the 24th Foot, with hundreds of miniature Zulu figures attacking the gallant British infantry company in an accurate model of the Rorke's Drift post.

Below Royal Artillerymen of 1815 from the Airfix OO/HO series, sold in boxes of about 48 plastic pieces.
Right American astronauts in the same series.

Period selection

The last important decision involves finding a period of interest and sticking to it; this will prevent your interest petering out because your collection lacks a theme. The choice of models is so large that it is easy to get side-tracked or confused. A collection usually demands some research, and so it's best to keep to a specific period and concentrate on it. The Napoleonic Wars, World War Two and the American Civil War are all popular, and there are plenty of books which give details of the uniforms, equipment and battles of these periods; uniform books are very important for the colouring details for unpainted figures. Other collectors choose more specialized themes – bands, German regiments, British regiments of the twentieth century, World War One, German troops in World War Two, and so on, for instance. Of course, there is nothing to stop you collecting several different types of figure simultaneously.

Top 54mm plastic assembly figure of a standard-bearer from George Washington's army.
Left guardsmen converted to 1914 Royal Fusiliers.
Above 54mm soldier of the Boer War converted from a plastic figure and army nurse made from Milliput filler over a wire armature. Her dress and umbrella are made of paper.

Polythene

Let's look at the merits and demerits of polythene Airfix figures. For a start, the range is good and new figures are added each year. Almost without exception the figures are very accurate anatomically. Though they are sold as cheap toys for youngsters in the first instance, the manufacturers very wisely take no short cuts as far as scale accuracy is concerned. Polythene is used partly because it is easy and quick to mould the complex shape, and partly because of its durability in juvenile hands. The figures are supplied unpainted, usually in a single colour such as sand, grey or khaki. From a scale modeller's point of view there are a few snags, but they are very simply dealt with. For a start, the soft plastic cannot be sawn, cut or cemented like the hard polystyrene plastic of a conventional construction kit. The only way to cut soft polythene plastic is with a very sharp (ie new) blade in a craft knife. The cut must be firm, hard and clean. Carving away with a sawing or chopping action will only mean that the cut edge takes on a rough fibrous appearance which will spoil the work. Sanding or filing is impossible.

The next problem is glueing. The figures are not intended to be cut up and glued together, but it is necessary if you wish to convert a model. Since ordinary plastic cement or other types of glue fail to 'stick' to polythene, the safest and easiest adhesive to use is a Five Minute Epoxy (such as Britfix 19), which is sold as a two-tube pack in model shops. A single pack lasts a long time. With this you can chop up and re-assemble polythene figures at will and you can also glue parts made from other materials, eg polystyrene and metal, to the polythene-type plastic.

Last we come to painting. Polythene has an inherently 'greasy' surface on which ordinary model paint won't adhere for any length of time: it either flakes off or rubs off with handling. The quick solution is to give each figure a base coat of clear PVA medium (eg Unibond), which can be bought in art shops. Apply it with a paint brush, let it set to give a hard 'skin' over the model, and then paint the model with ordinary model paints just like any plastic kit.

All that remains to be mentioned are the moulding limitations on these polythene figures. Because in the main they are one-piece mouldings the designer has to take a few liberties. Thus you may find an unrealistic 'web' of solid filling between a figure's arm and its side. For added realism, this needs to be cut away. Similarly such items as packs or water bottles may be very closely moulded to the torso, giving no impression that they are separate items. In real life there would be a slight gap between the back and a haversack; as this is missing on the model, you'll have to cut away some of the plastic to create the impression. Items such as rifles and entrenching tools may be warped or 'bendy' and may need replacing. Some figures also have 'flash' or mould marks which have to be cut away.

The next point to remember is that each figure must be considered on its own merits. Some may not need to be changed at all. But if you are contemplating conversion, any relative figure can be used purely as a basic item: cut off all his equipment (rifle, haversack, water-bottle and so on) and substitute new items glued on with Epoxy. You can swap heads by cutting the head from one figure and cementing it to another or you can cut two figures at the waist and cement the opposite halves together to give poses unlike any in the original set.

Right this group of polythene soldiers have all had minor conversions carried out on them.
Top above and above right each figure is shown in its original state on the right and converted on the left.

Polystyrene

Hard- plastic figures are much easier, for they can be assembled and cemented just like any other plastic kit. The scope for alterations is endless and will be limited only by your skill and imagination. The Multipose figures by Airfix are actually designed so that all the heads, arms, torsos, etc. in a given set are completely interchangeable, thus giving great individuality to your model making. Historex offer similar facilities with their figures: their horse components, for example, allow for over eighty variations depending on the parts selected. Further changes are possible if you use plastic putty to make up further accessories, such as rolled blankets from paper. Indeed, one model figure need never be quite the same as another.

Painting is a most important skill, for clever conversion and assembly work will count for nothing if the model is indifferently finished. For this reason choose figures with fairly simple uniforms and colours to start with, rather than those with highly intricate full dress uniform; World War Two figures in plain drab uniforms are good beginners' projects. It is usual to add artificial shading and highlighting to model figures so that they have added emphasis when seen from normal viewing distance. You can do this by adding a touch of black, grey or white as required inside creases or shaded areas while the main colour is still wet. Then work highlights and shadows in with the brush. Faces need similar highlights and shadows, shade in eye sockets and under chins and highlights on cheekbones, for example.

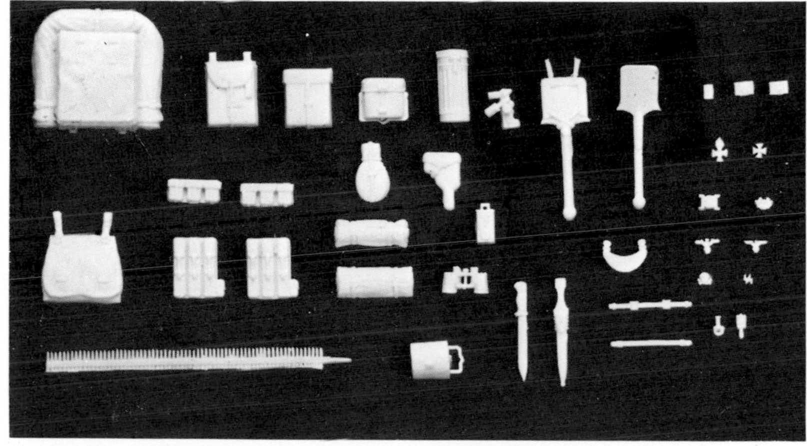

German Second World War personal equipment in plastic, useful for conversion work.

Above British soldiers of 1815. A variety of poses can be given to figures from the same kit.

Historex plastic horses are available in over 80 different positions.

Converting a Napoleonic figure

There are so many ways of assembling and converting plastic soldier figures that it is difficult to pick a typical example. It is worth pointing out, however, that many articles on conversion appear in monthly modelling magazines and will give you plenty of ideas. As an example of what can be done, here is a conversion showing all the stages and processes. A 1:12 scale Airfix Imperial Guardsman was used to make a soldier of the 3rd regiment of Grenadiers (formerly Grenadiers Hollandaise) at the time of the Napoleonic Wars. Exactly the same conversion could have been done with the 54 mm scale version of the same figure.

Needless to say, whichever way you build this kit there are plenty of options in the manner of assembly and the order of dress; the model depicts just one of them. Use the numerous books on the period to carry out some reference work.

Above the unaltered figure and the completed conversion (opposite).

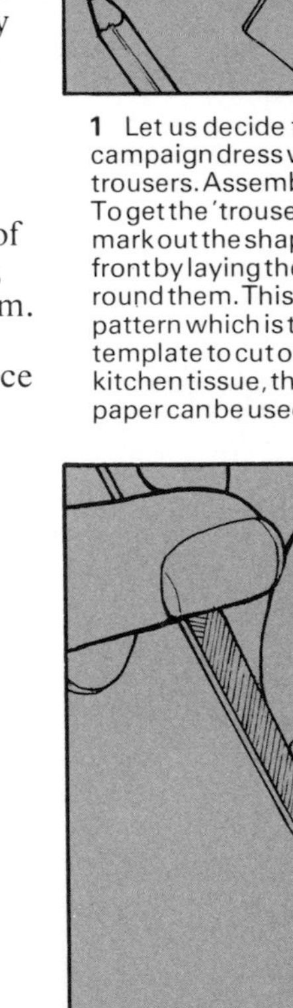

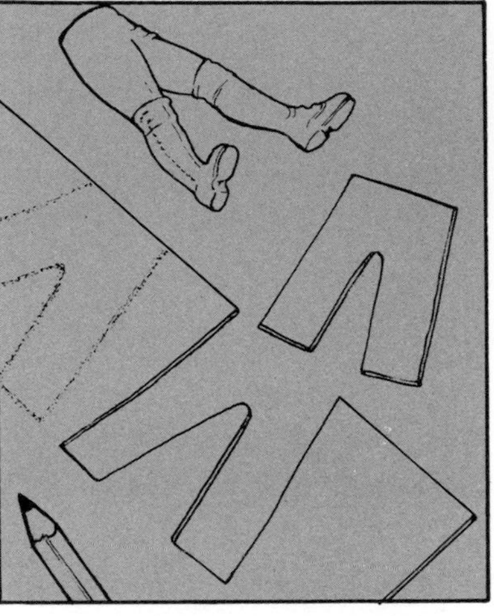

1 Let us decide to make the figure in campaign dress with loose coverall trousers. Assembly starts with the legs. To get the 'trousers' as snug as possible, mark out the shape of the legs back and front by laying them on card and drawing round them. This gives a front and back pattern which is then used like a template to cut out a front and back from kitchen tissue, though any other soft thin paper can be used.

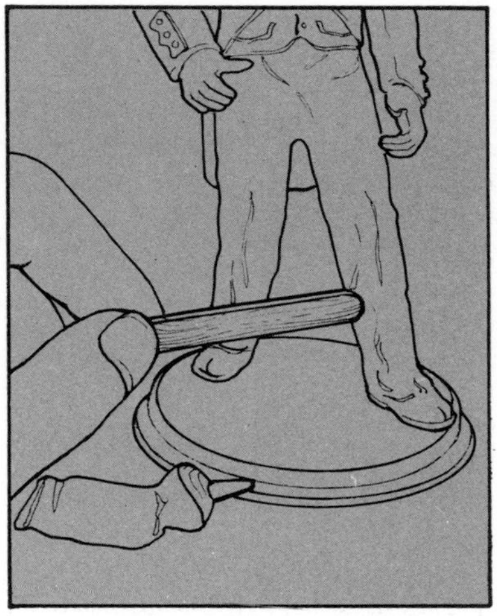

2 Then smear liquid cement liberally all over the plastic legs, and stick the front and back sections of the trousers in place, shaping them with the tip of a lolly stick to take up realistic folds and creases. Then 'paint' more liquid cement over the tissue paper, do the final shaping, and set the leg section aside to dry hard.

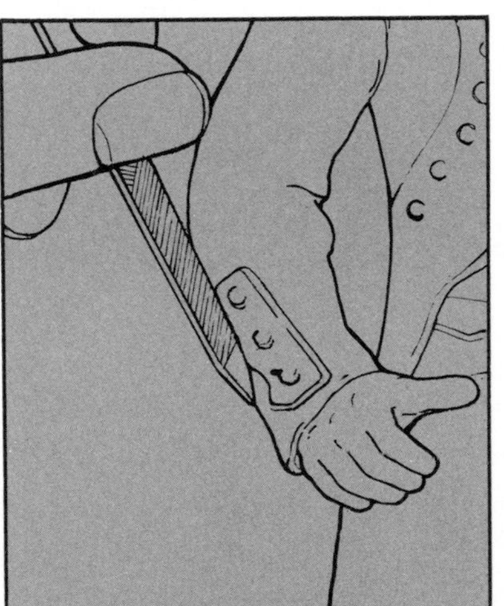

3 Meanwhile, assemble the upper torso and the arms, head and sundries, but don't join them up. The cuffs need special attention. In the 3rd Grenadiers, these were of Brandenburg pattern whereas the Imperial Guardsman had pointed cuff slashes. You can convert these to Brandenburg type by simply filing away the points until the slash has parallel edges.

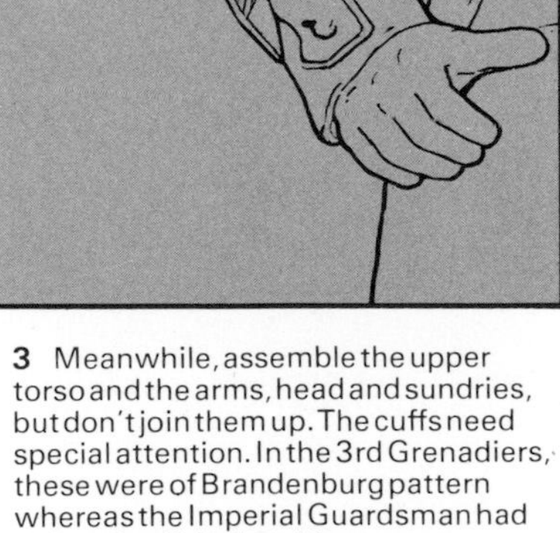

4 The bearskin as provided in the kit has a brass front plate, while the 3rd Grenadiers had a plain front. You can achieve this effect most realistically by filling in the front section with Green Stuff or similar fillers such as Plastic Padding. Using a pin, work the rough texture of the fur into the putty while it is still wet; when it is set and painted the filler is not apparent. On campaign the plume was not worn, so it must be sawn off the socket before the latter is affixed to the bearskin.

You can now assemble all the parts. This is a good moment to alter the position of the figure and make it look really different. The figure as supplied can be positioned so that he holds his musket in a carrying position; if you cement the arms at a slightly higher angle and turn the hands at the wrist, he can be placed in what I think is a more realistic and credible position, standing 'easy' and holding the musket at the 'order' position. A few dry runs will show yet more variations on this. Cement the head turned slightly left, though it could go in any other desired position.

Now that the standing position has been finalized and all the cement has set, carry on and add the equipment, exactly as described in the kit instructions. You can make the musket strap about half as long again as the given template length, so that it can be doubled back and given extra 'sag'.

All is now ready for painting, to the following scheme:
Trousers: Dark blue, or lightened to give a washed out effect.
Gaiters: White
Boots and pouch: leather (black), very slightly gloss but not highly polished.
Waistcoat: White
Surtout: White with Crimson turnbacks, cuff, epaulettes and collar. Mix Humbrol Crimson with Scarlet in about equal parts and add a touch of blue to get the best Crimson. The Crimson as supplied is rather too light.
Bearskin cords: Silver
Braid, buttons, buckles etc: Brass
For all the remaining parts, follow the kit instructions.

Even the figure as converted can be varied: he could, for instance, be left in full dress with breeches and gaiters as supplied in the kit and with the plume (Scarlet) left on the bearskin; in this case both breeches and gaiters would be white and the work involved in adding the trousers could be omitted. Yet another alternative is to make him up as a NCO.

Wienerwald
Gastlichkeit
Wienerwald
Gastlichkeit

PLASTIC BUILDINGS AND STRUCTURES

Model buildings provide one of the widest selections of all in the plastic kit construction field. Among the manufacturers who offer kits are Pola, Faller, Vollmer, Heljan, AHM, Aurora, Revell and Airfix. The output is so large, mainly because the kits are sold as model railway accessories. Thus the predominant scale is 1:87 (matching OO/HO railways) and 1:160 (to match N scale), though there are a few at 1:120 (to match TT) and some at 1:100 for 'background' use. There are some large scale (1:22) buildings for use with LGB's garden railways.

Obviously these building kits are of equal value to all kinds of modellers, for they can be used in any dioramas of appropriate scale and are thus ideal for, say, a street-fighting diorama using tanks and figures in 1:87 or 1:76 scale. Because buildings vary in size in real life, the precise scale is not too critical so long as the proportions match reasonably. Hence buildings matched to HO size look perfectly reasonable with the slightly larger 1:76 (OO) scale models.

Opposite page selection of the many pre-coloured building kits available in card or plastic for model railway layouts.
Below American station building being assembled from a kit of plastic parts.

For military modellers kits are now available intended specifically for military scenes – complete OO size buildings (such as a 1:76 scale Japanese jungle outpost) and 1:32 scale buildings, suitable for 54 mm scale figures, among them. Many of these military buildings have built in 'battle damage'. All this means that virtually everyone is catered for in plastic building kits. Quite apart from structures, there are engineering features such as bridges and scenic items such as trees, bushes and scatter material for ground surfaces. So whether your interest is railways, cars, commercial vehicles, aircraft, or military models, more than enough building and structure kits are on sale for full scenic settings for your work.

With a few exceptions, building kits come largely pre-coloured, in as much as roofs, walls, doors and window frames are all moulded in appropriate colours to exclude the need for painting. This is particularly useful when it comes to tiny and delicate parts such as window frames and bargeboards. Sometimes, however, the colours are a little too bright and glossy and need toning down with a wash of dilute brown or black. A little extra touching up, whitish grey 'dribble' marks to depict overflow from drainpipes and guttering for instance, gives that extra element of realism which will make the model stand out from other models built straight from the kit. Most of the better kits have sheets of cut-out curtains for the windows (again this allows much variety), while models

of stations and public buildings usually come with cut-out advertisements and notices as appropriate.

There are endless ways of giving extra individuality to models made straight from the kit. For example, glue smeared up the side of a house with appropriate scenic scatter material added will give the effect of clinging ivy. Doors and windows can be glued in place half open – even this simple change makes a world of difference – while potted plants outside doors, or bicycles propped against the front wall, give a true lived-in look. A favourite device is to set a house on a scenic base with a fully modelled garden made from model railway scenic materials. A clothes line (made from heat-stretched sprue), with tiny paper garments attached, flower beds and borders and so on, all contribute to a believable and homely setting.

Some buildings, those made by Faller for instance, allow you to install a bulb to give a lighted effect in the dark. To take advantage of this device you must either paint all the inside walls of the model matt black or line them with black paper cut to fit inside. If you don't do this, the light will glow through the inherent translucence of the plastic and give an altogether unrealistic effect.

A fairly recent idea is the 'combi' kit; this is half plastic, half card. It not only helps to keep costs down but also utilizes the great range of shades which colour printing can give to achieve the subtle colouring of building materials. A typical 'combi' kit might have base, roofs and window frames of plastic, with all the walls in coloured pre-cut card. The actual building procedure is virtually the same as for a standard plastic kit.

There is enormous scope for

Below girder bridges such as this are very useful on dioramas and layouts. **Bottom** standard OO/HO railway box girder bridge assembled from Plastruct girder and angle iron components.

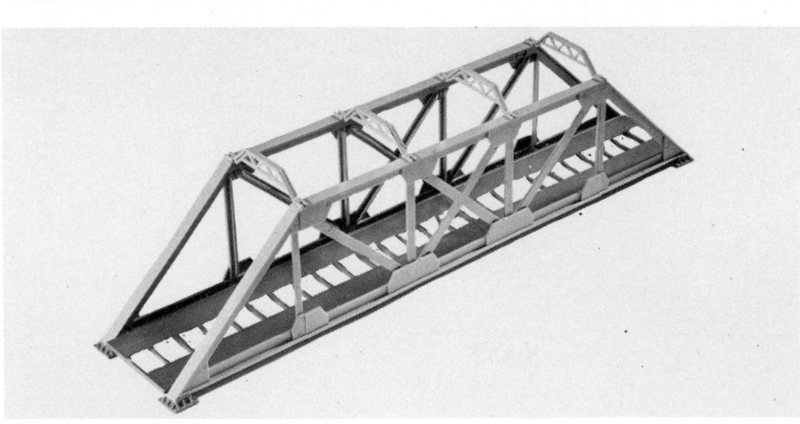

Skeleton building on a new site made entirely from Plastruct parts. Plastruct's huge range of miniature building accessories includes fencing, girders, flooring and sheet styrene.

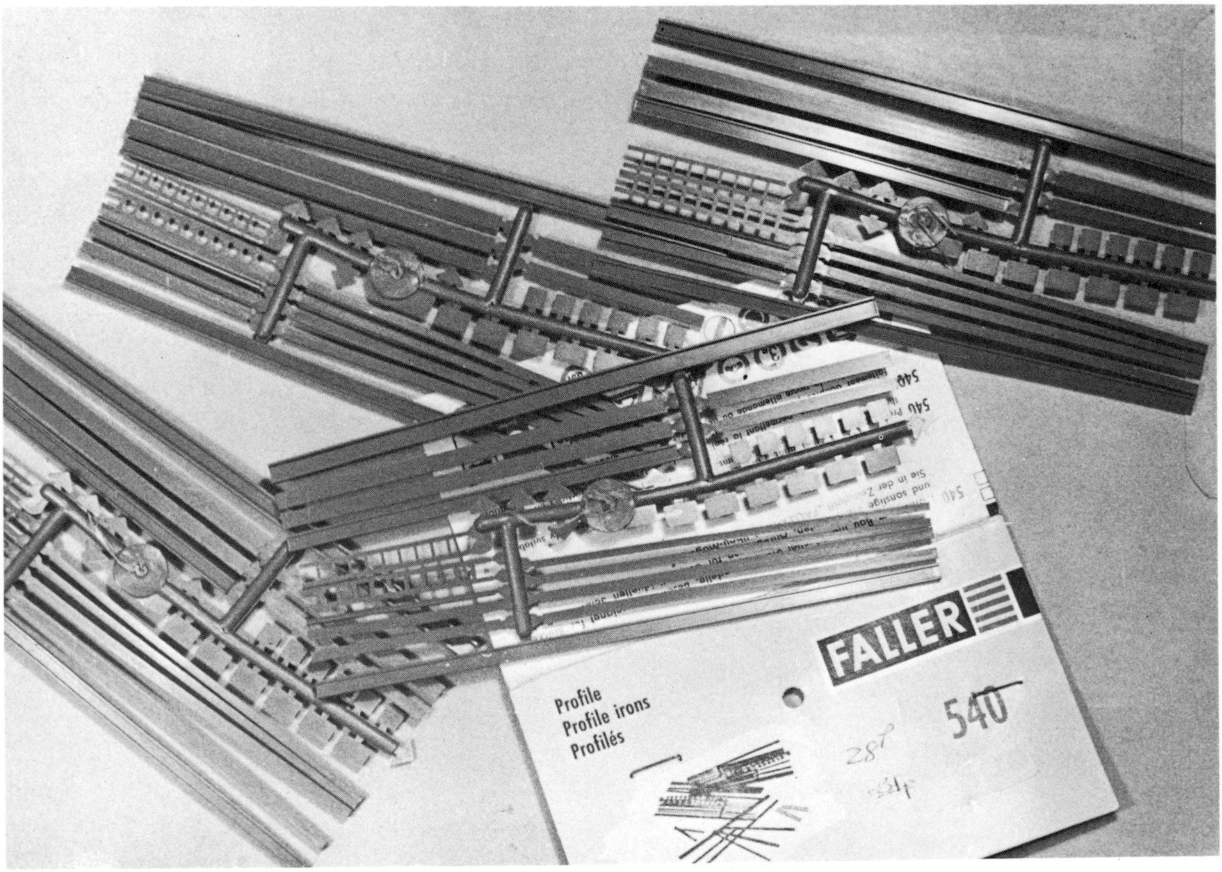

Above set of girders, ladders and drain pipes. Several building kit manufacturers market sets of accessories for conversion and scratch building works.
Right 1:200 harbour scene.

conversion work with model buildings; indeed the wide range of models available makes it a good way of achieving individuality. Conversion work with buildings is actually quite easy, because most surfaces are flat or at least simple. By switching station walls around, say, you can completely alter the appearance of a station; or try adding a hut to the side of a cottage to give a 'lean to' effect. Two long buildings can be stuck together at right angles to make a more imposing structure. Loading platforms can easily be fashioned from balsa or plastic cards and added to factories. A popular trick is the 'low relief' building: in effect this is rather like scenery on a stage; only half a building faces the viewer. If you are operating a railway layout or diorama it is a great space saver and also has visual advantages. Cut the model in two parts at the centreline using a razor saw and then cement the two half buildings side by side to give a double length frontage.

You can also get immense variety by 'cross-kitting'. You either mix parts from two kits or use parts from one kit to alter the look of another. A simple example is the well-known Airfix signal box. This is a classic old-time wood-frame structure: but if the upper floor (the cabin itself) is cut from the lower floor (the switch room) and built instead on to a new switch room made from brick walls (say from an engine shed kit), the effect will be altogether different.

Any model building not used on a large layout really does require a small diorama base (an offcut of chipboard works admirably) which can be given scenic ground treatment. A golden rule here is to make it look as though the building is really built into the ground and is not just standing on it. To do this, ensure that you take the material you use to represent the ground surface, whether plasticine, patching plaster, Hydrozell or papier mache, right up to the structure.

Though this water tower is intended as a model train accessory, the kit is a useful source of parts for conversions.

Put a grey-wash over all the walls in those kits where the parts are moulded single colour. This will run into the coursing most realistically. Wipe off the surface before the wash dries, leaving the bricks as they are. For white or grey moulded walls, paint the walls with a fairly dry brush. The indented coursing will show through as the light plastic.

Careful grouping alone can work wonders for realism: instead of just one house, try two or three, forming a portion of a village street. Vary the level with extra layers of baseboard, and add miniature trees and bushes in 'believable' positions.

CARD MODELS

Card is the most basic of all modelling materials, and card models long pre-dated plastic or cast metal. You can make card models from almost literally nothing more than scrap card, your only expenditure being on glue. Card can, of course, also be purchased in the form of good quality art board or Bristol board, but in most households almost all the card you'll ever need is all about you, most of it being thrown away as old packaging or other domestic rubbish. A good deal of this is usable in modelling; things to look for are shirt stiffeners, writing pad stiffeners, old post-cards, toilet tissue 'cores', kitchen towel 'cores' and good quality boxes in which such items as cosmetic products and plastic kits are supplied.

Given a selection of scrap items, a surprising number of simple building models can be constructed quite easily. Anything with storage towers makes an imposing start – grain silos, farmers' silos, gas tanks, fuel tanks, grain elevators, lime kilns and so on. Select any tubular cores or containers such as kitchen towel rolls. If they have spiral seams, cover them first with plain matt paper to facilitate painting later. The only glues required are white PVA children's or household glues or 'universal' tube glue.

How to make a grain elevator and loading bay is described on pages 114-115 in detail. This will give you the idea of how quick construction is – and, that aside, it gives you an instant 'industry' for a model railway.

Right scratch-built offices in wood and plastic card on a gauge 1 model rail layout.
Below station building made from a card die-cut kit.

Simple scratch-built buildings

Small buildings and huts are also easy to make. Just mark them out in pencil on card of suitable thickness, preferably not the pulpy kind, and cut them out with craft knife and steel rule. Use a new sharp blade at all times to prevent tearing. For a wood structure you can simply score groove and tongue type boarding on to the surface of the card and stick paper strips up and down the roof to depict roofing felt. However, the more realistic alternative is to cut thin card or thick paper into individual strips for lapboarding and then start at the bottom, glueing strip after strip in place, each lapping over the lower strake. The result is most pleasing and convincing. Do the same with roof tiles, cutting them partly through. For a concrete or pebble dash building use fairly rough card of the sort used in shirt stiffeners, rough side out. When these are painted with white or off-white poster or powder paints, in particular the latter, a good lime-wash pebble-dash effect is achieved. To make it even better, dab white powder paint freely over the surface while the paint is still wet.

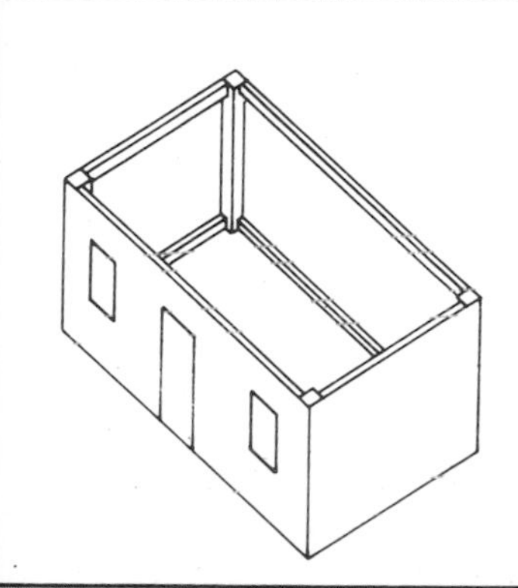

1 Build up box section from card, reinforced with strips of balsa.

2 Cut lap-boarding from strips of paper or thin card.

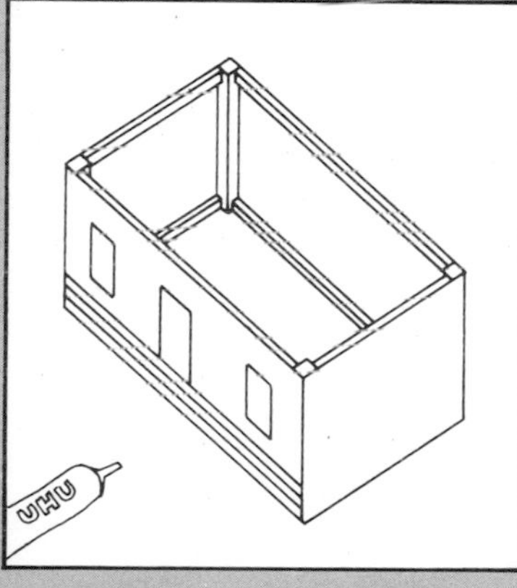

3 Glue overlapping strips in position. Cover apertures and cut away later.

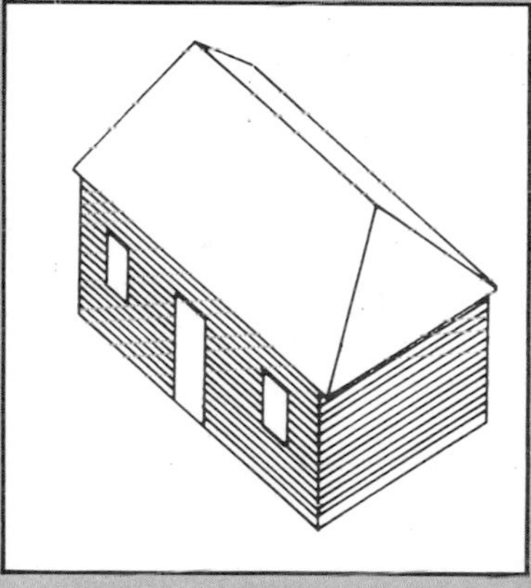

4 Cut the roof from plain card and glue in position.

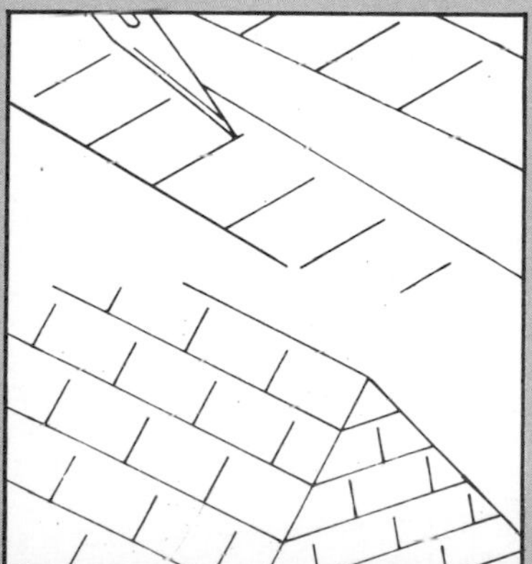

5 Cut strips of paper partly through and glue in position from the bottom.

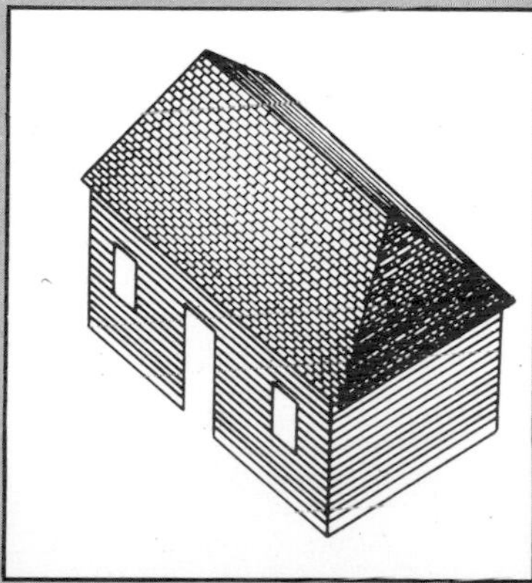

6 Cut ridge tile strip to double width to finish apex of roof. Finally add doors and windows glued inside.

Surface materials

If you want a brick or stone finish, the easiest method is to use the printed brick papers which are available under names such as Builder Plus or Modelcraft and with every sort of finish – red brick, blue brick, weathered brick, random stone, Cotswoldstone and so on. Cut the walls out and glue them to the paper. The sheets themselves include arch sections, sills and corner stones to take care of windows, doors and neat corners respectively; you should cut these parts out and cement them in place after all covering and assembly work is complete. If you lack sills, door arches and corner stones, you can, of course, draw them out on paper (tinted stone colour for choice) to any desired style.

As supplied, brick paper is simply flat printed paper. To enhance its texture and give an impression of relief (admittedly a bogus one), lay the sheet face up on a large new sheet of glasspaper. Rub over the entire surface with your finger in a cloth (as you would to polish metal) and the sandy texture of the glasspaper will be impressed on the brickpaper, giving a quite realistic relief effect. This will give a greatly improved appearance to the finished model. (see opposite page).

Another allied model product is embossed building card, of which the major manufacturer is the German firm of Faller. This comes as brick or stone in various forms, but with all the coursing embossed out and everything in full colour. The construction technique is as for card. Also made by Faller is a delightful embossed paving stone, cobble stone and random stone tiling which is ideal for courtyards and backyards. Though this embossed card is much more expensive than printed building papers it is certainly worth the money in terms of enhanced realism.

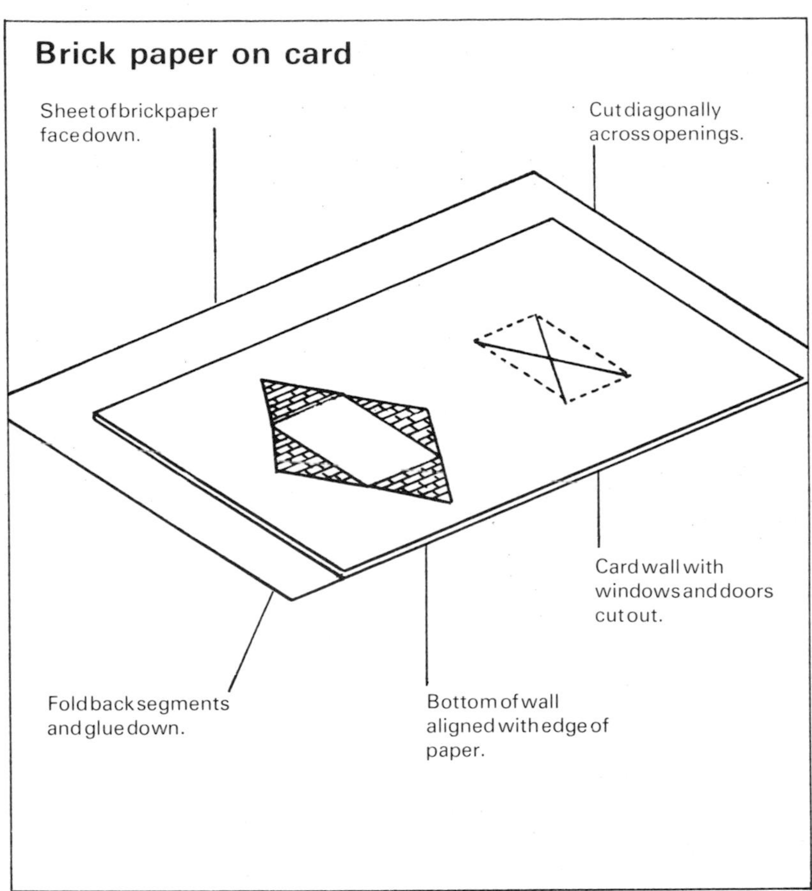

Right attractive 1:76 scratch-built house; the modeller has used embossed brick and tile card or plastic sheets.

Numerous different types of brick paper are available and can be used to simulate a multitude of different finishes. Shown here from left to right are red brick, sooty black, yellow brick, random sandstone, grey roof slate, grey slate, red tile and paving stones.

Texturing brickpaper

To obtain a textured finish on brick paper, place it face up on a sheet of new, course glass paper and rub hard with your finger or a cloth. The contrast between untextured and textured brick paper can be seen, right.

Making a scratch-built elevator tower

Scratch-building is an excellent test of inventiveness and the ingenious use of everyday materials. Demanding though many of the kits mentioned elsewhere in this book are, some modellers believe that the greatest challenge of all comes from scratch-building. Whether you agree or not, it certainly proves the value of recycling as much packaging material as possible.

Materials

3 cardboard tubes

2 sheets of card one at least 1/6 inch thick

toothpaste tube carton

flat carton

2 cartons for buildings

drinking straws or refill ball point tubes

a paper towel

a tall thin carton for elevator tower *or* 4 strips of wood

scrap wood to brace same

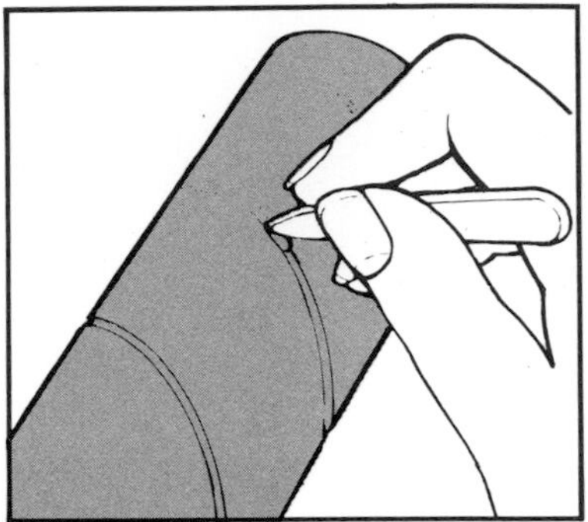

1 Choose the best tubes you can find, bearing in mind they are usually made of low grade card and some have very wide 'candy strip' join seams spiralling round them, which must be filled.

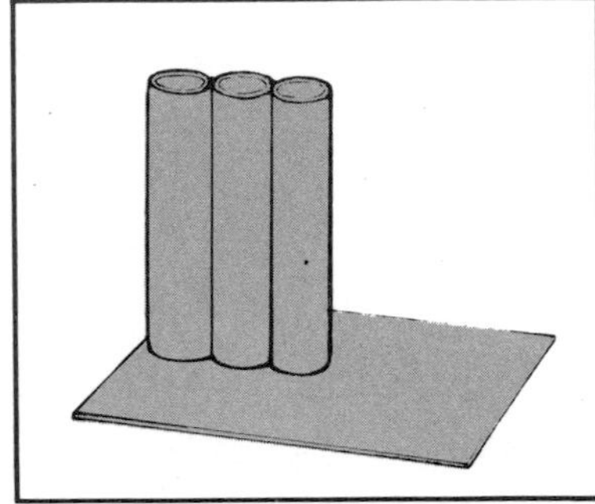

3 Choose a good sheet of card – mine came from a shirt box – as a base, glue the three tubes vertically to it, and use a good rigid carton as a set-square to support the tubes while the glue sets.

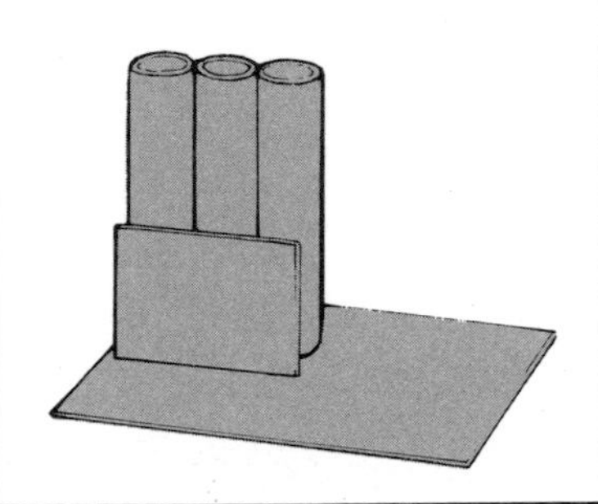

4 Glue the inner curtain wall of the covered loading bay directly to the three tubes. On my model the tubes (bins) are 9 inches high, and the inner wall of the loading bay measures about 5 inches long by 4 inches high. Use the thickest card you can find.

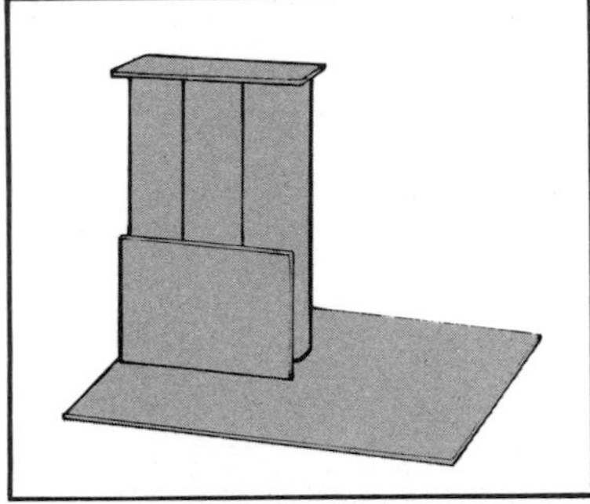

5 Cut a rectangular roof for the top of the bins, again from the 1/16 inch card, and make it wider and longer than the overall length and width of the bins by at least 1/16 inch; glue this in place.

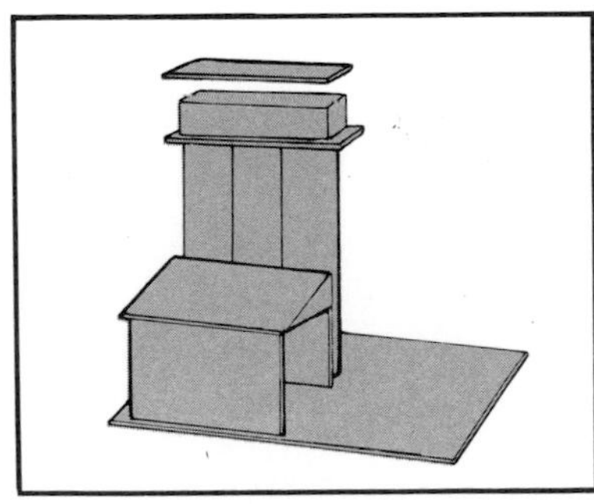

7 Securely glue shut the end flaps of a toothpaste tube carton (or similar item) and glue this centred above the roof of the bins. Then cut yet another roof to match the bin roof, overhanging the carton top.

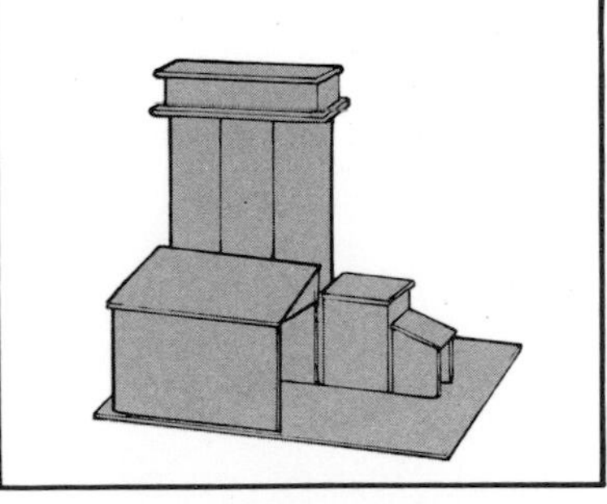

8 The scale house at the foot of the elevator tower comes next and on my model is simply a thick car carton again with a flat card roof. To obscure the lack of a detailed entrance I built a lean-to-porch-type entrance. Make sure this porch is wide enough for OO/HO size trucks to back in.

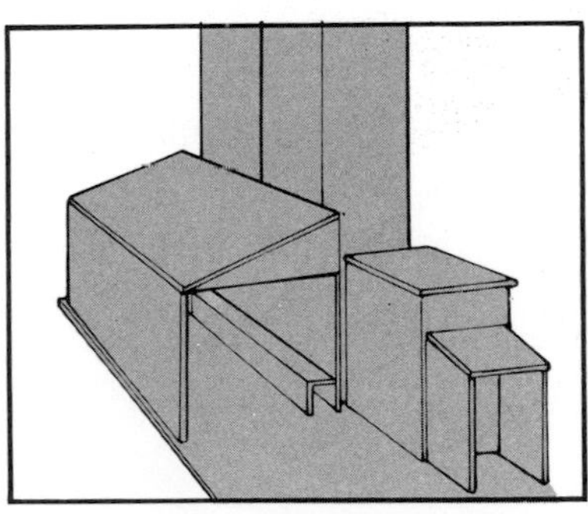

9 A platform to give workers floor height access to freight stock was fitted into the the covered loading bay, and this was simply the tuck-in flap of another carton trimmed to height (about ½ inch) and glued in place.

2 Glue three tubes side by side with 'universal' adhesive, using a flat surface like a table top to get them 'square' to each other in both the vertical and horizontal planes.

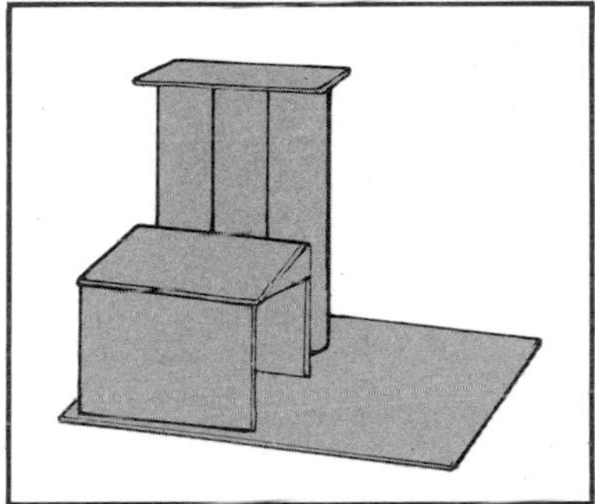

6 Cut an outer curtain wall, a sloped roof, and two right angle triangle ends for the loading bay canopy, glue these in position and reinforce with wood strips on the inner portals each side. I also glued a paper towel over the roof to depict an asphalt covering.

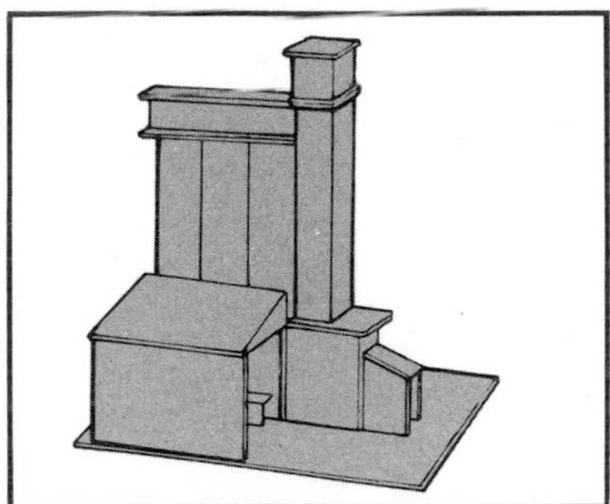

10 Trickiest part of all is the actual elevator tower. Use another long narrow carton for this. The little structure topping off the tower was a section from yet another carton, again given a flat roof and ends cut from the embossed material. This is braced internally with wood scraps.

That just about completes the description. The vacuum pipe and grain spouts, often seen externally, are assumed to be inside the tower, with a swinging gantry type filler pipe inside the loading shed, but drinking straws or ball-pen refills could be used for external piping.

Painting this model with powder paints was an interesting experiment, as the structure might well have collapsed in a soggy heap if too much water was used. Do one overall coat of off-white applied in the normal way, but leave the elevator tower unpainted for the moment. Later it can be painted pale yellow or some similar shade. While the basic fairly thick coat is still wet, apply as much white and black as will adhere to the brush in powder form, working it over the wet surface of the model. This is a sort of 'texturing' procedure which results in a very realistic weathered 'ferrocrete' finish, both in looks and actual feel, and the powder paint obviously absorbed most of the surface moisture from the original coat of paint.

Weathering and shading is done by the judicious application of black. Paint the inside of the loading bay as dark as possible so that the absence of interior detail will not be too obvious.

To keep the spirit of this cheap modelling theme, I cut the Kelloggs' trade names from the breakfast cereal packets. The outer curtain wall of the loading bay needed a large panel, in particular, to break up an otherwise large expanse of plain uninteresting surface. The other additions made were the Agrico name panels, cut from old magazine advertisements.

A revival in card soldiers

One recently marketed innovation revives an idea extremely popular in Victorian times – press-out card models of famous regiments. They now come complete with plastic stands for the figures. Shown here are, right, one of the original Victorian figures together with its modern replica and, below, a complete set from the current range.

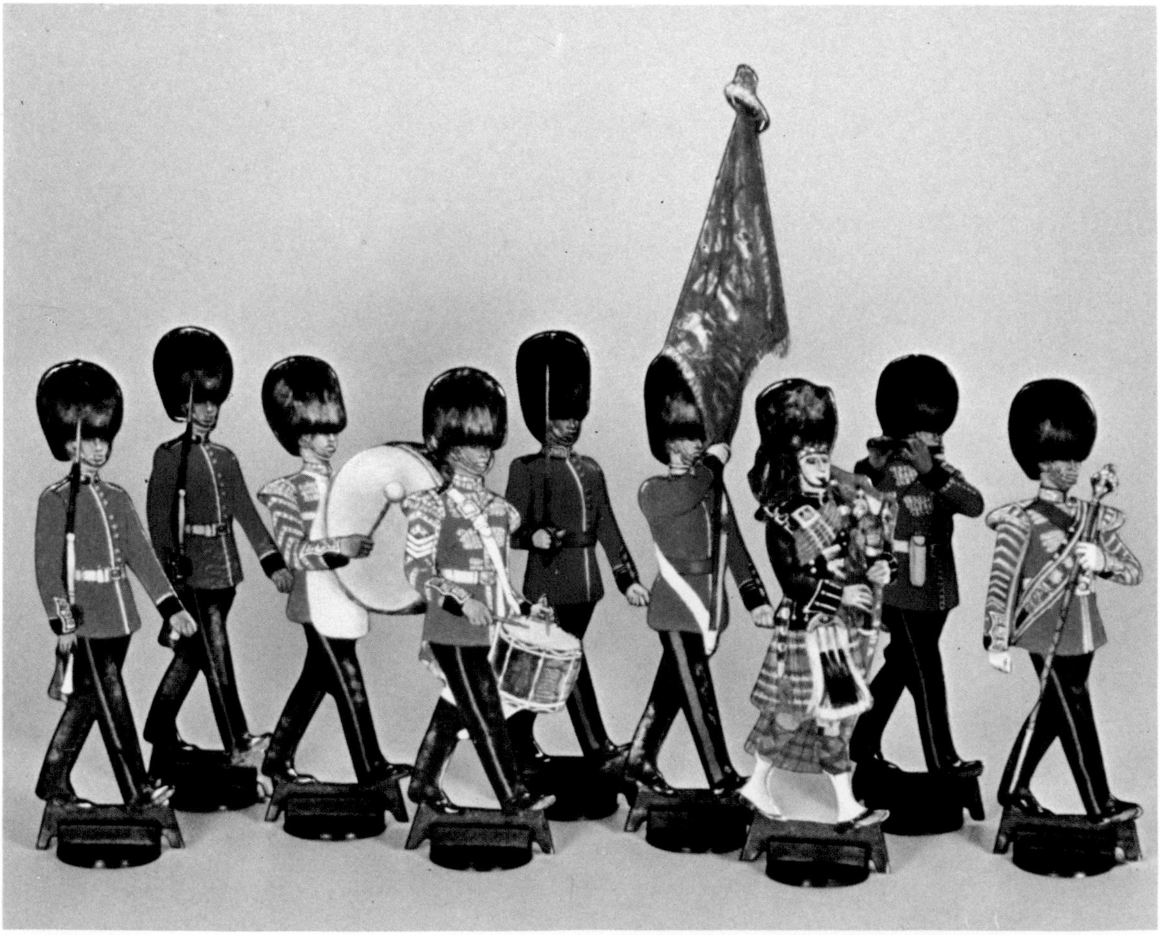

Card kits

Sheet balsa of various thicknesses is needed for card kits. These are now widely available; the majority are buildings of various sorts scaled for OO, HO, TT or N gauge railways. They can be used for non-railway purposes, too, of course, such as military dioramas. Builder Plus, Superquick and Bilteezi are major producers. There are many German companies in the business, too, and in Germany card kits have become very exotic. Apart from buildings they include airships, aircraft and ships – and even a complete old-time fairground. Some kits are die-cut so that components may be pressed out from the sheet, while others have to cut out completely from the printed sheet.

In general these card models are straightforward assembly jobs and full instructions are given with each set. However, care and competence are still essential for success. It is particularly important not to smear glue on the outside of the structure, since glue reflects light very noticeably and can ruin an otherwise fine model.

A favourite ploy is to ignore the manufacturer's method of cutting and glueing tabs and instead cut out each face of the model glued to thin balsa sheet. This results in a very strong, perfectly rigid model which will last literally for ever in a normal domestic atmosphere.

Detail of cardboard model of the Tower of London showing the White Tower and, inset, the whole model.

Strengthening a card building

Card and wood modelling complement each other. Structures made from card alone tend to warp or bow eventually. This can be avoided if wood is used to reinforce the card; in particular, it helps to reinforce all the corners and edges with strip balsa, so ensuring square assembly and a strong and rigid structure.

Some card buildings are sold as die-cut sheets with the main components ready to be pressed out. Cut-out buildings printed on thin good-quality card are more common, however. Ships, fairgrounds, aircraft, etc., are also available in this form.

The cards are usually printed in colour. Some items, though, are printed in black outline only and have to be painted first of all. Pin the card to a drawing-board, and use water colours.

Almost all card cut-out models are simply assembled by folding and gluing scored flaps and tabs, following the instructions provided. Large models made in this way will need to be braced to prevent warping and distortion. A good way of doing this is shown here.

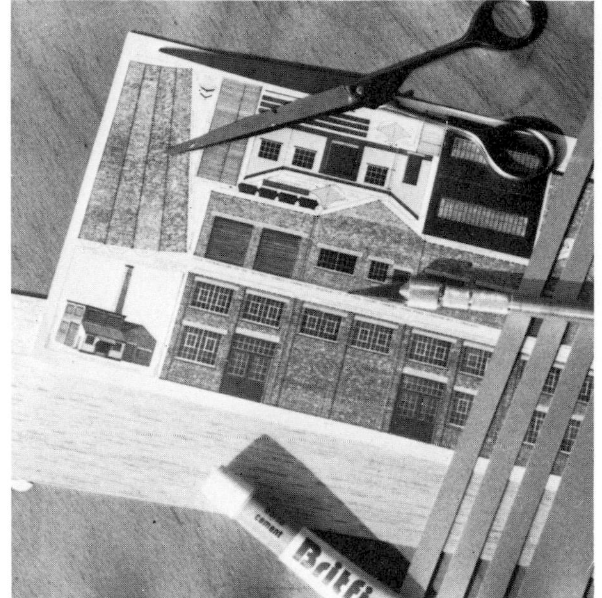

1 To make this small cut-out factory, you will need the card cut-out sheet, glue, a sheet of $\frac{1}{16}$ inch balsa wood, craft knife, metal rule, roller, emery board, set square, and scissors.

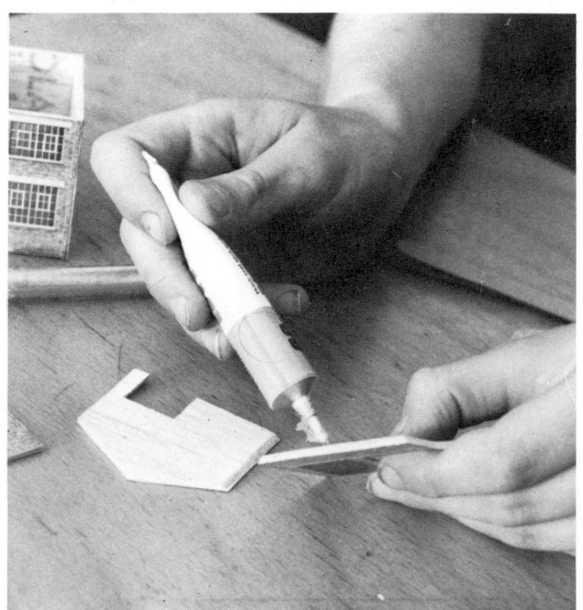

4 Apply balsa cement to the mitred edge prior to assembly.

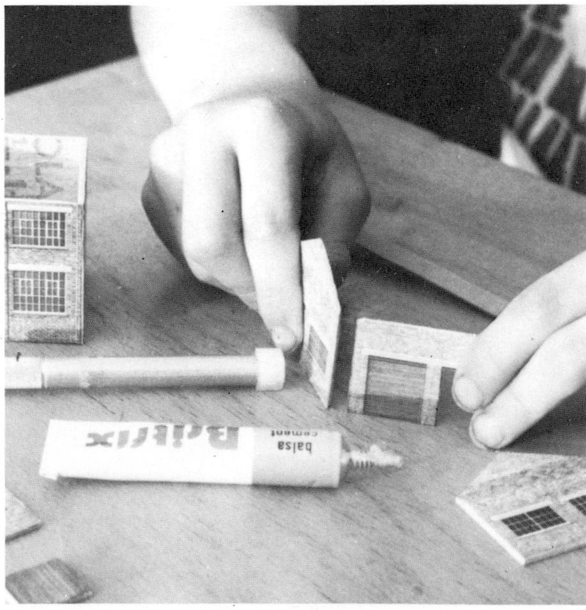

5 When assembling the finished pieces, use a set square to ensure that all the walls are upright. Work on a flat surface.

2 Roughly cut out the main components. Then with the knife and rule cut to the outlines, cutting off the printed flaps and tabs. Then glue each individual part to the balsa sheet.

3 Use an emery board to file a 45° camber on each cutting edge, and test for a square joint. Leave the printed windows in, though on a larger-scale model you could cut them out and 'glaze' them with clear plastic.

6 Use a coloured felt-tip pen or water colours to touch up any white edges and joins and also to add wear or weathering – such as soot on the chimney top.

7 The completed model in position beside a model railway. The flat roof is scrap strawboard painted grey, the loading platform consists of unused parts covered with 'brick' card.

Scratch buildings

Using this card and balsa combination you can make models of almost anything. Though card cutouts of tanks, trucks and cars are available, there is nothing to stop you making your own. One well-known modeller, John Sandars, has built up a huge collection of 1:32 scale tanks and trucks and guns, all made entirely from scrap card and wood, working from scale plans and reference photos. Even if you don't aspire to this sort of thing, scratch-building in card and wood can enable you to supplement models made from kits and to build your own where no kit exists of a particular subject.

1:24 modern British AFVs made entirely from card and wood, with the exception of the wheels and tracks, some of which are from plastic kits.

'Scratch-built' windows

Many building kits in card include glazing for windows, while others simply have the windows printed on them. For a background model, or in a very small scale (such as N), this may be acceptable, but usually glazing is required.

1 Pin a sheet of clear acetone to a suitable hard board, score frame lines in with a knife and ruler.

2 Rub white (or any other) poster paint over the whole lot.

3 Then wipe a damp cloth over the sheet. This will remove the excess paint and leave only the frames coloured.

This locomotive shed is made from a die-cast 'press-out' card kit, in which the inner and outer walls can be glued together to make a rigid structure; there is no need to use a balsa sheet. The glazed window material is sandwiched between the inner and outer walls.

Balsa kits

Finally we come to all-balsa models. Strictly speaking, these are mostly outside our definition of scale models, but nevertheless there are kits for a few flying scale models, gliders and simple fighting planes, and they serve as a good introduction to flying models generally. Some of the more recent kits are largely of sheet balsa, usually printed and die-cut. Assembly of these models is generally quite straightforward.

In general all these flying models are built up with a frame structure of balsa wings and stringers. Use the plans given with the kit as an assembly pattern: pin it to a large sheet of chipboard, cover it with a clear polythene sheet, and then use pins to hold ribs and stringers in position while you cut the parts and assemble them over the full-size plan. Balsa cement is, of course, the adhesive to use.

Balsa strip and sheet can be used in their own right to scratchbuild such things as trestle bridges. In general the style of structure follows that of full-size bridges of this sort. Build up bents of strip to the required height and glue them *in situ* on the terrain; the job is held together by the deck of the bridge and the cross-supports, which you should add between the bents last of all.

There is also a whole range of wood kits, made of bass wood rather than balsa, which duplicate real-life wood structures. Builder Plus and Campbell are among the manufacturers in this field. Logging camps, coal hoists, shanty town houses, timber yards, hotels etc. are all available in this form. Assembly is quite straightforward, since all parts come cut and milled to shape, and as wood models of wood structures they offer unsurpassed realism.

Building a balsa flying model

Most balsa flying aircraft are miniature aircraft built to give a good performance in the air, *not* scale models as such. There are a few, however, that combine the virtues of both: they fly and are also scale models, within the limitations of balsa and tissue construction.

Such models are assembled along the lines shown here. The model under construction, a Prefect glider, is typical of the simpler flying scale models available.

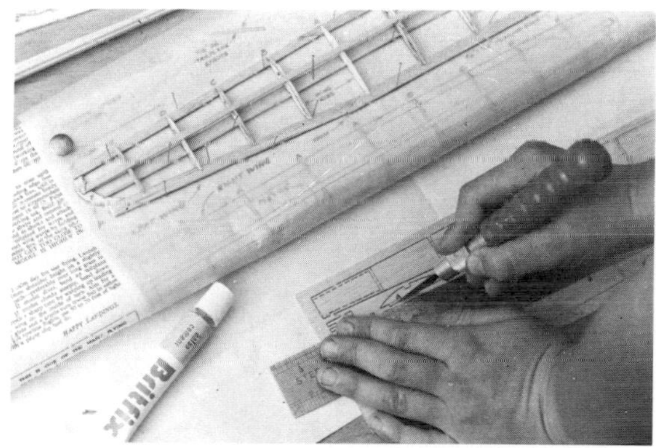

1 Pin the plan up and assemble the wings and, where applicable, the other parts, too, using it as a pattern. Cut all the longerons, ribs, etc., from the balsa strips supplied. Hold the parts in place with pins while the balsa cement dries. Here, wing ribs are being set from a printed sheet.

2 The two wing halves have been made separately and then cemented together. Balsa blocks support the wing tips at the correct angle while the cement dries.

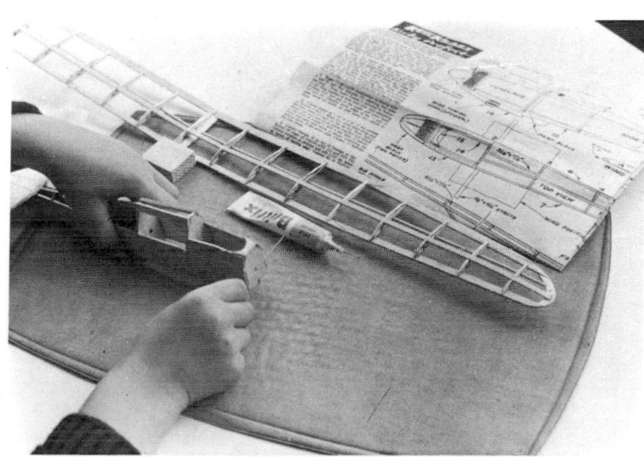

3 Fuselage assembly follows a similar pattern. Here, sheet balsa has been used to simulate the wooden fuselage of the original. Pins hold sections in place while the cement dries.

PAINTS AND BRUSHES

More models are ruined by faulty painting and finishing than are spoiled by clumsy workmanship. Conversions which have taken much careful work or the most expensive plastic kits can just as easily be ruined by poor finish as the humblest small model. Crooked markings are only too common; so are inaccurate markings or colour schemes, transparencies daubed with paint, tyres which aren't even painted as such, edges which have been overlooked by the paint brush, and internal areas visible through hatches or cockpit covers.

Poorly applied markings can all too easily spoil models. See that your models don't have shiny transfers on an otherwise matt surface, or transfers with transparent areas round them, or brush marks which reflect as ridges in a strong light, or hairs from the paint brush.

Faults usually sound worse than they are on the actual model, but as your own standards improve, and after you've seen models better finished than your own, you'll become more and more dissatisfied with your own efforts.

When it comes to painting it is absolutely vital to know what you are setting out to achieve. If you have made a warship, did you paint the deck a different colour from the superstructure, or did you just paint everything grey? Are your straight demarcation lines really straight, or did you make do by painting them free-hand?

In conversions, research material is needed all the time. Even if you intend just to finish the model as it comes in the kit, it really is essential to decide which full-size aircraft, tank or car your model is

Even a simple paint finish, like this all-black model Mosquito night fighter, can be effective when carefully and accurately applied.

to depict. Ships, planes, tanks and so on change more frequently than you might expect. Some aircraft, for instance, have never been photographed twice in exactly the same markings or colour scheme, while radar aerials, masts and so on vary, not to mention non-standard or unofficial modifications.

Time spent on these considerations is time well spent, since it is only too easy to paint a model in inaccurate colours or make a mistake with the markings.

Accuracy doesn't necessarily mean finishing the model just as the manufacturer supplied it. The markings and painting schemes given in a kit may not always be fully accurate, though recently standards have improved considerably. But to keep prices of commercially produced plastic kits reasonable, limitations are always necessary, so be prepared to improve or modify the markings and finish suggested.

For plastic models you need oil-based enamel paints; the label usually indicates that they are suitable for use on plastic. Humbrol, Airfix, Joy, Pactra, Testor and so on are among the well-known brands. One or other of these will have produced all the colours and types of paint that the enthusiast requires for the most popular model subjects. All you need to do is stir and apply straight from the tin.

Do not use cellulose paint on plastic models or plastic parts – it melts the plastic. Some hobby shops sell cellulose paint (dope) for use on flying models, so check that you are purchasing the right kind of paint. Cellulose paint can be used on wood or metal models, as can ordinary oil-based paints in-

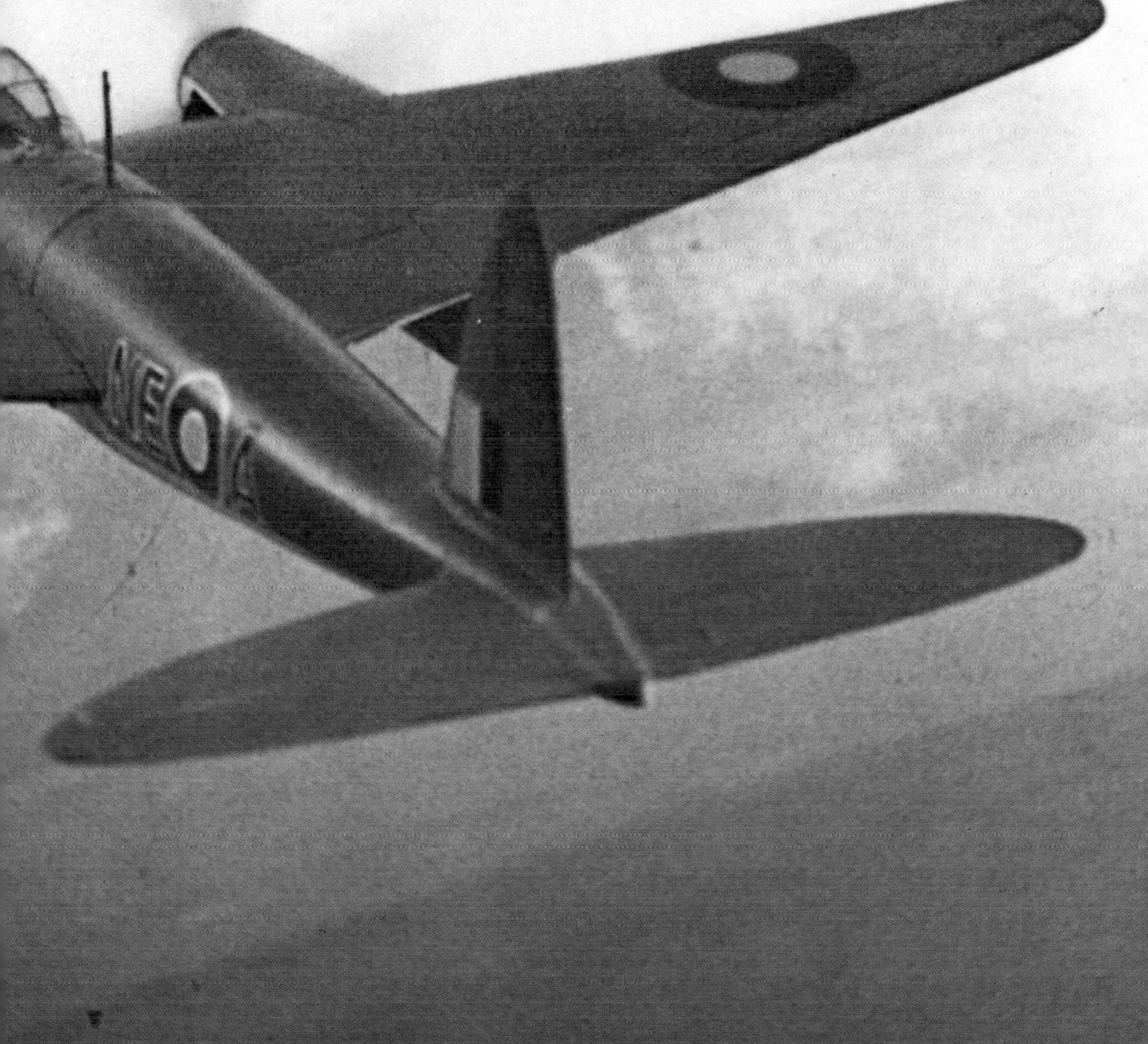

tended for plastic models.

Other sorts of paint are commonly used for modelling purposes. On metal models, some sort of primer is required. The larger model paint makers include metal primer in their ranges, though usually it is only sold by the biggest hobby shops. Polyurethane clear varnish is a more recent and popular paint used for priming on metal models. It must be worked well into all corners and crevices of the model to give an overall air-tight 'skin'. With this varnish you can use ordinary matt model paints as an undercoat; matt emulsion paint of the domestic sort also gives a very smooth finish ready to take a top coat.

Ordinary oil paint as used by artists is also extremely useful for models, notably model soldiers. Sets and tubes of colour are readily available at all art shops. Oil paints are easy to mix, give an infinite range of subtle shades, and are easy to work and apply. Model horses and flesh tones can be done particularly realistically. The main thing is to avoid diluting the paint with linseed oil, since this could adversely affect a plastic model. Oil paints take a day or two to become touch dry and a few weeks to become really hard, so models must not be handled for some time after painting.

One other sort of paint worth mentioning is Polly S, a water soluble paint made specially for modellers. It is rather more expensive than conventional paint but has great flexibility and can be mixed and applied using only water.

After the paint, you will need brushes. Cheap brushes shed hairs, and soon you'll be picking hairs out of wet paintwork. Worse still, you may not discover them until after the paint has dried.

At any shop specializing in artists' supplies, however, you'll find a rack of squirrel or sable hair brushes of various sizes and by reputable manufacturers. Three of these brushes should suffice for the average modeller's requirements, though if your particular models, miniature soldiers for instance, demand more intricate painting then a bigger selection is desirable. Three good quality brushes will give better value than six cheap brushes. For most of your painting you can use an OO and a number 1 size brush; the OO size is small enough for most detail work on small scale ships, tanks and aircraft etc. If you do need something

An economical way of painting a model is to buy a finishing kit containing small vials of enamel paint, a brush and cement. Each kit has the appropriate colours for a particular subject.

Silver finishing

Many jet aircraft and metal monoplanes of the late 1930s were left unpainted in bare aluminium. Although silver paint will give a satisfactory result, a much more authentic effect can be achieved by using one of the paper-backed, self-adhesive foils available to the modeller. As long as the foil is applied in strips along the panel lines of the aircraft, you will find the technique quite simple. It is important to remember that the material will not bend round a compound curve.

Right Northrop A17 finished in gleaming 'Metalskin'.

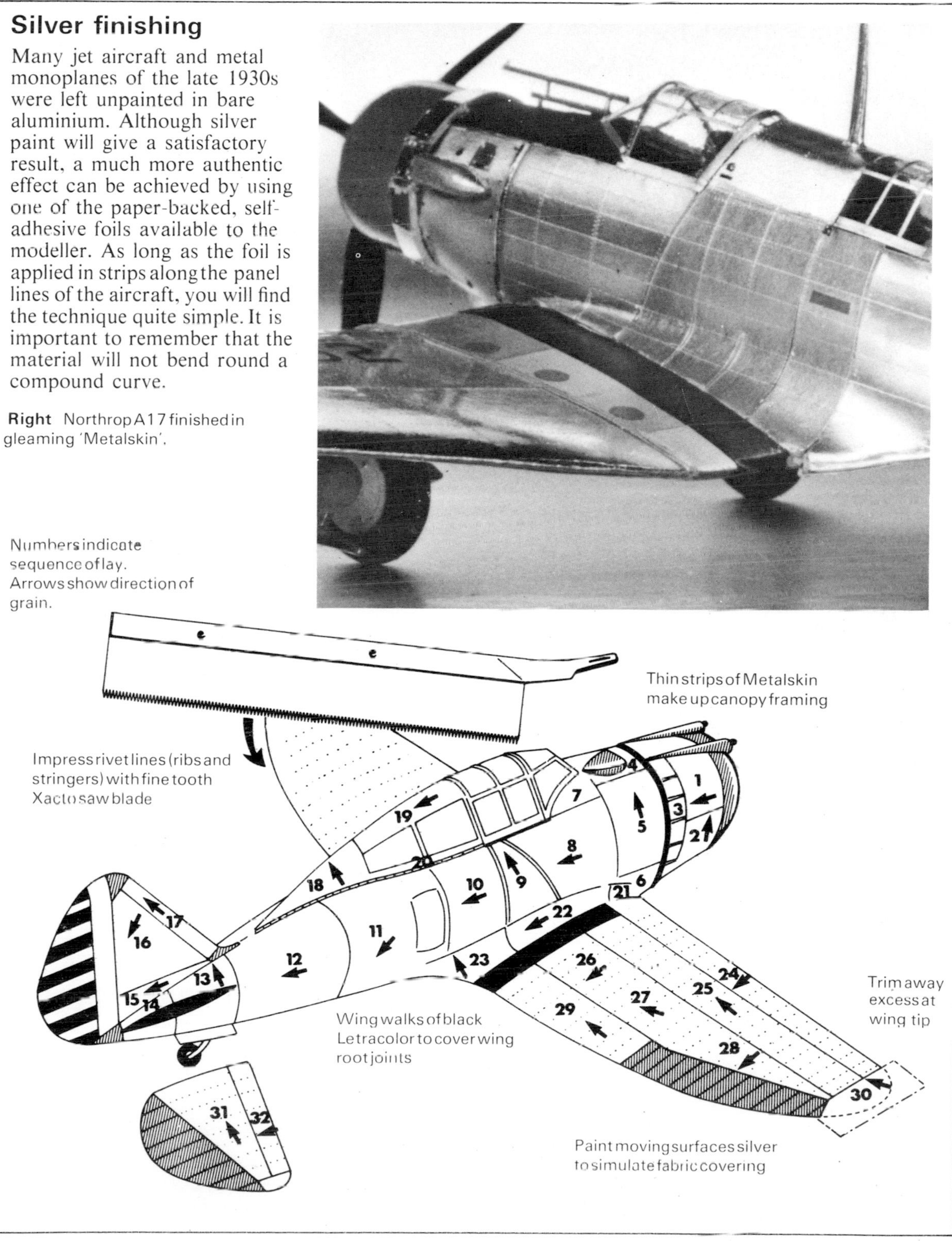

The basic range of Humbrol paints: with these, there is virtually no effect or markings the modeller cannot obtain.

smaller, buy the OOO size. The sizes go up in numbers 2, 3, 4, 5 and so on.

A number 2 size chisel-edged brush is also very useful. This, as its name implies, is straight edged and is invaluable when painting a smooth edge between the two adjacent colours in a camouflage scheme, for instance. Chisel-edged brushes also come in a range of sizes.

Whichever brushes you choose, don't overlook the important fact that they must be kept clean and tidy.

Buy a small bottle of turps or white spirit and keep it exclusively for cleaning brushes. When you've been painting large surfaces, pour a little turps into an old saucer or dish and work the paint brush out thoroughly by pressing it against the bottom of the saucer in a twisting motion. If this doesn't get all the paint out, knead the brush with your fingers. Then dry the turps out with an old rag and wash the brush through again, this time in another saucer of slightly soapy water. Then dry the brush off and it should be as good as new.

If a variety of colours is being used to paint in the final detail parts of a model and only the tip of the brush is being dipped into the paint, you can clean the tip off by just dipping it into the turps, drying thoroughly with your rag, and then going straight on to the next colour. At the end of your painting session, however, give the brush the full cleaning treatment. After cleaning, always stroke the point back into the brush with your rag and return it to store; never rest it on its tip or stand anything else on it that might crush it out of shape. It's a good idea to keep your brushes in a pencil box or upside down in a jar.

It is never necessary to have the whole brush overflowing with paint, nor should you find your brush dropping big blobs of paint *en route* from tin to model. It it does, you're dipping your brush too far into the paint. As a general rule, always pick up less paint on your brush than seems necessary. You can always go back and take another dip; this is far cleverer than having to wipe surplus paint off the model. To avoid taking too much paint from the tin, just wipe the tip of the brush against the inner rim of the paint tin after you've dipped it in; any excess paint will get knocked off the brush.

The Humbrol specific kit range contains about six colours suitable for specialist modellers.

Brushes

The best brushes are made from sable and are expensive. However, as most modellers only require two or three brushes, it is worth the extra investment in sable brushes. Cheaper and far less resilient brushes are made from squirrel or ox hair; these simply do not compare with pure sable.

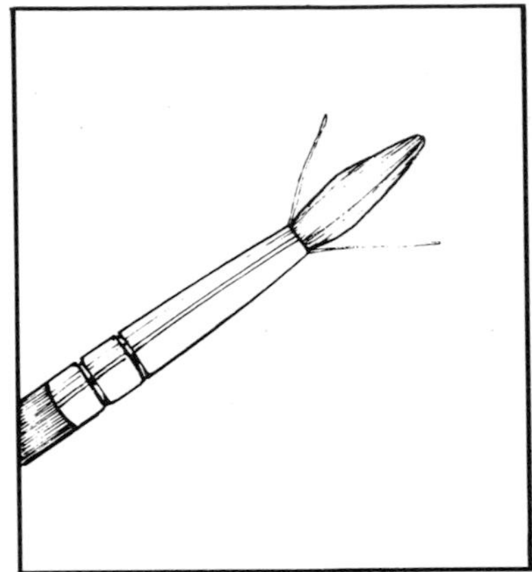

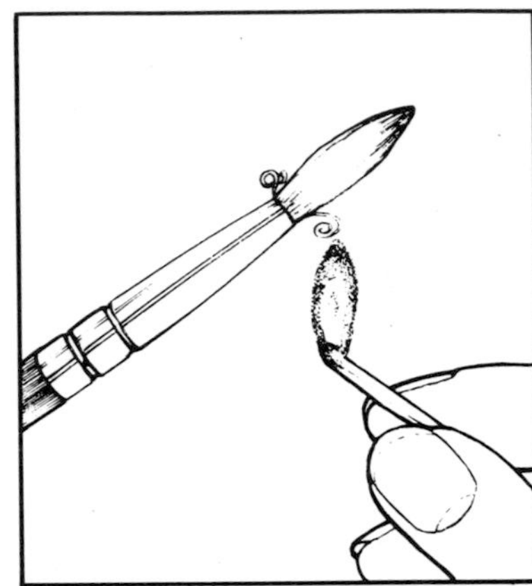

If a brush has the odd hair that will not lie flat with the rest, do not try to pull it out. Wet the brush in water and shape the hairs together and very quickly pass the brush over a flame. This will burn off just the outstanding hair.

The ruling pen

The ruling pen, sometimes called a drawing or bow pen, is useful for drawing fine lines of constant thickness. This would be almost impossible with a brush. To allow the paint to flow consistently, it will probably be necessary to thin the paint with a little white spirit. It is best to practise on some paper to become accustomed to the technique and to test the thickness of the line.

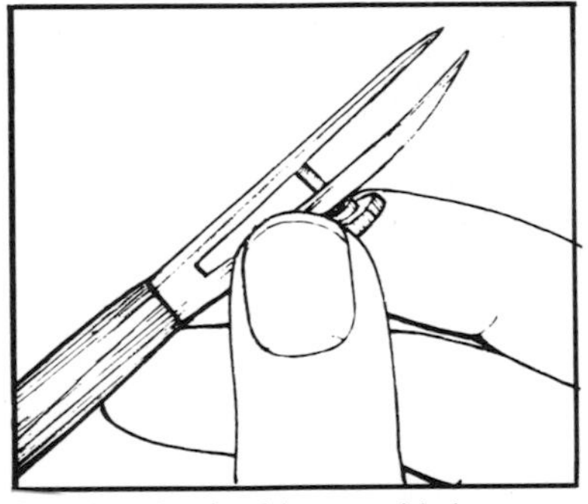

1 Adjust the tip of the pen with the knurled wheel to the required line width.

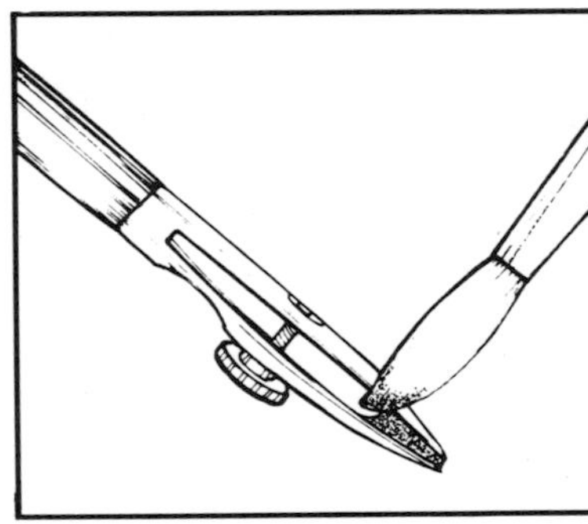

2 Load the pen with paint using a brush and test on some paper.

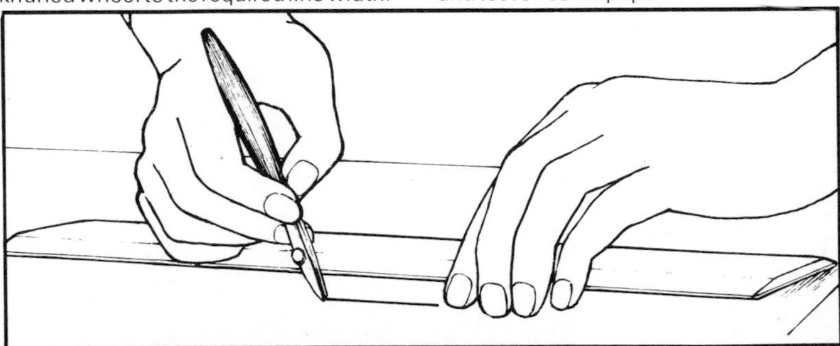

3 To draw a straight line, hold a ruler clear of the surface with your fingers under the front edge and your thumb pressing down on the back edge.

000 M.GRUMBACHER BEAUX ARTS 190 IRELAND
00 M.GRUMBACHER BEAUX ARTS 190 IRELAND
0 M.GRUMBACHER BEAUX ARTS 190 IRELAND
1 M.GRUMBACHER BEAUX ARTS 190 IRELAND
2 M.GRUMBACHER N.Y. BEAUX ARTS 190 U.S.A.
3 M.GRUMBACHER BEAUX ARTS 190 IRELAND
4 M.GRUMBACHER BEAUX ARTS 190 IRELAND
5 M.GRUMBACHER N.Y. BEAUX ARTS 190 U.S.A.
6 M.GRUMBACHER N.Y. BEAUX ARTS 190 U.S.A.
7
8 M.GRUMBACHER BEAUX ARTS 190 IRELAND
10 M.GRUMBACHER N.Y. BEAUX ARTS 190 U.S.A.
12 M.GRUMBACHER BEAUX ARTS 190 IRELAND

AIRFIX
GLOSS
PAINT
G8 SILVER

Preparing to paint

Wood models need extremely fine finishing before they are painted; the process can be laborious. Priming and undercoating are of the first importance. With balsa wood you will need several coats of balsa filler; rub each lightly down before the next application. One useful trick for getting a really smooth finish is to add talcum powder to clear dope and then add two or three coats of the mixture (rubbing down between each application) after each of the filler coats.

On hardwoods, use several coats of ordinary primer paint and undercoat as sold in hardware shops. Rub each coat down until smooth. A less orthodox but effective alternative is to apply grey cellulose car primer paint (available from motor shops) very thickly, rubbing it down between coats. Up to five or six coats may be needed for a really good finish.

Plastic models have further problems of their own. There is a great temptation to cut corners by not painting the whole model, but the sheen on unpainted plastic fails to give the slightest suggestion of the painted metal, wood or fabric of the real thing. Plastic also has static properties which attract dust quickly; the longer the plastic stays unpainted the more and more ingrained the dust seems to become. So always make it a rule to paint the whole model, however near the plastic may be to the finished colour. An unpainted model is never really finished, because no matter how skilled and clever you are it is rarely possible to conceal join lines without a coat of paint. Working parts such as the wheels and motion of a locomotive can however be left unpainted. Some very small models may be left unpainted if the plastic is correctly coloured, but they must be coated with clear varnish once they have been completed.

Painting small OO/HO figures with a fine brush. Soft plastic figures such as these do not react to paint well; however, an undercoat of white PVA glue produces a hard shell which will accept paint.

Oil-based enamel paints take very well on plastic kits even on an unprepared surface. In most cases you can paint straight on to a model you've just made without any special preparation at all. However, you are likely to catch up all the bits of filings, dust and grease from your fingers, so don't be surprised if you achieve a bitty finish.

Before putting paint to plastic, stand back and study the finished model at eye level to check that you haven't forgotten any important addition or detail. Then survey the model very closely, looking along each surface to see if there are any nicks, particles of plastic, scratches etc., and treat them straight away. Imperfections that are hardly noticeable on an unpainted model will be very apparent from under a coat of paint. Then dust the model thoroughly to remove any filings or dust; a good idea is to use a big soft number 5 paint brush which gets right into corners and crevices with no risk of damage. Check joins and moving parts in particular – wing roots and wheel hubs are just the places where dust gathers and gets overlooked.

Now all you have to do is remove the grease. The most effective way of doing this is by washing. Notice how greasy plastic kits are. Some of the grease comes from the moulding process, which leaves a very fine film over the entire surface; a lot more comes from your fingers. Ordinary oil-based enamel paints such as Humbrol adhere perfectly well to a plastic model which has not been de-greased. It is not really necessary to wash tank models before painting unless they are obviously dirty. In real life tanks usually have a very rough finish which you can capture by putting paint straight on to an unprepared surface. Aircraft, cars and ships are a different matter. Much more care is lavished on painting them in real life – whether in the interests of efficiency or looks, or both – and this must be reflected in the model. A lumpy rough surface may look lifelike on a tank model; it looks awful on a model aircraft.

Washing will give a nice smooth plastic surface free from greasy ridges and specks of dust. But don't rush off and hold your model under a tap: this may get the grease off, but all the most inaccessible places will fill with water and it'll leak for days. The easiest way of washing a model is with a soft number 5 size (or similar) brush and a saucer of cold water in which just a tiny drop of washing-up fluid has been dissolved. Wash the model by brushing it with the soapy solution as if you were painting it, a section at a time. Then follow up with a small piece of bath sponge and another saucer of cold water, drying off each section before proceeding to the next. This may sound laborious, but on a 1:72 scale plane it will take about five minutes work so long as you are not over-liberal with water. Dry it off completely, however, or additional smears will dry on to the plastic which will defeat the whole object of the exercise. A little rubbing with a sponge should remove any really dirty patches.

Painting Polythene

There is one plastic you really can scrub. This is the polythene-based plastic in which Airfix OO/HO size figures are moulded. It is so greasy that oil-based enamels won't adhere to them if you paint them straight from the box. The procedure here is to remove any flash when you take the figures from their sprue, toss them into a bowl of cold, slightly soapy water, scrub them with a nail brush, and wash them off under a running cold tap. Then dry them in an old towel or tea cloth. Enamels will then take more kindly to these little figures than you ever supposed.

Finally, I must stress that you should always use cold water with any form of plastic: hot water will distort or soften your model, as will any form of heat, so don't place it by the fire to dry either!

PAINTING TECHNIQUES

Getting a really good surface by brush painting depends on good brushes, a judicious amount of paint on your brush, and a grease- and dust-free surface. If you use an enamel paint such as Humbrol, the natural flow of the paint will do most of the rest for you. Provided that the paint itself is in good condition – you should throw away any that has become lumpy or has lost its smooth consistency – you'll find that brush marks disappear as the paint dries. There's no particular magic about it so long as you paint in one direction only – ie along or across, but not haphazardly in both directions at once. There may well be brush marks when the paint is freshly applied; they'll run into each other after a few moments, so don't be tempted to brush the other way so as to eliminate them. This, incidentally, explains why you should not overload your brush; the brush marks left behind at each stroke will not only run into each other,they'll also run over each other and you'll get 'weeping' or 'curtains' – 'teardrops' of paint or ridges which will only stand out when the paint sets; then the only way to eliminate them is to strip the paint off and start again.

Be careful and patient as you paint. If the surface of your model

does flood with paint, skim off the excess with a dry brush while the paint is freshly applied. Once it has had time (just five minutes) to set it will form a surface which your brush will disturb, leaving ridges in the surface. If this does happen, the best remedial action is to remove the paint before it sets any further and then start all over again. The quick method of doing this is to pour a little turps into a dish and with an old clean cloth apply it to the painted area with a circular motion. Once the first area has been cleared, move your finger to a clean patch of the cloth and repeat. Use just the lightest dab of turps, as excess may harm the plastic surface. In addition, keep turps well clear of transparent plastic.

For maximum control hold the brush on the metal part near the head and keep it in contact with the surface all the time rather than dabbing it up and down.

Never rush things while painting. Putting a second coat on top of a coat of paint which has not dried thoroughly, for instance, will lead to disaster. Unless you are putting a dark coat on a dark plastic, you'll

1:96 scale 'Flower' class corvette, an excellent example of straightforward brush painting.

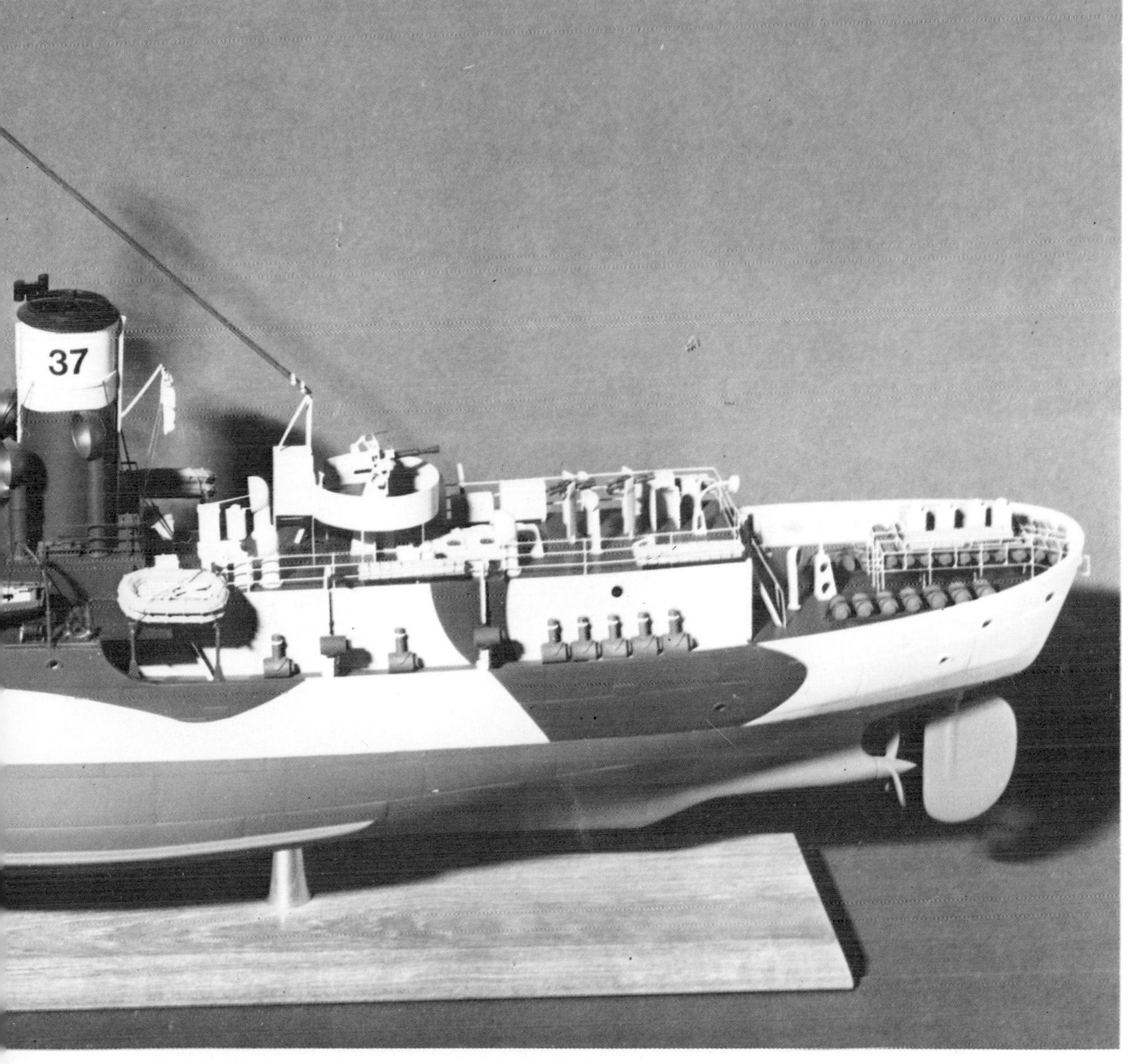

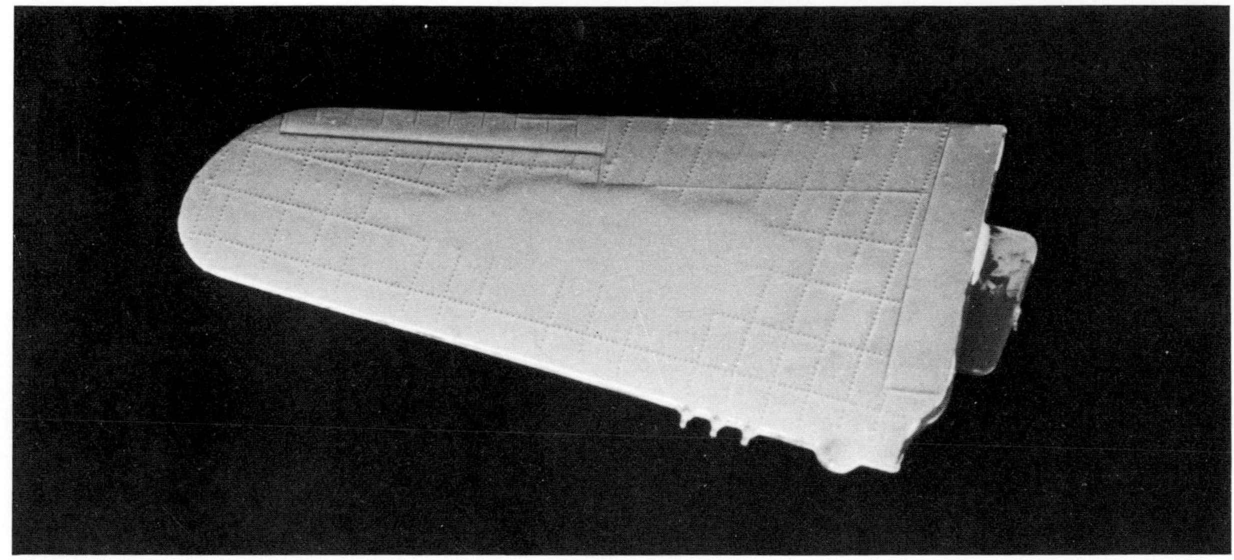

Above an example of careless and haphazard painting where blobs have built up to obscure the surface detail.
Right a useful technique for emphasizing and giving depth to detail, such as control surfaces, is to work in a black wash with a brush, wiping off any surplus after application.

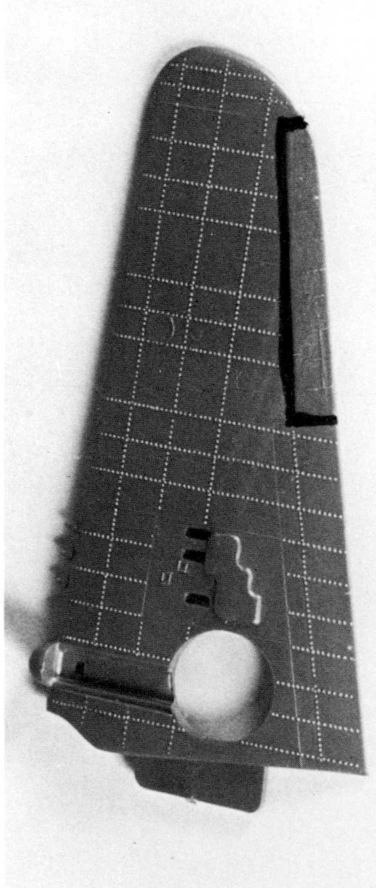

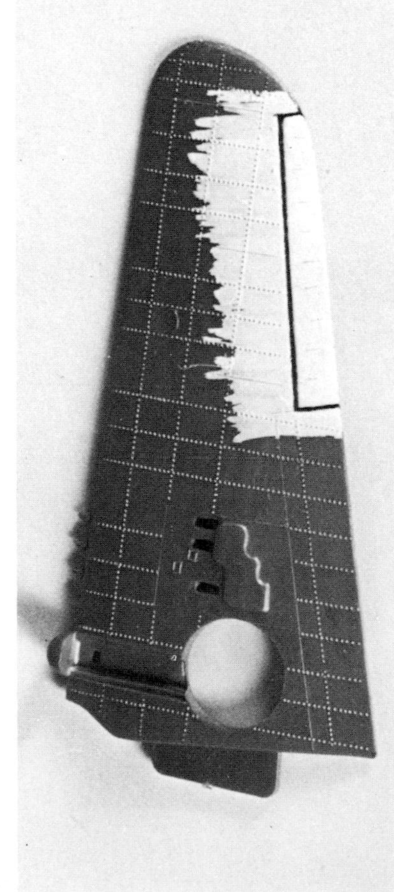

almost certainly need to do two coats or even more to get a perfect surface. Oil-based paints are inherently transparent. Painting yellow over green plastic is a good example: green-yellow streaks will be the first result; beginners will then be tempted to put on more yellow paint straight away. But if you wait overnight and then paint it all over again, you should achieve just the finish you hope for.

Paint as much of a model as you can before assembling it, for many areas become progressively more inaccessible as the model progresses towards completion. So paint such parts as wheel-wells, cab interiors, cockpit walls, seats, wheel hubs, tyres, oleo legs, pilots, chassis members, suspension, wheels, bogies, coupling rods and so on at an early stage. In fact, it's easiest to paint them while they're still on the sprue, since you can hold the sprue and thus avoid getting paint on you fingers or finger marks on the paintwork. Obviously the main structural components such as wings, fuselages, hulls or boilers, for example, can't be painted until after assembly; painting all the small parts is a useful way of utilizing time while waiting for cement or putty to set elsewhere. To avoid having to hold on to the sprue until the paint has set, stick it upright in a jam jar, paste-pot or block of plasticine. When you cut the painted components from the sprue a little unpainted area will remain, but it can be touched up during the main painting session.

When painting a model in more than one colour – for instance, an aircraft camouflaged dark green and dark earth – the easiest procedure is to paint the lighter colour first and then apply the darker pattern after the lighter colour has set.

For camouflage patterns which are irregular, use your chisel-edged brush, since any lobed pattern of this nature can only be applied free hand. If you've painted the light colour first, it is a simple matter to mark out the pattern very lightly with a soft pencil as a guide.

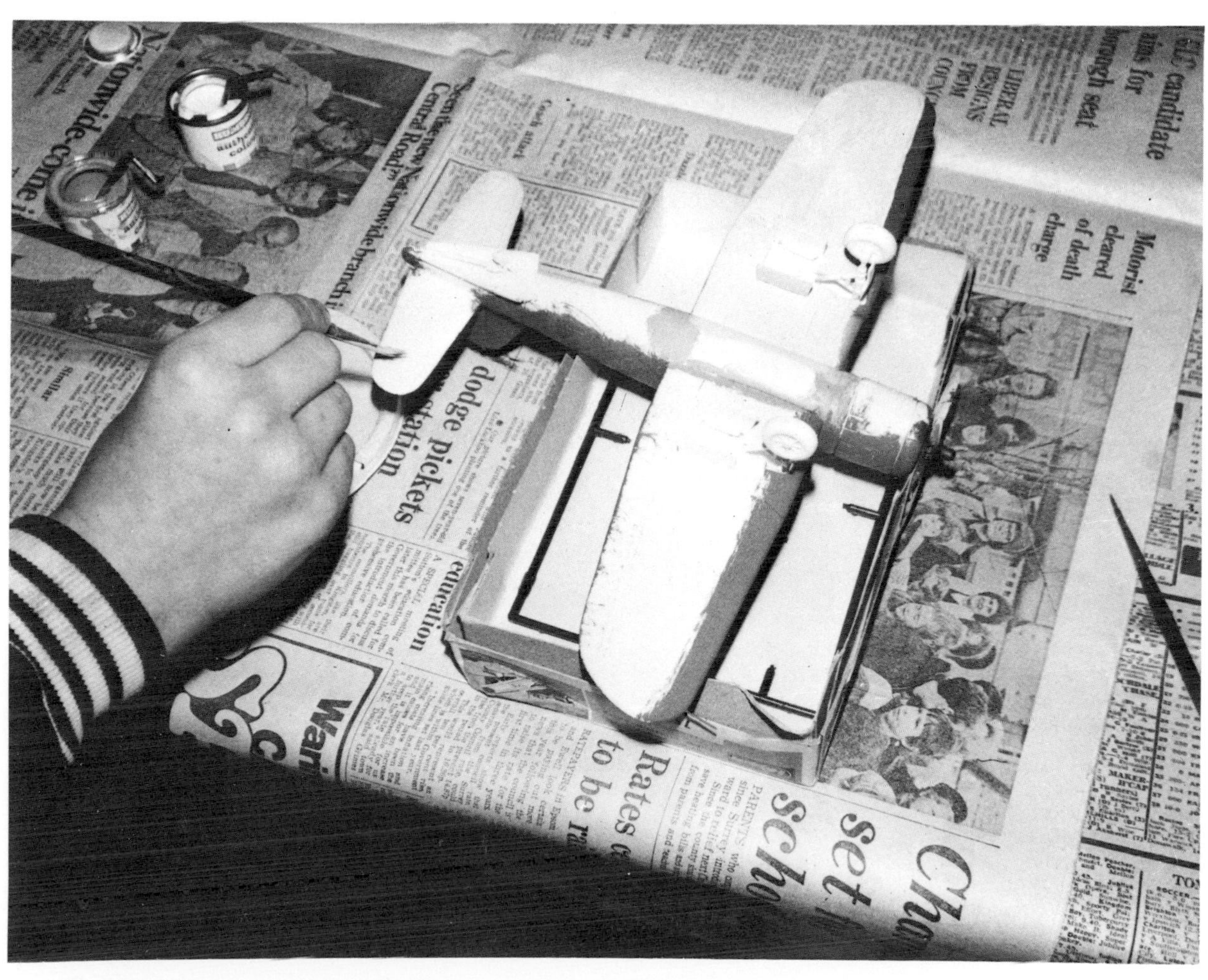

Use a suitably sized cardboard carton, such as a shoe box or the kit box, to support the model when painting.

German camouflage

The task which puts many modellers off First World War period model aircraft is the exotic and intricate lozenge-pattern camouflage carried by many German warplanes of the time. On the real aircraft this effect was obtained by using fabric on which the pattern was printed, in an endlessly repeated pattern, rather like curtain material. You can use the system shown here to draw out and paint in an accurate lozenge scheme without too much trouble, though careful marking out is necessary.

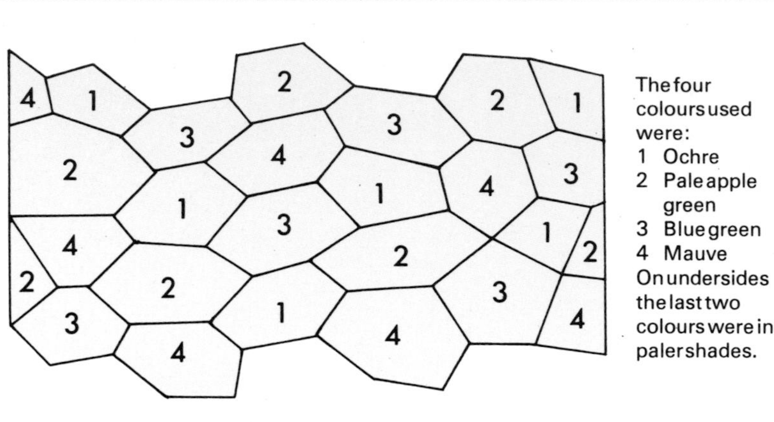

The four colours used were:
1 Ochre
2 Pale apple green
3 Blue green
4 Mauve
On undersides the last two colours were in paler shades.

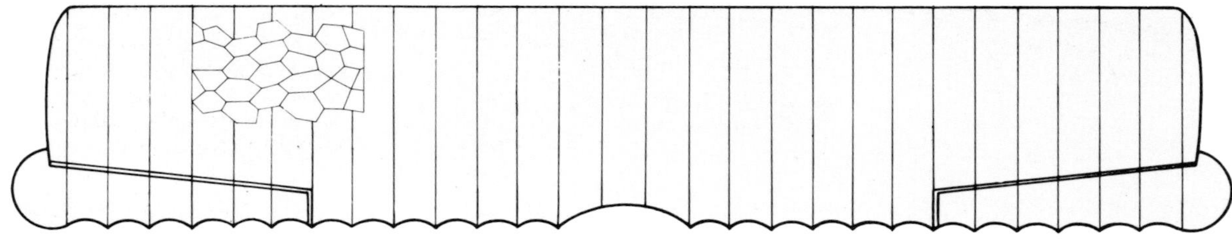

Make a master pattern to the scale you require; this corresponds to the width of the fabric panels in the full-size aircraft. Pattern lines are 1 $\frac{1}{8}$ inch apart for 1:48 scale, $\frac{3}{4}$ inch apart for 1:72 scale, and 1 $\frac{11}{16}$ inch apart for 1:32 scale.

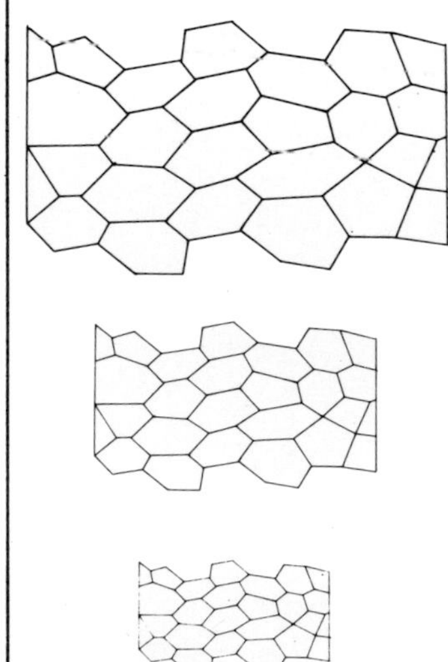

After painting the entire wing surface with one of the pale colours, trace the master pattern on the tracing paper. Draw a series of lines across the wing to depict the panel lines, place the tracing paper master in position to line up with the wing lines, then use a sharp pencil to trace the pattern through to the wings. Move the pattern up one section and repeat. Do this for each set of panel lines until the wing is covered. Then choose the next easiest colour to identify, say the green, and fill in the lozenges which should be green, making sure the repetition is in regular sequence. Then apply the remaining two colours, also in regularly repeated sequence. It is a long repetitive job but worthwhile for the end result.

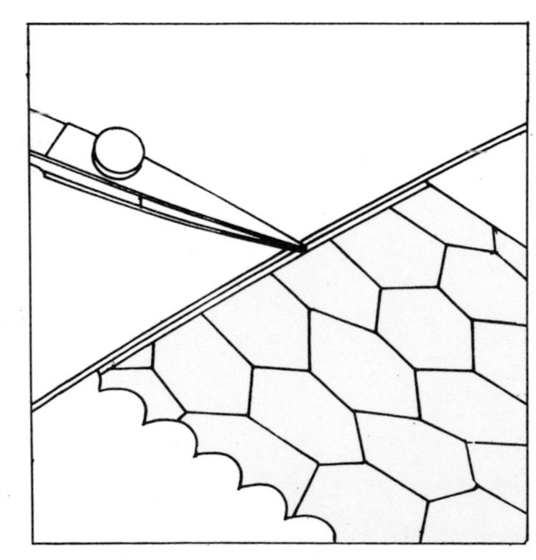

Finally add the rib tapes which were fitted on most aircraft. These were usually light blue. Cut a piece of card, Perspex, or transparent plastic to the appropriate width for the model ribs, hold it over the wing, and draw the tapes in with a stroke of a draughtsman's pen. If this is too complicated, use a good make of blue ball pen with fine point and draw them this way instead—not quite as good, but visually effective.

In the Second World War, as in the First, the Germans excelled themselves in the great variety of camouflage schemes and patterns applied to their aircraft. One reason for the great popularity of German warplanes in model form is undoubtedly because of the fascination of the widely differing styles of camouflage and markings. Don't be put off by the seeming complexity of it all, however. All modern kits of Luftwaffe aircraft come with camouflage patterns and markings fully illustrated in the instruction sheet. But if you want more variety of originality, look up some of the reference books and choose your own subject.

Above a Junkers Ju 88 in Italy in 1944 in characteristic 'ripple' camouflage pattern presenting a good challenge for the modeller. **Left** a close-up of another machine revealing a closer spaced and denser version of the same camouflage, applied by spray gun. **Below** 1:72 scale model of a Fw 189 on the Russian Front in 1943, carrying a further variation of the 'ripple' pattern, in this case green over white, applied by brush, as snow camouflage.

Masking

It is tempting to try painting straight demarcation lines freehand. Lots of people do, and the result is generally disastrous unless they happen to be skilled painters or have a very steady hand. The really easy way to get good straight demarcation lines is to use ordinary masking tape to mask off the edge you require. A simple example is the boot topping of a model ship. Since the hull is the lighter colour, you'll have painted this first, terminating roughly below the level of the boot topping upper edge. When the hull colour has had time to dry thoroughly, preferably overnight, simply take a strip of narrow masking tape and lay it along the hull side with its lower edge along the line of the upper limit of the boot topping. You may need to mark the limits lightly with a pencil as a guide to the precise positioning; some manufacturers etch the boot topping line on the hull, which makes positioning still easier. If the model is big or the hull has a lot of curvature, you won't be able to mask it all with a single strip of tape. In this case use 3-inch lengths, or even shorter ones, taking care to keep the line straight when seen from the side.

Before your start to paint the boot topping, however, rub your finger along the lower edge of the tape to ensure that it is adhering firmly to the plastic. If any part is lifting, the boot topping will creep under the tape and defeat the whole object of masking. Now you are all set for painting; the time spent putting on the masking tape will be amply rewarded by the resulting excellent straight edge. Paint away from the masking rather than up towards it. If you paint towards it, the paint will pile up against the edge of the tape and when the masking is removed a ridge of paint the thickness of the tape will stand out in relief from the model's surface. Occasionally such an effect is desirable, but you certainly don't need it if you have been painting a model car in a two-tone scheme.

Right a Revell 1:72 scale model Haygate (Frank) fighter with subtle wear and weathering applied by paint brush.
Below 1:32 Messerschmitt 109F in a plain two-colour scheme with straight demarcation lines; simple painting schemes are best whenever possible.

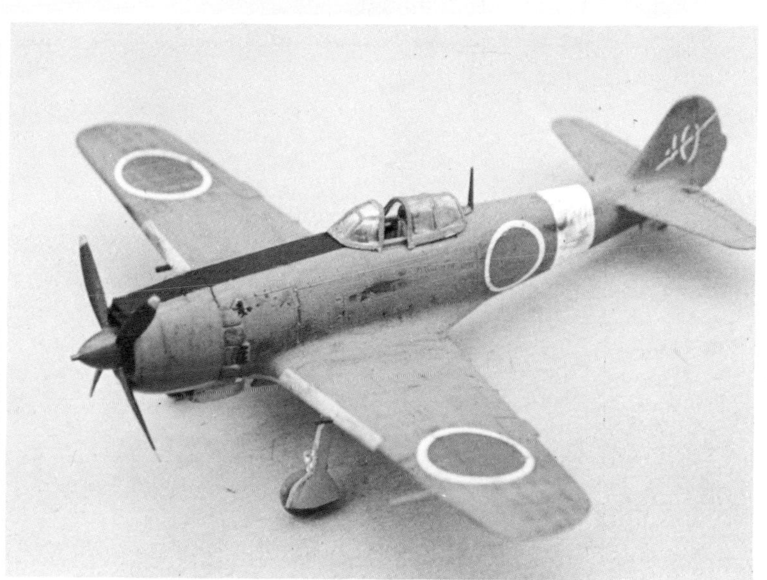

Above a beautifully painted chequered engine cowl on this P-47D, in 1:48 scale.
Right a P-38 Lightning with invasion stripes painted by the masking method.

Invasion stripes and chequered patterns

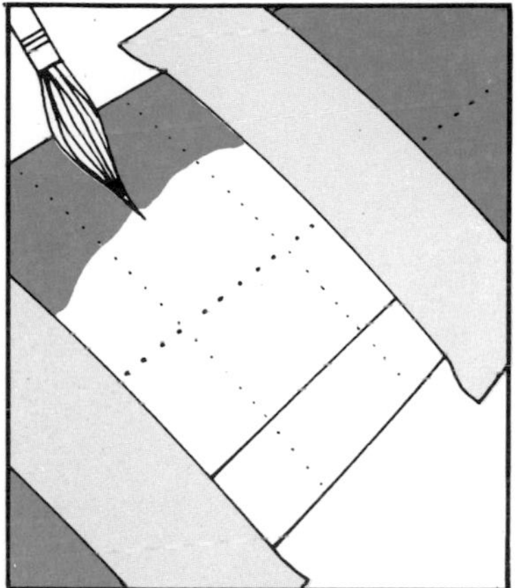

1 Mask off required area with tape. Paint white and allow to dry.

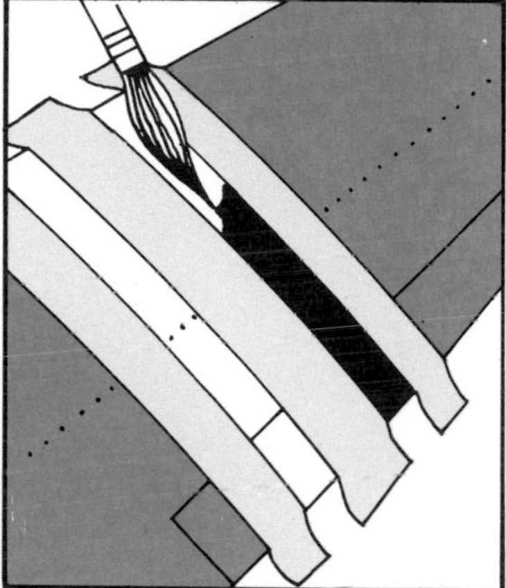

2 Remask with strips of tape the width of the bands and paint black.

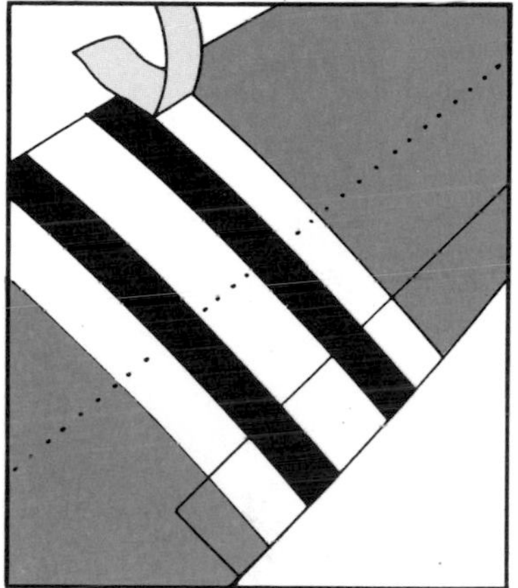

3 When black paint is dry, remove all tape.

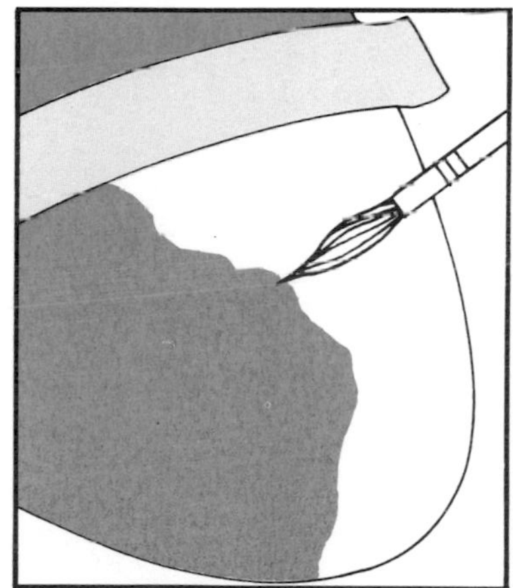

1 Mask off area required as above. Paint white and allow to dry.

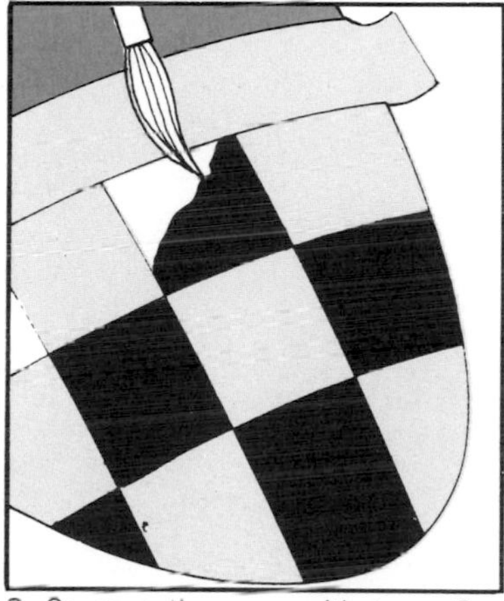

2 Cover entire area with tape. Cut squares with a knife. Peel off every other square. Paint black.

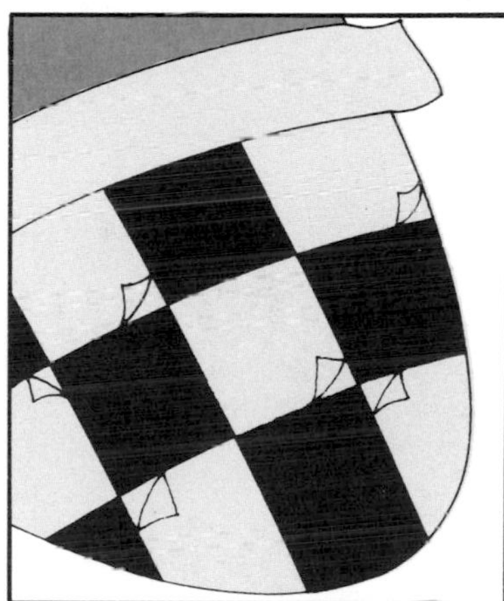

3 When black paint has dried, remove remaining squares of tape.

Having left your boot topping to dry, you can now remove the masking: simply take one end of the tape and peel it gently away. If any small areas of paint come away with the tape you can touch them in afterwards, though if the base colour has been properly applied and allowed to set thoroughly this should not happen.

Follow the same procedure for the demarcation line between upper and lower surface colourings on the fuselage of an aircraft, anti-dazzle panels on cowlings, certain unit markings with straight edges, identification bands or stripes and de-icer boots or coloured leading edges on wings. Simply add another strip of tape at right angles to the main strips where a panel terminates. For invasion stripes of the kind used in Normandy in 1944, simply paint the entire area of wing white, when this is dry, mask off the areas which are to remain white with strips of tape, paint the whole lot black then strip off the masking: you will have perfect black and white striping.

Masking tapes come in varying widths. If you need only a narrow strip, simply cut your tape along the middle line and use only half.

Obviously, you should use the straight outer edge of a split length of tape as the masking edge. Wide masking tape is also a help when painting other shapes such as the lobed camouflage patterns on warplanes. Draw the precise shape of the demarcation in pencil on the tape, then cut it out and put it in place on the model. If used carefully, masking tape can be used several times. Keep special lengths and shapes by sticking them flat on a scrap offcut of Formica.

Mottling

Though most painting is straightforward brush work, quite often there are variations. For example, you may want a mottle finish on, say, a German aircraft model or a tank. What happens then? There are three simple ways of going about it.

The easiest method of all is to stipple the mottling on with a dry splayed-out brush. Don't use one of your good brushes, rather an old cheap brush that is past its prime. Splay out the end (if it's not already splayed) by pressing it on your palm or trimming it down with scissors to a splayed out stump. Then take the colour you are using for the mottle, dip the end of the brush very lightly in the paint – so lightly that you scarcely touch it – 'stab' it lightly against a scrap of plastic to ensure that there's not too much paint on the brush, and start stippling the brush over your model. With a bit of practice you will get an excellent realistic mottle effect.

Start from the top of a model and work towards the bottom, since in most mottled aircraft the actual mottle peters out as it gets lower. The secret of success is to be very sparing both with the amount of paint in your brush and the amount of mottle you apply. It is always easy to add more mottling, much less easy to get too much mottle off again, though this can be done with a cloth dipped in turps. Use the same technique for tanks or vehicles for this sort of finish.

The method of mottling most people favour is with a piece of old sponge. Put a little of the desired colour in a suitable receptacle, take a piece of sponge, dip it very gently into the paint, barely skimming the surface, and apply it by dabbing the sponge over the base colour on the model. Both pressure and amount of paint should be even more sparing, otherwise you'll end up with big smears and no mottle.

The final method is spray painting. Take a piece of card, the backing from an old writing pad for instance, pierce some small holes in it with a fork or knitting needle, hold it about 2 to 3 inches from the model and start spraying from the other side of the card. A certain amount of spray will penetrate the holes and land on the model, thus giving the mottled effect. Of course, the card must be large enough so that it completely conceals the model, and a lot of practice is necessary to get the knack.

Of these three mottling methods, the first is by far the easiest and most foolproof.

Above using a chisel-edged brush to achieve a 'feathered' demarcation line on a model Fw 190.

Opposite page top an Me 262 finished in mottle camouflage achieved by dry brushing.
Below reference to actual photographs helps to gain an authentic effect as with this Fw 190, opposite.

8

Wear and weathering

Weathering is the next technique to think about. Aircraft, tanks, ships and other forms of transport vehicle don't stay in mint condition for long, and it is quite easy to give a 'used' look to a model. Models in a scenic setting must certainly receive suitable treatment, even if you feel that a clean look is better for showcase models. Aircraft tend to be more carefully maintained than most other subjects, so there is some justification for an impeccable finish on all the aircraft models you make. Once you study the real thing, however, you will start to realize that even aircraft get weathered and worn, especially warplanes.

Quite frequently pictures of real aircraft show paint flaking off the wing leading edges and shiny bare metal showing through underneath. Paint may also be wearing away on the wing root where the pilot climbs in and out of the cockpit, and damage in the wings or fuselage may have been patched but not painted, or painted with a darker finish. Again, the patching may obliterate part of the squadron markings. Almost certainly, too, there will be a sooty patch aft of the exhaust manifolds, and possibly dirty oil dribbles under the engine cowling. Paint may also have worn on the cowling covers, where mechanics have been carrying out maintenance, or perhaps they've replaced an elevator which hasn't been painted to match the rest of the colour scheme. All these small points and many more will become evident from a close study of prototype pictures – and all of them can be incorporated into your model.

The track and bogies of a tank may be caked with mud. The identification signs on its turret may have been deliberately smeared over with clay or oil to render them less conspicuous, the exhaust manifolds may be sooty and rusty, with oil patches on the engine covers, to say nothing of the leaking jerricans which have allowed water to stain the hull sides. Buildings have discoloured stonework, water 'runs' down the roof, sooty trains, trucks and cars all come in for similar treatment, and everything wears or weathers with time: all this can be shown in the finish of your model.

Study the extent, direction or form of wear or weathering on your prototype. Then visualize your model as the full-size original and work out your approach from there. To take an aircraft as an example: bare metal showing through the camouflage can obviously be depicted by silver paint, which you may be tempted to apply after you've finished the rest of the painting. But on the real thing the paint was applied to the basic metal surface, so the really effective way of portraying bare metal is to put the silver paint on first and leave it showing through when you apply the camouflage. This doesn't mean painting the whole model silver: if only the wing roots and leading edges are involved, simply paint these areas initially, covering a larger area than will show as bare metal. Then, when you paint the camouflage finish, bring the camouflage over the silver areas, using the splayed brush technique previously described to get an uneven edge depicting the flaking paint. This method can be used on virtually any model on which bare metal is to show through a top coat.

Use matt black paint suitably diluted in turps or thinners to depict exhaust stains and dribbles. Fill your brush with turps and squeeze it into whatever receptacle you use for mixing; then mix in a tiny dab of black and a watery black solution will result which can simply be 'painted' on to the area to be treated. Only the tiniest amount of staining should be applied – as with mottling, apply less than your imagination deems necessary, and use the tiniest strokes of the brush so that you avoid getting a black patch with a definite outline; if this happens you won't get the effect you want at all. You can avoid any suggestion of a definite outline by carefully wiping your brush dry and working it over the sooty area. Take the brush strokes in the direction of the exhausts, aft in this case.

If you look at anything sooty or dirty, you'll rarely find pure black. Most often, staining or soot marks are a dirty mixture of black, brown and grey. So put a little brown with the black in your original mix; this sort of mixture will represent almost any kind of staining or discoloration. Add more or less brown, black or grey as necessary, according to whether the original staining involved oil, soot or just plain dirt. The major precaution is to use a minimum amount of turps; if you use too much you might dissolve the main coat of paint, which would be something of a disaster.

A sooty finish can be obtained with nothing more complicated than a charcoal pencil, available at art shops. Just lick the tip of your finger, rub the end of the pencil on it to give a watery black solution, and then work it in to the required area of the model.

There are several other ways of depicting wear and weathering; the method you use necessarily depends on your particular model. White or black powder paint rubbed well over the model gives a good 'dusty' effect. A dilute black or brown wash (made as suggested for exhaust stains) most effectively makes a model look generally worn, and since the wash runs into recesses, hinge and panel lines for instance, it helps to emphasize detail beautifully. 'Dry brushing', which is like mottling except that it is applied locally, is a good way of applying paint to represent rust streaks or water dribbles etc. Just whisk the brush lightly in the area needed. Brown, mushroom, grey etc. are all suitable colours for this sort of discolouration.

A muddy finish on tanks and trucks is easily got by using the turps or thinners dilution method. This time, however, use dark earth or brownish paints as the main constituent. Humbrol make an

Above and left modellers should always try for as realistic an effect as possible, and this means showing the dirt and wear evident on all planes, including these B17 Flying Fortresses and, left, a Fairey Swordfish.

Above 1:35 Chevrolet truck with realistically mud-spattered windows.
Below Centurion tank, with rain marks on side and front achieved by 'dry brushing'.
Opposite top the rust and water marks on the USS *Olympia* obtained by brush painting.
Right Exhaust stains on a 1:32 scale Grumman Hellcat.

excellent grimy-rusty colour called 'Track Colour' which is also ideal for depicting mud or dirt.

Another good way of depicting mud is to use plastic putty roughly worked in with a screwdriver tip wherever you need it. Just leave it to set, and then touch it up with dark earth or brown paints. Another trick is to add talcum powder to matt dark earth or brown paint. This again gives a rough, lumpy texture which can be worked in where required with a brush.

For rust, dilute a red-brown oxide paint as for the sooty solution and apply it in the same way. The shade of the matt red oxide in the Airfix range is ideal for rust and is also the best miniature shade for depicting the 'Red Admar' paint used on the bottom of ships.

If you make a lot of models, you may well find that the special aerosol spray paints produced by Floquil are a worthwhile investment. They produce a 'grime', 'rust' and 'soot' already mixed which you simply spray over your model where required. It's particularly effective on tanks, railway rolling stock and buildings, on which weathered areas tend to be large. An hour's work with a brush and a selection of paints or mixes takes ten seconds. These aerosol mixes are not suitable if you are solely interested in aircraft models, however, as the spray effect really does blanket the model with more grime than would be seen on a real aircraft. When using spray aerosols, take account of where the 'grime' comes from: for instance, on a vehicle it is largely thrown up by the wheels, so apply the spray upwards from the wheel area.

Choosing the right paint

Kit instructions normally suggest which paints to use. But if all else fails, simple observation is all you need to avoid choosing the wrong type of paint. As a general rule, cars, locomotives, railway rolling stock, woodwork on buildings and jet planes have a gloss or semi-gloss finish, at least when new, and military vehicles, warships, buildings, clothes, animals and a lot of aircraft types have a matt finish. Many materials have predictable finishes; leather is usually gloss, rubber either gloss or matt according to age and so on.

If you are making World War Two aircraft, the chances are that you will hardly ever need gloss finishes, except in the case of highly polished fighters. But the finish on modern aircraft is nearly always polished, even if it's camouflage. As a rule, matt paints are easier to apply by brush and give a better 'look' to a model simply because they are non-reflective; a speck of dust trapped on the surface of the paint may not even show on a matt finish but would most certainly stand out on a gloss finish, perhaps even throwing a reflection. Gloss tends to dry with a more streaky look than matt; good red and yellow are particularly difficult to put evenly on plastic. Finally, most paint sold as gloss is too gloss for models. In real life even a highly polished car doesn't shine as much as its equivalent in miniature when gloss paint is used straight from the tin, so the really wise modeller will avoid using neat gloss altogether, except perhaps for small details such as the leather seats of a car or a soldier's boots.

Fortunately, however, some paintmakers, notably Humbrol, give admirable help to the modeller. First of all, they make a range of semi-matt paints under the name of Railway Enamels; every modeller should have some of these, whether or not he makes railway models. The significance of the brand name is that the colours are matched to actual railway company colours – but as railways used a lot of colours there is quite a close match with other colours even if you use the Railway Enamels straight from the tin; and of course you can always mix them to provide other shades. Apart from being perfect for railway models, Railway Enamels are excellent for anything – cars, trucks and airliners – which is gloss in real life. In fact they give a perfect 'scale reflection'. In addition, they are fine for jet aircraft; several of the colours are very close to standard camouflage colours.

The modern modeller needs to do little mixing, because the vast range of shades now available means that at least one manufacturer makes exactly the colour you need. Occasionally, however, you may feel inclined to mix the odd shade for yourself, or you may read a magazine article which tells you how to mix a colour omitted from all the paint ranges. It is also sometimes necessary to tone

down a shade, especially if you are painting a supposedly weathered building, when you would add a little black or white to the basic colour. In these cases go ahead and simply mix the paints, one colour into another.

Most plastic paint is compatible, but to be on the safe side restrict the colours you mix to those of the same make. Obviously, do not mix the paints together in the tins but use some suitable mixing

Superb 1:32 M3 Lee tank made not from steel – despite its appearance – but from a plastic kit; the realistic 'steel' texture of the parts has been enhanced by careful painting.

Top the finish on this 1:25 scale Jaguar SS100 has just the right reflective quality.
Above Javelin night fighter with semi-gloss camouflage.
Below 1:72 Curtiss Helldriver painted to depict a brand new plane.

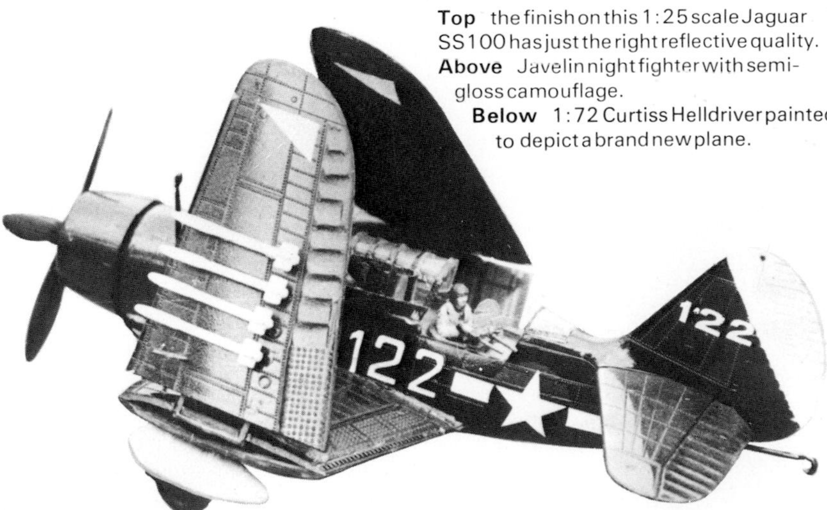

receptacle, such as the foil dishes which come with oven-ready pies.

It is particularly useful to be able to measure paint precisely. Mixing instructions often refer to 'four parts of matt red, two parts gloss brown' etc; guessing doesn't really help. An old salt spoon or small plastic ice cream scoop will enable you to ladle the paint in very precise quantities straight from the tin or bottle into the mixing tray. This is simple, but you must clean the spoon with a clean rag between colours, of course, to avoid mixing the paint in the tins as well as in the trays. Use old cocktail sticks or bent paper clips for mixing, but again wipe them off before trying to mix another colour. Clear varnish is another essential painting aid. Several manufacturers, including Humbrol and Airfix, produce clear varnish in both matt and gloss forms. This is used either for matting down a gloss coat of paint or for painting over a complete model once the transfers have been affixed. It is a most effective medium, especially for getting the very slight sheen on a polished World War Two fighter model or the polished effect on a tank that has been cleaned up for a parade. It is most important, however, to stir matt varnish vigorously for at least ten minutes before you apply it, otherwise it may not dry properly.

Modellers do not generally use gloss varnish much, but it is particularly good for coating cockpit transparencies; indeed, in my opinion it is a 'must' as it gives an excellent 'glass' look and removes the plastic texture. It also saves you buying gloss paint when only small quantities are required and is ideal for putting a 'wet' look on ships' waterlines or on waterfalls.

It's easy to spend much more than you need on paints, so make it a rule to look after what you do buy.

Always put the lid back on a tin; don't leave it standing open to be knocked over. If paint solidifies round the rim of the tin or bottle, scrape it off with an old knife blade

False shading can give added depth, as with the black shading around the engine fittings on this 1:72 Short Singapore flying boat.

and ditch your scrapings – don't let them fall back into the paint. Solidified paint will stop you closing the tin properly, thus letting air inside. If a skin should form on the paint, remove it with a cocktail stick and throw it away. Paint which has stood unused for many months is suspect; if the pigment has solidified at the bottom of the tin, dispose of it and buy some new paint. Get rid of any paint that gets lumpy in normal use. Finally, if tins of paint are standing unused for a long period, invert them occasionally to prevent the pigment from settling.

Stir all paint vigorously before use with a cocktail stick, wire or old sprue. Make sure all traces of streaks disappear before applying. If a tin is in use for any length of time, stir the paint again frequently.

Make sure that everything, clean rags, tùrps and thinners etc., is to hand before you begin painting, and that you have somewhere to stand models while the paint dries. Old box lids are very useful. Paper or some other coverage is essential to catch spilled paint.

Keep paints safe when not in use. An old wooden box or tin which gives room for brushes and rags as well is ideal, but a cardboard box does just as well and catches any unexpected leaks. Always wipe the sides of paint tins or jars before returning them to store.

Dust is the big enemy of drying paint and settles and sticks on the surface. Bedrooms tend to be dustier than other rooms because of blankets and daily bed making, so, if you can get permission, use the kitchen or bathroom for painting, as there is generally enough damp to lay most of the dust. But check first that your kitchen or bathroom doesn't suffer from condensation problems: if the ventilation is adequate and the walls don't run with damp you will be all right. Leave the model to dry somewhere where it won't get moved or knocked, putting a 'wet paint' notice by it if necessary. One idea is to cover models with a shoe-box (or something larger if necessary) until the paint is thoroughly dry.

Always leave paint to dry overnight. Some paints dry faster than this, sometimes in a matter of minutes. But always leave them longer than the manufacturer indicates and never touch them before you are sure that the paint is rock hard. If you must satisfy your curiosity, paint a 'test patch' on scrap plastic when you paint the model and touch that rather than the model itself. Last of all, never paint a second coat or a second colour before the first coat is dry.

If your eyesight is not too good, or if you have some tricky detailing to paint, ensure that the model is well illuminated and try examining the area you have to paint under a magnifying glass. You can also buy magnifying glasses on stands; this leaves your hands free to get on with the painting.

Finally, always paint in daylight whenever possible. It's only too easy to leave tiny areas uncovered when you paint in artificial light and not notice them until after the paint is dry. If this presents problems, do your main coats in daylight and leave smaller areas and details till later.

AIRBRUSHING

The airbrush is one of the most recent painting aids for modellers. It's not a new idea, though, for airbrushes have been used in commercial art for many years. But it was only in the 1970s that small airbrushes came on sale at prices and sizes modellers could afford. Badger, Humbrol, Paabst, and De Villbus are among those who manufacture airbrushes.

The old type of airbrush was driven by a motor-compressor. What made the airbrush more suitable for modelling work was the introduction of the aerosol 'bomb' in place of the motor compressor. Of course, the 'bomb' has a limited running life, but when it is exhausted it can simply be discarded and replaced by a new can. 'Bombs' come in various sizes; the more elaborate have pressure controls.

The airbrush is a small instrument about the size of a fountain pen and not unlike it in shape. It is held exactly like a pen. Where the nib would be there is a nozzle, a fine tube which is adjustable on the more expensive models. A reservoir to hold the paint is either incorporated in the holder or takes the form of a bulb near the nozzle. An air tube connects the airbrush to the aerosol 'bomb'. When the air supply is switched on the air rushes through the nozzle pulling a fine spray of paint with it.

For small scale models, the airbrush is still something of a luxury,

The *Mauretania* receiving a basic grey undercoat with an airbrush; the table is protected by brown paper.

The modeller's airbrush

A top quality airbrush and mechanical compressor, as used by commercial artists, can involve a very large financial investment. However, over the last few years, airbrushes with aerosol type power units designed specifically for the modeller have been available quite cheaply. Although this type of airbrush is not capable of the same fineness of line and subtlety of tone that can be achieved by a more sophisticated model, it will fulfil the needs of the average modeller.

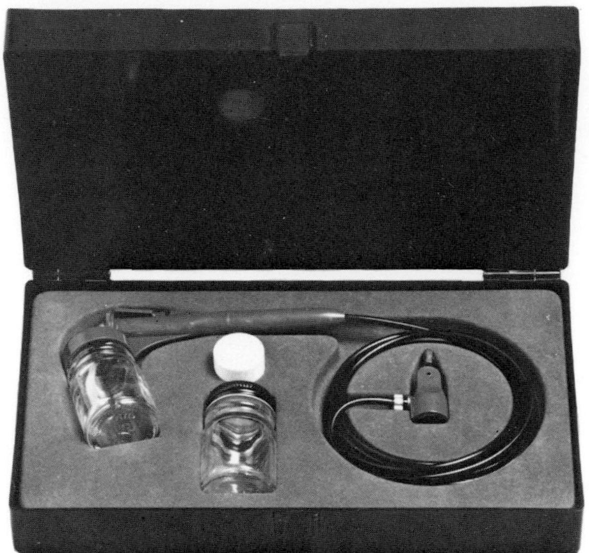

Right a modeller's airbrush kit complete with two paint jars and power unit.
Below the parts of a modeller's airbrush.

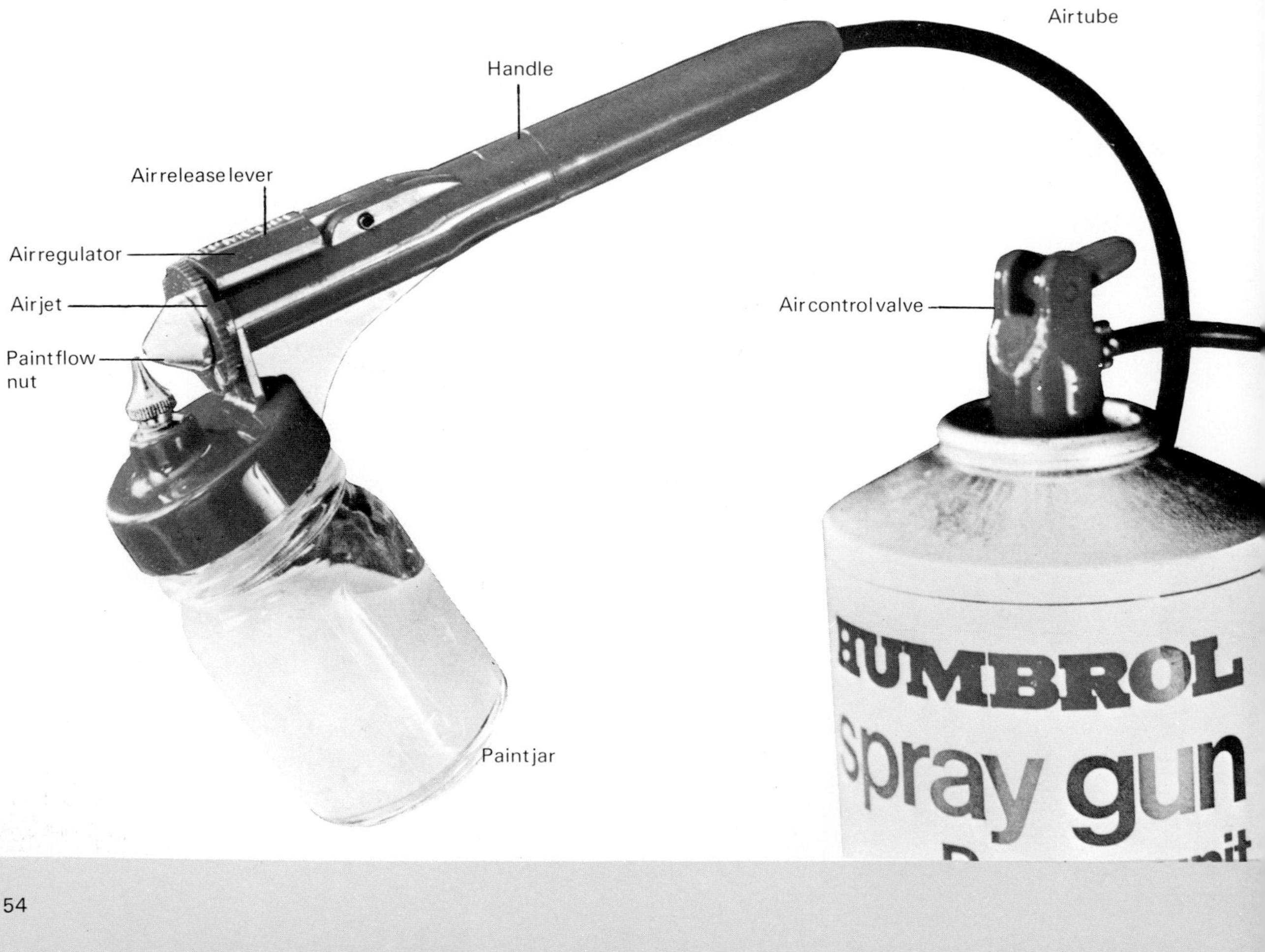

Air tube
Handle
Air release lever
Air regulator
Air jet
Air control valve
Paint flow nut
Paint jar

1
2
3
4
5
6
7
8
9
10
11
12
13
14
15
16
17
18
19
20
21
22
23
24

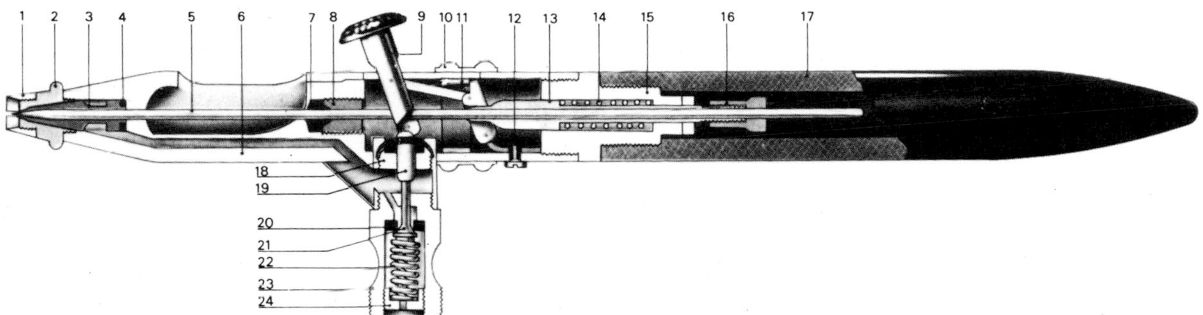

The parts of a conventional airbrush

1 Air cap guard
2 Air cap
3 Nozzle
4 Nozzle washer
5 Fluid needle
6 Model body assembly
7 Needle gland washer
8 Needle packing gland
9 Lever assembly
10 Cam ring
11 Cam
12 Fixing screw
13 Square piece
14 Needle spring
15 Needle spring box
16 Needle locking nut
17 Handle
18 Diaphragm nut
19 Diaphragm assembly
20 Air valve washer
21 Air valve stem
22 Air valve spring
23 Air valve box
24 Air valve spring retainer

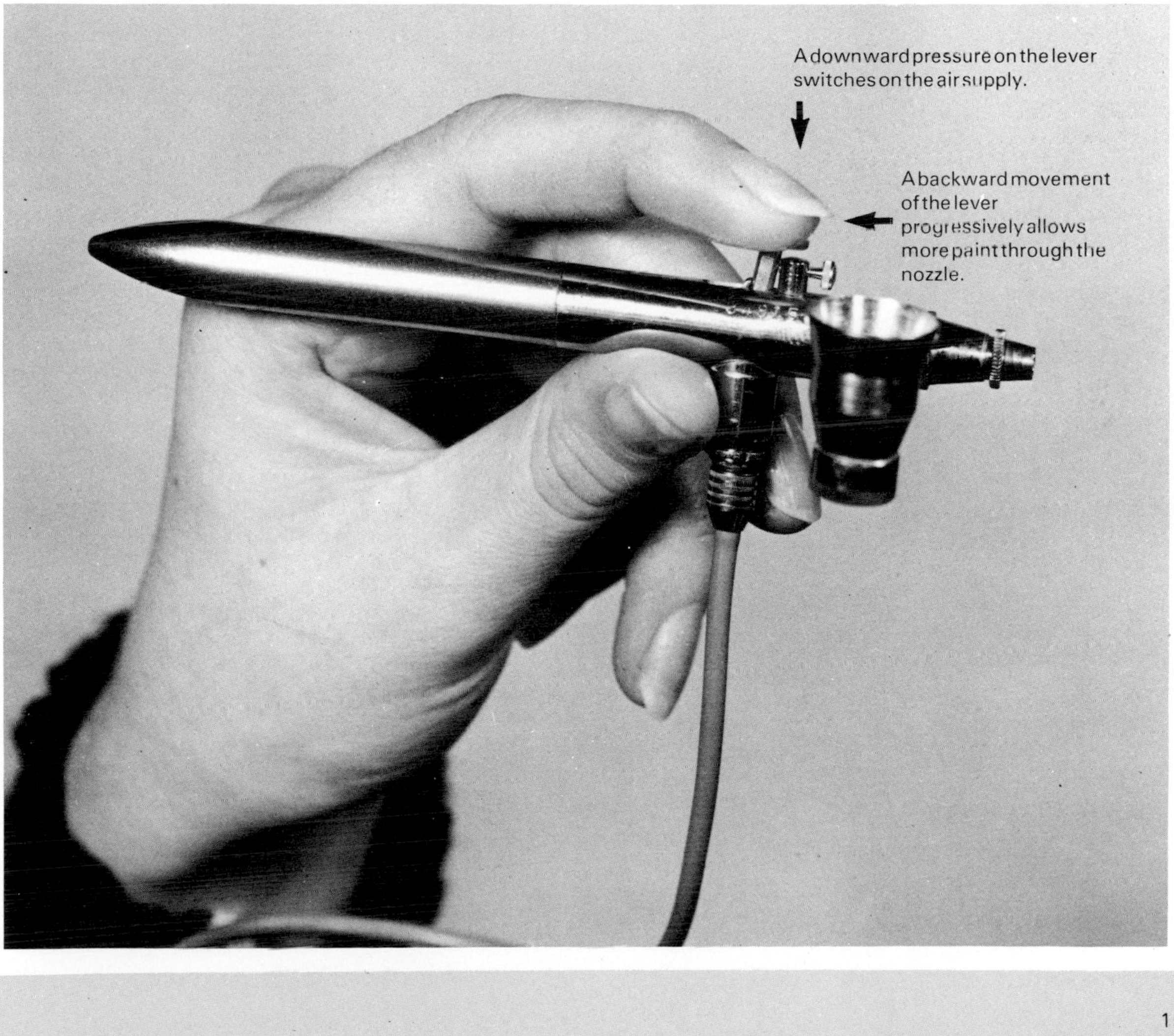

A downward pressure on the lever switches on the air supply.
A backward movement of the lever progressively allows more paint through the nozzle.

Airbrush effects

Airbrushing is a quick and easy way of painting large areas, and a wide variety of effects can be achieved.
Right He 219 night fighter with a lightly airbrushed mottle finish.
Below start with simple colour schemes, as on this Ju88 A-4 fighter, which is basically sand and light blue; the realistic green mottle can be added by airbrush.
Opposite top a soft, gradual division between upper and lower colour schemes, as here, is best achieved with an airbrush.
Opposite bottom underside view of an airbrushed P-47 Thunderbolt; very subtle streaks of weathering have been added to tone down the overall finish.

3

Right if you paint camouflage regularly on your models, make and mark card templates so that you can use them time and again for masking; hold them lightly in position either with tape or by hand, using the tabs.
Below airbrushing has achieved a soft division of camouflage on this 1 : 72 scale Phantom F-4.

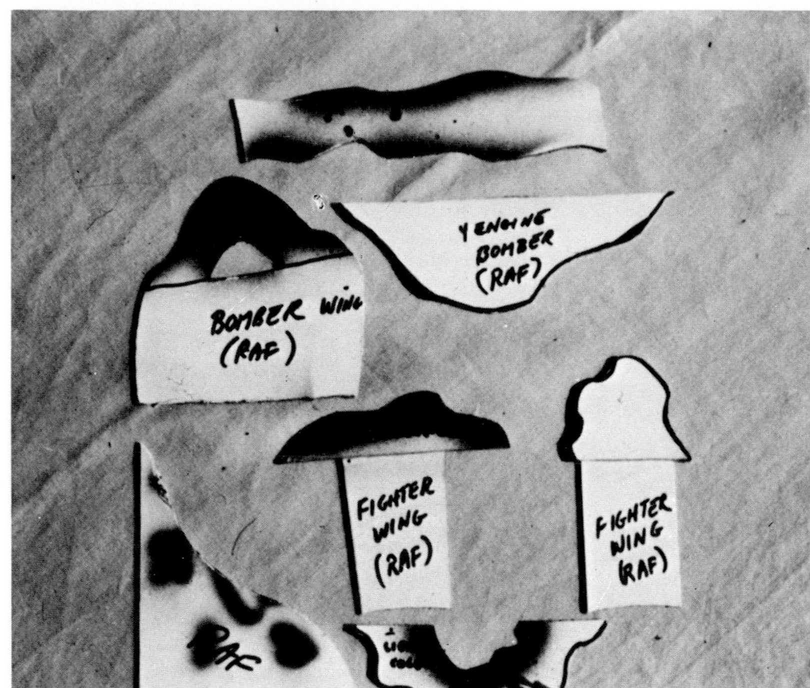

and on many sorts of models, model soldiers for example, you may never need to use one. However, there is no denying that an airbrush allows you to tackle ambitious paint schemes with excellent 'professional' results, especially on model aircraft and tanks. If you do either buy or borrow an airbrush, however, it is essential to practise with it first on glossy card or better still on plastic scrap parts. Observe the fine spray of colour and the way in which areas can be covered with minimum fuss.

Theoretically, airbrushing can be done indoors, but a novice would do better to work in a garden shed or garage, at least until well practised. Good ventilation is essential. The paint used in an airbrush should be 'milky' in consistency, according to manufacturer's instructions; this means that ordinary model paints need to be thinned a little with turps or thinners. In practice, however, the pressure of the airbrush tends to separate the original pigment and the thinners, and you might find it better to use fresh paint straight from the tin after thorough mixing. It is essential to ensure that there are no impurities or lumps in the paint (hence the need for fresh paint), for the nozzle is all too easily blocked and proceedings come to a halt until the equipment is stripped and cleaned. The best rule is to load the reservoir little but often. If the paint round the nozzle begins to look dried out, just load some more fresh paint into the reservoir, either poured straight from the tin or decanted into a small bottle first.

Changing colour is easy on most good airbrushes. Just pour the next colour into the reservoir when the first is sprayed out. Spray on to scrap card or plastic until the new colour comes through strong and clean, and then apply the second colour to your model.

With some forward planning, you should be able to take two, three or even more models to the painting stage. Then they can all be painted together. It helps if they are similarly coloured, a batch of Luftwaffe fighters or a group of military vehicle models which are to depict 8th Army types, for instance.

Left mask off areas not to be painted before you start work; use masking tape for flat areas, and stuff orifices and openings with tissues.
Below Centurion ARVE conversion with an airbrushed camouflaged finish; a similar, more extensive dust effect has also been achieved.

The real value of the airbrush is that it enables you, with practice to come up with a really professional looking paint job. Certain items such as aircraft or tanks have a sprayed finish in real life, so that demarcations between camouflage colour have soft 'feathered' edges rather than hard edges. Similarly, many camouflage schemes have 'feathered' mottle patterns. These effects can be duplicated to perfection by airbrush work. Use card masks to shield painted areas while the second colour is worked up to the masked area to give the 'feathered' edge look.

A purchaser must read and follow all the literature put out by airbrush manufacturers and practise all the procedures before starting on painting proper. And, whatever else you do, it is most important to clean all airbrush equipment after use and to store it carefully.

MARKINGS

Almost every kit comes with some sort of markings. The sheet on which they are supplied is sometimes called a 'transfer' sheet, sometimes a 'decal' sheet; the latter term is most common. In an aircraft kit, the sheet will probably be quite comprehensive, with national markings, codes, serials and other markings, if it is a warplane, and registrations and possibly decorative coloured panels if it is a civil aircraft. Tanks may have WD numbers and unit markings, ships will probably only have pennant numbers and their name, locomotives the running number, lining and name, and so on.

Just as transfers vary from subject to subject, so the quality of the transfer varies from manufacturer to manufacturer. Much depends on the actual age of the kit and its country of origin.

Kit transfers are almost always of the waterslide type; this consists of the appropriate colours printed on a soluble base which dissolves in water and provides adhesion when the transfers are located on the model. They are 'fixed' by a clear varnish covering.

The prime rule for applying waterslide transfers is to trim your transfers. The varnish fixing which covers each transfer subject is almost always larger than the marking itself. A group of code letters may be fixed by a rectangle of varnish which simply covers the whole area of the group; and even a simple roundel or cross will have a very slightly bigger varnish covering. When you soak the transfer in water, the whole lot, varnish fixing and all, slides off on to the model – hence the varnish surround. You can avoid this by simply trimming

round each transfer close up to the actual figure or emblem. On an ordinary national marking, for example, cut carefully round the exact edge; cut round each and every letter of squadron codes and soak, slide and position each individually, however easy and tempting it may seem to slide off the whole string of letters as they appear on the transfer sheet. A small pair of nail scissors is ideal for cutting out transfers like this; any really awkward shapes such as the inside corners of Es can be nicked out with the tip of your craft knife before you do any of the main cutting.

It is not always practical to apply this rule to very tiny transfers of serials, aircraft names, maintenance stencilling or tank WD numbers. The procedure here is to treat the whole group like an individual letter and trim close up along the top, bottom and ends. You must take special account of the ends. Though the varnish fixing remains between the digits of the group, the fact that they are small and close together renders it virtually unnoticeable so long as all the edges are closely trimmed.

Application instructions for transfers are usually printed on the back of each sheet. You will need a saucer of water. Always use tweezers to remove the complete transfer, backing as well, from the water, and then hold the item on the model adjacent to its position. Use a matchstick or cocktail stick – not your fingers – to slide the subject

A fine example of model finishing using a combination of kit markings and hand painting, the latter being used to give the eagle motif on the cowling side.

Applying transfers

One of the main problems with waterslide transfers is the reflective carrier base, as can be seen on the Martin Marauder below. There are three ways of coping with this problem: soaking the transfers in a softening agent, covering the entire model with a matt clear varnish or trimming the transfers as illustrated, right. The Rufe floatplane on the opposite page has had its transfers trimmed and the complete model coated with matt varnish.

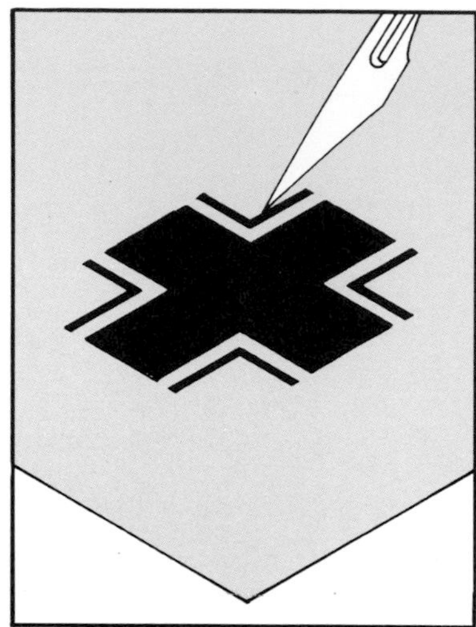

1 Trim round the transfer with scissors or a craft knife as closely as possible to the image.

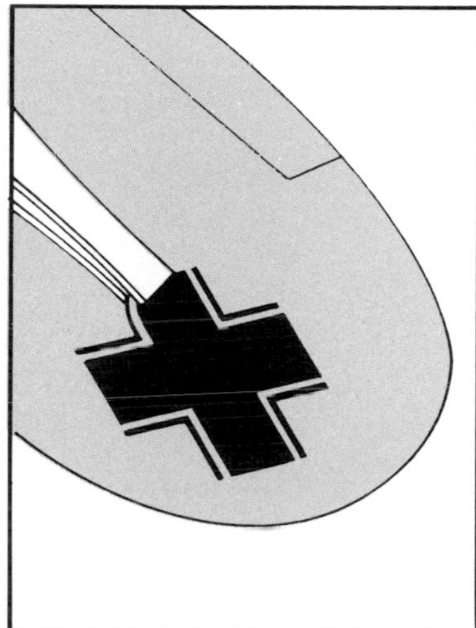

2 After soaking, place the transfer on the surface with tweezers.

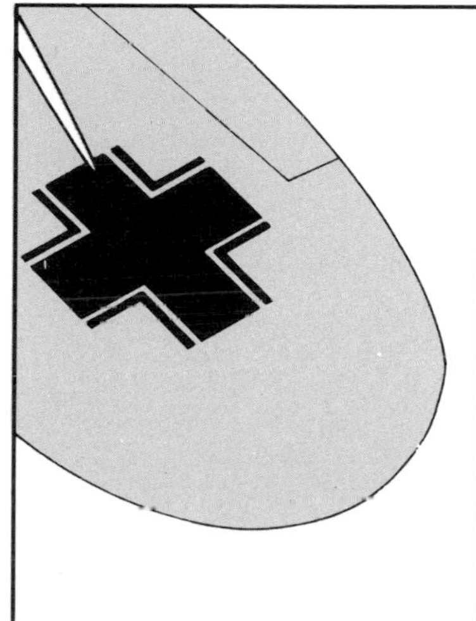

3 Position the transfer with a cocktail stick, using panel lines as a reference.

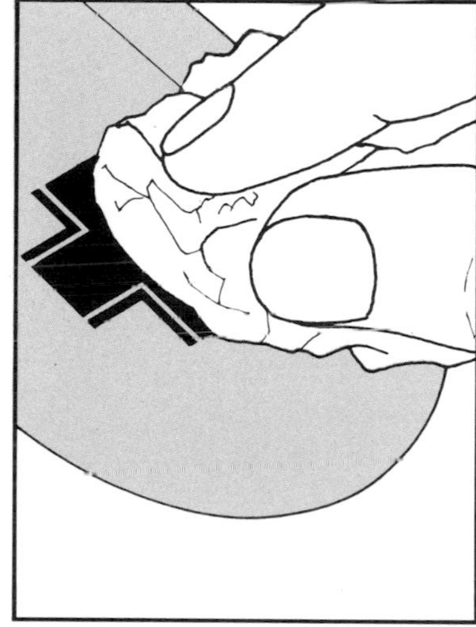

4 Remove excess water by gently dabbing with a dry cloth.

from the backing paper, and on no account make any attempt to slide the transfer before it is really loose on its backing paper. Broken transfers or transfers which stick to your fingers will result if you fail to take these simple precautions. Tweezers are vital, since when you have trimmed close round the subject there will be no backing paper protruding to pick up. When using tweezers, be very gentle. A hard grip may well crack or chip the transfer and land you with work repairing the damage. At worst, your transfer may be ruined completely.

Some water will come away from the backing paper; this provides 'lubrication' on the surface of the model for sliding the transfer so as slightly to adjust its position. When all is in place to your satisfaction, simply press firmly and gently with a clean cloth to squeeze out the air and soak up the water, taking care not to shift the transfer under pressure.

One American transfer manufacturer produces a useful 'softening agent' for use with any make of transfer. It is known as Micro Sol and is merely added to the water.

Needless to say, never apply markings until all the painting is finished to your satisfaction, except for any final touching up you may need to do. Ensure all paint is thoroughly dry.

Once it is in place, check that the transfer is straight or correctly lined up. Compare your model with the kit instructions, drawings and pictures. Very often panel or rivet

lines will act as a good positioning guide, assisting you to check that roundels on each side of the fuselage, for example, are lined up with each other. Faint pencil marks can also be of use when positioning.

Quite frequently a transfer becomes separated from its backing paper while still in the water; if this happens, don't try to marry them up again. And don't be tempted to pull out the transfer on its own. Get a sheet of fairly glossy paper and dip it in the water, lifting it to capture the loose transfer. Then proceed as usual.

If you have wrongly positioned a transfer you can move it again by placing a few drops of water on it and spreading it round the area until the transfer shifts under gentle pressure. Don't attempt to force it. This normally works for a short period after original application; if you do it too often or too long, however, the transfer may well come off and stay off for good. If for any reason a transfer refuses to adhere naturally, it can often be affixed by carefully lifting the edges with the tip of a craft knife and applying a very thin smear of office glue. This is not a guarantee of success, but it often works.

If transfers disintegrate while being soaked, which is not unknown, leave all the pieces floating and fish them out one by one on a strip of glossy paper. Then 'assemble' the broken pieces *in situ* like a jigsaw puzzle, treating each

Press the transfers down hard to ensure that rivets show through the decals, as on this Spitfire IX.

individual piece as if it were a separate transfer, and follow the usual drying out and positioning procedure. Extra special care is needed to line all the pieces up, but with care you should not be able to see any joins. Any measures other than these are liable to lead to further disintegration.

Where the transfer is applied over simulated riveting or panel lines which stand proud from the main surface, it is essential in the drying-off process to press the transfer firmly and decisively over the raised projection. If you don't do this, your transfer may well end up standing clear of the surface like a ridge tent; even worse, any air or water left beneath it round the rivets or panel line will cause loss of adhesion and the eventual loss of the transfer.

When applying a transfer on this sort of surface, rub it down very hard as if you were doing a brass rubbing, so that the rivets show clearly through the transfer with no suggestion of air bubbles. This is a prime example of how forward planning eases your work: the wise modeller will have rubbed down over-prominent rivets in the assembly process, especially in the precise area where transfers are sited. The older kits still available often have overscale rivets; in these kits too the transfers tend to be thicker than current ones.

If a transfer gets chipped or cracked during the process of trimming, wait until the model is finished. Then simply touch in any small imperfections with paint of the appropriate colour afterwards. This also applies if you trim a transfer over-closely; if you accidentally nick a tiny portion off a letter or number, you can remedy it afterwards with a fine paint brush.

Some transfers in old kits are excessively glossy because of the thick varnish used in the carrier film. If you paint the model with matt clear varnish this problem will be overcome. If you don't intend to varnish the entire model, however, the transfer can be given a matt finish by placing the transfer sheet on a firm, flat surface and rubbing gently with 'wet and dry' paper; this skims off the gloss surface.

Once you have applied the transfers you may consider the model finished, apart from any last-minute touching up. This may well be the case, but very often the model can be improved with an overall coat of clear varnish, matt or gloss as may be appropriate. The point to remember here is that varnishing should take place after the transfers have been affixed. An overall coat of clear varnish is almost always desirable on aircraft models as it fixes the transfers permanently and disguises the shadow-throwing edges that transfers sometimes have. Aircraft have more transfers than other models and they are more essential to overall appearance than the one or two small transfers you may get on a tank or a car. Some transfers are much less adhesive than others, and these need a coat of varnish to 'seal' them in place.

In some old kits still available, the transfers may be out of register. In other words, they may look distorted, because the central red of, say, an RAF roundel is slightly off-centre or because different colours overlap. This is because the paper has stretched between runs of different colours during the printing process. More care is taken with modern transfers.

If the distortion is only very slight, it can often be overcome. For instance, in an RAF roundel on which the red centre is slightly out of true, it is possible to cut out the central spot altogether, trim it and apply it to the model separately. Basically the method is simple: fold the roundel in half while it is still on the transfer sheet and use nail scissors to cut away the complete red and white sections, leaving only the blue band of the roundel. Mark the roundel position lightly with pencil on the model and paint a white patch slightly smaller than the outside diameter of the blue ring

but larger than the inner diameter. Trim down the red and white section of the roundel to leave only the red spot; then apply the blue ring over the painted white patch and the red spot last of all, positioning it centrally on the white patch. Out-of-register tail flashes can be remedied in the same way.

An even better solution, however, with these old transfers is to replace them completely, either by using spare left overs from other kits or by buying new ones from a specialist transfer manufacturer such as Microscale or Modeldecal.

The other problem that often arises, particularly in kits first released some years ago, is basic inaccuracy in the markings themselves. In its simplest form on an aircraft model this might involve

Left often, complicated markings in the more elaborate kits may be provided in decal form, as was the case for the entire tail fin colouring in this 1:28 Spad XIII. **Below** Frog/Novo Buccaneer SZ on which the kit markings have been discarded and replaced by those of 809 Squadron, Fleet Air Arm.

the right markings in the wrong colours – white instead of light grey code letters is a typical error for instance. If you have a careful hand you can touch them up after they are in place and add the correct colour with paint. If in doubt, however, replace them.

If the markings supplied with an aircraft or tank kit are very inaccurate, your best plan is to find another marking scheme altogether and finish your model with it. With good research, this should be no great problem: find reference photos or colour schemes of another aircraft of the same type for which you can find suitable markings, then forget the kit maker's ideas and finish the model with the scheme you have researched.

TANGERINE

Of course, you can also finish a model with markings of your own choice. At its simplest, this may involve merely changing aircraft codes, squadron markings and serials; here you might retain national markings if their style is still applicable to the new squadron marking. At its most complex, such a change might involve a completely different colour scheme, different national markings and different codes and serials altogether: you might wish to finish a P-51D Mustang as a Korean Air Force machine, for instance, not as a 1944 USAF aircraft. Similarly, you might wish to finish your T-34 tank model as a vehicle captured, re-painted and used by the Germans; or a destroyer as a sister ship with different pennant numbers; or a locomotive as a similar engine with a different running number or livery; or a racing car as another car in the same team.

This becomes ridiculously easy if you have a stock of spare transfers at your disposal. Most kits these days offer some sort of alternative markings. For example, the well-known Matchbox Fury fighter kit has two sets of transfers, one for a Royal Air Force finish, the other for a Portuguese finish. If you finish the model as a RAF machine you are immediately left with an unused set of Portuguese markings which can be used on another model later, a Hurricane or Beaufighter, for example. This will in turn release the transfer sheets from the Hurricane or Beaufighter kits for use elsewhere. If you later buy another Fury kit and complete it as a Portuguese machine, you are then left with a set of pre-war RAF markings which can be used with another model. And so it goes on. In no time at all you are on the way to a collection of spare transfers which will enable you to ring considerable changes over the years.

If your spare transfers do start to accumulate like this, life will be easier if you file your transfers just

Opposite and below fine 1:48 model of the Mustang 'Tangerine'. All the markings have been made up from odds and ends, and the name and the white, yellow and red areas have been hand-painted with a fine brush.

as you file your research material. This may seem unimportant, but two or three years hence you may be glad you bothered. A lot of valuable modelling time can be lost while you sift through a heap of bits and pieces of transfer sheet trying to find suitable code letters or roundels or a tiny piece of an old transfer that can be turned into a unit emblem.

Cut up any left-overs from a kit transfer sheet into separate components (unless they form matching sets), and place each piece into an appropriately labelled box or envelope. Thus aviation modellers might have boxes marked in such categories as : RAF roundels – B type; RAF roundels – C type; White Code Letters; Black Code Letters; Black Serials; White Serials; Small Maintenance Stencilling (eg 'No Step' etc.); USAAF Stars; Pre-war USAAF Stars; German Crosses; Swastikas; Miscellaneous emblems; Japanese roundels; Coloured sheet or patches, and so on.

Similarly, military modellers might keep categories labelled

Above two Me262A models made from the same kit but with different colour schemes and unit markings made up from left-overs from other decal sheets.
Right reference illustration from a Spitfire kit showing alternative markings and paint schemes.

ZX M
MT928

WFD
JF814

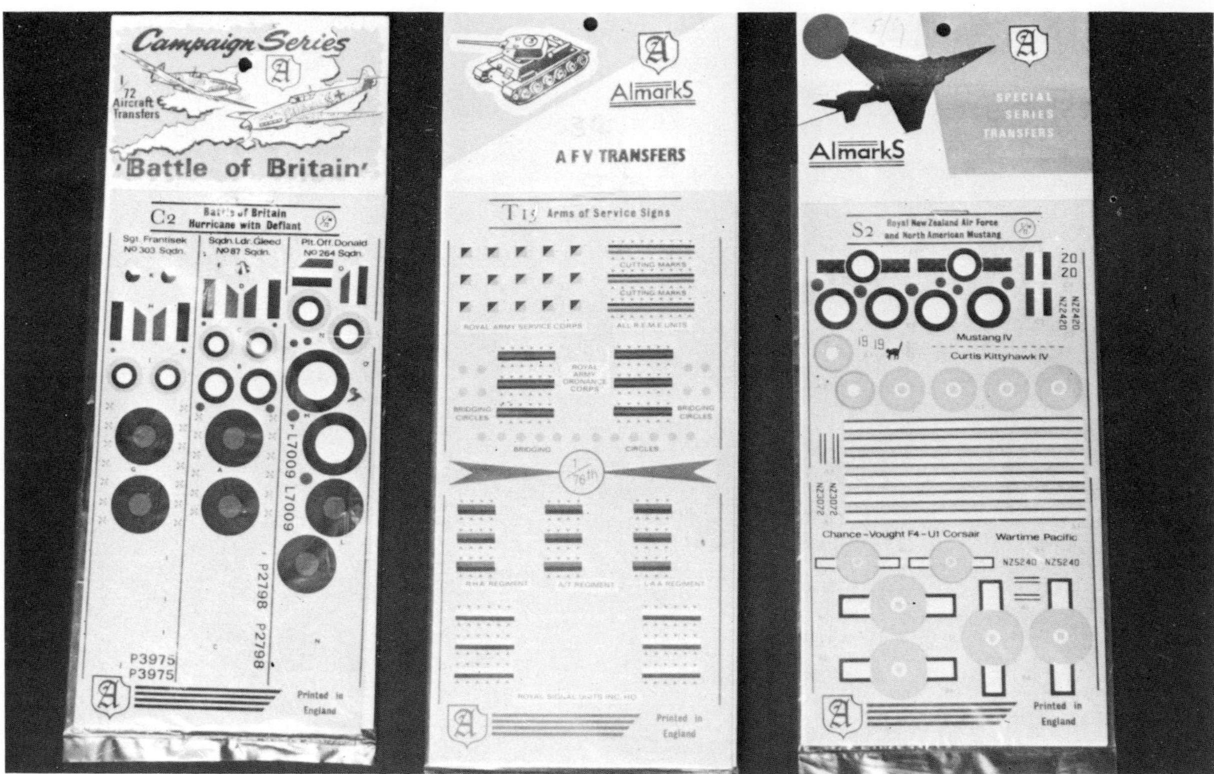

Above waterslide transfers (decals) of this sort can be purchased from specialized hobby shops to give variety to markings supplied in kits.
Right this Tyrrell-Ford racing car comes complete with all the markings necessary to complete it as Jackie Stewart's car. However, spare markings of this sort are available or can be made up from colour magazine advertisements.
Opposite top a good example of hand painted markings on a 1:35 scale Sherman, finished as a French vehicle.

German Turret Numbers; British Formation Signs; Vehicle Serial numbers in Black; Ditto in White; Squadron Markings, and so forth.

Once your transfer collection begins to build up, the scope for adaptation becomes enormous. Simply by using scissors or a craft knife, you can re-arrange existing serials or even cut up two figures to make a third. Obviously, however, you must be careful to match styles.

Very often, too, it is possible to adapt letters or digits by a brush stroke or a crafty snip of the scissors; simply cutting the appropriate parts away transforms a capital 'E' into an 'F' or an 'A' into a 'V'. With a very fine (OOO) brush or pen and thinned down paint you can carefully alter a 'Z' into the squared-off kind of '2' or add a serif to an 'l' to make an 'I'. Inverting a '9' makes a '6' (though not always), and there are thousands of other simple possibilities.

Dry transfer

The dry transfer system evolved by Letraset and made by them and several other firms, notably Blick Dry Print, consists of pressure sensitive transfers on a transparent sheet which are transferred by rubbing on the opposite side of the backing sheet with a ball pen or pencil. They leave no surround and are of negligible thickness. In many cases they are available in a range of colours, including red, blue and yellow, as well as black and white.

The Letraset range is vast and comes in hundreds of styles. It is expensive for the modeller though a sheet lasts a long time. Apart from letters there are sheets which consist of nothing but black dots and dashes or stripes in a vast range of sizes. These cannot be bettered for exhaust ports, camera ports, portholes on ships, windows on airliners and for any kind of aperture which you want to represent without actually cutting out.

Most economical for the modeller are the small sheets made by firms such as Blick. These have fewer letters but are much cheaper than the big Letraset sheets. Most of the 'Gill' or 'Helvetica' typefaces in this range are suitable for serials or code letters. These cheaper ranges are sold at most stationers. Letraset is mainly sold by big art suppliers; stockists have a style book which you can consult before purchase.

A few specialist suppliers stock a limited range of dry-print transfers made specially for model makers. Among these are railway company lettering and some aircraft and tank markings. Because the runs are of a limited nature, supplies are not constant; check model magazine advertisements to find what is available. With such a prodigious range of dry transfers available no style of lettering should stump you completely.

Keep Blick and Letraset sheets in a folder. Application details are given on each sheet, and your main problem is merely to keep everything in line. A very fine pencil line helps; in tricky positions or with small models it is best to cut out the letters one by one leaving enough backing top and bottom to give you a grip while you hold the letter in place and rub it down.

Sometimes you'll find that tiny letters are difficult to transfer or are reluctant to leave the backing paper; in this case it is best to rub the back of the letter while it remains on the backing paper by pressing it down on the protective (and non-adhesive) paper cover that comes with each sheet. This loosens the letter, and only very light pressure is needed once the letter is in position to persuade it to adhere to the model.

Another good way of using Blick to make up names or serials in the smaller sizes and on small models or in awkward curved areas is to transfer Blick on to a clear waterslide transfer sheet and then apply it as you would a ready-printed waterslide transfer. This really simplifies your task, as it is far easier to line Blick up on a flat surface with plenty of working space than directly on to the model.

If all else fails, you can resort to hand lettering, but this can make a model worse if you do not have the draughtsman's touch. It's far better to find a finish for your model which will utilize the transfers you possess.

Carrier deck markings in kits are often a combination of decals and paint. It is difficult to provide waterslide decals of long white lines and, on this model of the Japanese carrier Taiho, they have been applied from strips of white dry transfer.

Using dry transfer lettering

1 Remove the backing sheet and position the required letter. Shade lightly over the entire letter.
2 Carefully peel back the sheet, making sure that the transfer has been completed.
3 Align the next letter with the first and rub down as above. Some dry transfer lettering has alignment bars beneath the letters.
4 Repeat until the word is completed. Then place the backing sheet over the lettering and burnish with your nail.
5 If you wish to remove a letter, simply press adhesive tape over the letter and peel off.

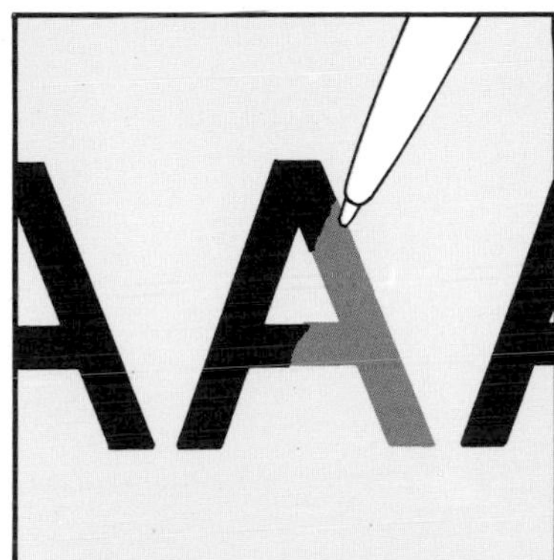

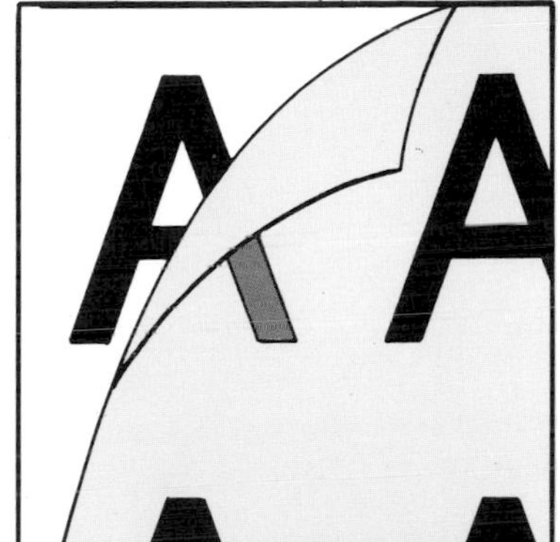

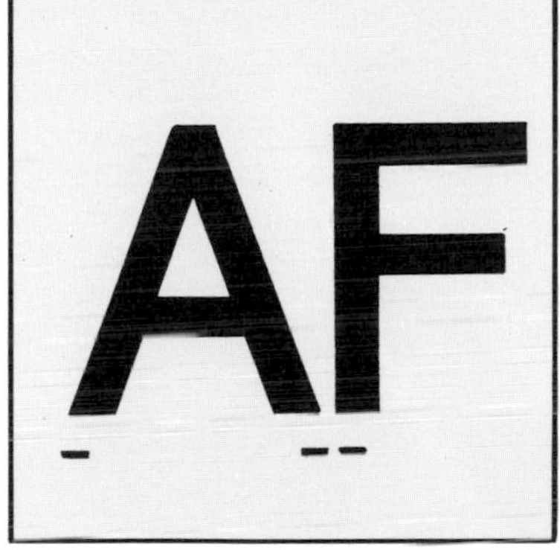

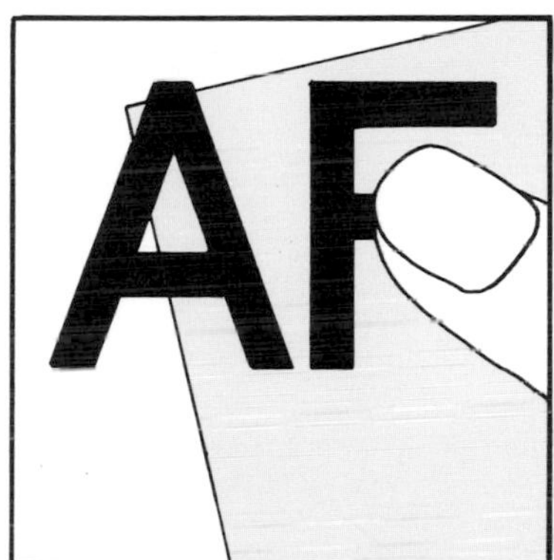

Helvetica and Univers type styles will fulfil most of your needs, however Superstar Shadow made by Letraset can be used on American warships.

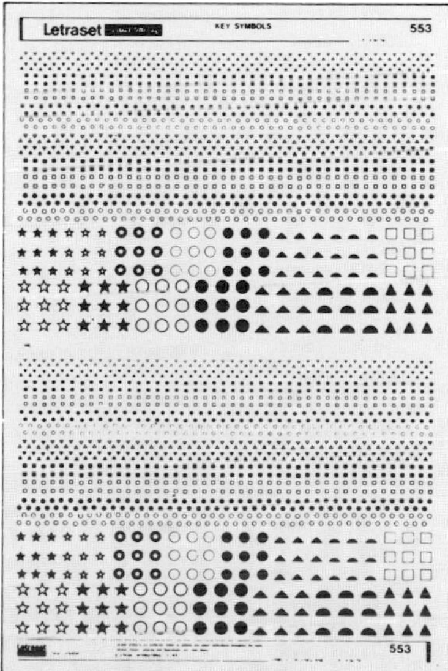

A wide range of miscellaneous symbols are available for various uses.

DIORAMAS

It is worth giving some consideration to the scenic display of your models: almost everyone who has ever made model aircraft must at some time have thought of an airfield setting for the models; similarly, everyone who owns model tanks or soldiers or a model railway layout likes to devise some sort of scenery.

Modellers today have a rich diversity of accessories at their disposal. So many kits, die-cast cars, railway accessories and even scenic backgrounds are available that almost everything you ever need can be purchased, adapted or made from something else. In addition, excellent books on scenic modelling are on sale which tell you all you need to know about making trees, hills, rivers and so forth, very useful for making up miniature battlefields, advanced airstrips or big airfields.

A visit to a big model railway shop will provide you with everything you need for any kind of scenic modelling, from plaster and lichen to simulated stone paper and

Above an effective display for a Luftwaffe F-104 Starfighter, with green baize, fine sandpaper for the runway, lichen 'trees' and crumpled paper 'hills'.
Right typical accessory set of the kind available in various scales for diorama and display work.
Opposite 'ripple' effect achieved by intricate brush work on a Fiesler Storch; the desert diorama is a good example of camouflage work.

5F
K

figures. Merit, for instance, make RAF personnel for model railway platforms which are sold as model railway accessories; this doesn't stop you using them on a miniature airfield. Airfix have an excellent wartime 'prefab' control tower and sets of airfield personnel figures. A few kits for airfield vehicles and small buildings are also available. The modeller's own ingenuity will furnish other airfield buildings and equipment.

Nor is there any limit to the range of figures which can be adapted to airfield personnel from other sets. Airfix World War One British soldiers make a good basis for RFC personnel, for instance. As these OO sets are very cheap, it doesn't cost much to try your hand at removing packs and rifles with a craft knife and altering arm positions with a couple of snicks of a knife to suggest a mechanic swinging a propeller or pulling away chocks.

You can make up an effective display area on a chipboard shelf or chipboard offcut. Incorporate proper scenery using Polyfilla mixed with sawdust as an earth mix, crumpled newspaper or canvas as a basis for contours, dyed flock or sawdust for the grass, and loofah or rubberized horse hair for trees and bushes. Some modellers build up a scenic section like this on any convenient piece of board.

Top and right simple miniature dioramas of Russian Cossack Horse Artillery and an SS despatch rider. The sign was made from scrap balsa and the ground from modelling plaster with string teased out to represent grass.
Above crew of a 1:35 PzkpfwIV(H) searching for hidden mines ahead of the vehicle; for this diorama, grass matt stretched over crumpled tissue paper has been used, with lichen for bushes and a little surface dressing.
Opposite page 54mm scale section of a First World War trench; French troops (converted from plastic 1944 Japanese figures) are firing a 37mm Hotchkiss gun made from a cast metal kit of parts. Styrene packing material was used for the trench, fuse wire for the barbed wire.

At the other extreme, if you do have a big showcase you can give the full scenic treatment to individual shelves, using model railway scenic background sheets to depict distant hills and houses etc. along the back of the showcase and finishing the shelves to represent grass or tarmac. Several firms make 'grass'-textured paper which is ideal for giving a most realistic finish of this kind. Small or large display areas of this kind which put the models in a scenic setting are known as dioramas.

If you are a military enthusiast, the same sort of scenic setting can be used to show off tanks, army

Opposite top 1:35 Sheridan tank in a superbly realistic setting.
Right accessory pieces for ruined buildings, available as individual items or as a complete set.
Below and opposite bottom 1:35 Flak 88 in a set on sand glued to a wood base.

Golden Hinde

Ships can be attractively displayed either on a stand, as in the model *Golden Hinde*, opposite, or in a realistic setting, as with the *Prinz Eugen* above; here, cellophane has been crumpled and spread over a sheet of blue-painted plywood or hardboard.

trucks or miniature soldiers. Tanks in the smallest scales are even more compact than aircraft, and a lot of people make up most convincing little scenes on nothing larger than an expanded polystyrene tile of the kind used for interior decorating.

Lastly, some ideas for scenic settings for ships. Impressive models such as those made by Revell, Airfix and Heller come with a display stand and are so large and so eye-catching that they don't really need scenery to go with them. But a lot of modellers who make up the popular series of warship kits like a 'sea' setting. This is surprisingly easy to create given a piece of board slightly larger than the model and a small quantity of Polyfilla. If the model is a full hull model you'll have to use enough Polyfilla, of course, to bring the level of your 'sea' up to the waterline, but models which come as waterline types to start with will need only the barest smearing of Polyfilla to break up the flat surface of the board. Build up the required wave formation with an old knife or spatula as the Polyfilla sets – but study pictures of real sea, as it's surprisingly easy to make an unconvincing job of imitation sea! Paint it with greenish-blue poster colours, leaving flecks of bare white according to how rough your 'sea' is.

Other ideas include complete groups of model ships in a common sea setting, so that you build up a complete flotilla or task force using the appropriate models. A battleship could be moored to a buoy with destroyers tied up alongside, a storeship on the other side, and even liberty boats and pinnaces fussing around the gangways, all quite possible in 1:600 scale, as even the ship's boats come as separate components in most kits.

The Airfix series of small sailing ship kits includes a sea display stand which can be discarded in favour of a larger board. With 'sea' made as already described it is quite feasible to make up an old-time sea battle scene complete with dismasted or sinking men-o'-war.

Modellers who favour the really small scales of ship model (1:1200 or 1:1000) needn't worry about Polyfilla, as a sheet of Cellophane crinkled over blue-green paper makes a quite realistic sea. In 1:1200 scale, the Hornby Company make a complete series featuring jetties, warehouses, cranes, a lighthouse and even a lightship, so making it possible for the 1:1200 scale fan to build up splendid harbour scenes.

Grouping models in scenic dioramas has enormous scope for impressive model display and makes a challenging and demanding exercise for the imagination.

SHOWCASE DISPLAY

Probably the first method of display that comes to mind is suspending plastic model planes from the ceiling on pieces of cotton. This is great fun for the younger modeller; but it does not provide protection from dirt, and the model is liable to break because of 'cotton fatigue'.

The cheapest way to provide a good cover for a limited number of models of whatever material is the so-called 'orchid box'. These are used by florists for protecting small flower arrangements or rare blooms and comprise a flimsy transparent plastic carton with either a cardboard or plastic base. They can be used either way up and stacked if necessary. The ones with cardboard bases look best with models inside. They are also relatively cheap, conveniently sized and virtually dust proof; thin plastic is exceptionally clear too, so visibility is good. Florists may not be willing to sell the box without a flower, though, and you may have to 'shop around'; bulk buying direct from a stationery supplier might be cheaper, particularly if a group of modellers gets together.

Any kind of clear plastic container is of course very useful, though few of the larger, heavier type are available today. They do scratch easily, however, and become opaque with use and age.

In recent years, various firms have produced showcases of all sorts and sizes specially for models, but supplies seem to fluctuate. Some are quite cheap plastic, others reach the highest standard with polished wood bases.

Once you have about a hundred models, plastic boxes become expensive and space consuming, and expenditure on a showcase is a reasonable proposition. You can, of course, build a showcase complete with sliding glass doors and strip lighting (see pages 186–187).

If you are limited in time, tools

Plastic kit of the *Cutty Sark* displayed as the traditional shipbuilder's half-model on a wall plaque.

ROYAUME DE COGUÉ
Calmou
Chaparangue
Mont Tanla
Sirinagar
Jengapor
Dely
Agra
Almer
Gualeor
Halabas
NAVARRI
ROYAUME DE NECBAL
ROYAU. DE TIBET
Bramson
Guerguon
R. D'ASEM
MOGOL
R. DE TIPRA
UDESSE
BERAR
ROYAUME DE BENGALA
D'ORIXA
R.D'ARACAN
Aracan
R. D'AVA
Bramas
R. DU PEGOU
Golconde
CARNATE
COROMANDEL
Negraille
R. DE SIAM
Tavay
Andamans
Ponto gale
ISLE DE CEILAN
aux Hollandois
Nicobar
Cutty Sark

Building a showcase

You may feel that to build a display case is beyond your capabilities, but the construction shown here requires only very basic skills and a few simple tools. The sizes and materials shown can all be changed to your own particular needs and taste, and lighting could be incorporated if required.

Materials

One 96 inch length and one 72 inch length of white melamine-faced chipboard, 9 inches wide by $\frac{5}{8}$ inch thick, for top, bottom and sides.

Two sheets of $\frac{1}{4}$ inch clear perspex or $\frac{1}{4}$ inch plate glass, 25 inches by $34\frac{1}{2}$ inches for doors.

Three sheets of $\frac{1}{4}$ inch plate glass, 36 inches by 8 inches for shelves.

Twelve 1 inch No. 8 countersunk screws.

Twelve $1\frac{1}{4}$ inch No. 8 countersunk screws.

Twelve white plastic screw-concealing caps.

Twelve white plastic shelf supports.

Two 48 inch lengths of white plastic sliding door tracks.

Four 3 inch triangular steel corner plates.

Twenty four $\frac{3}{8}$ inch panel pins.

IMPORTANT: All the glass used in constructing this display case must have the edges polished by the glass merchant.

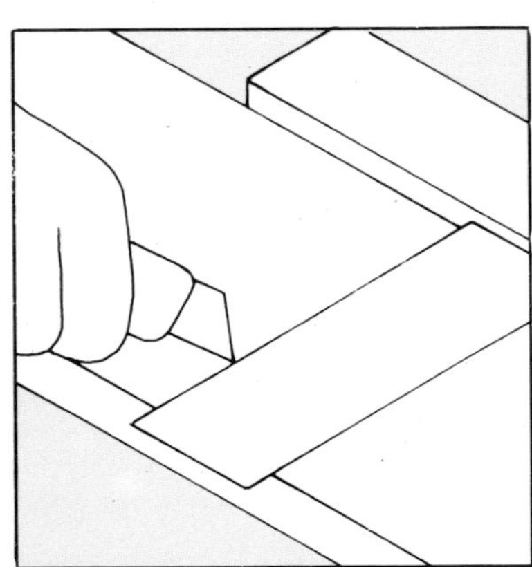

1 Accurately divide the length of both boards in half and score melamine with a knife on both sides.

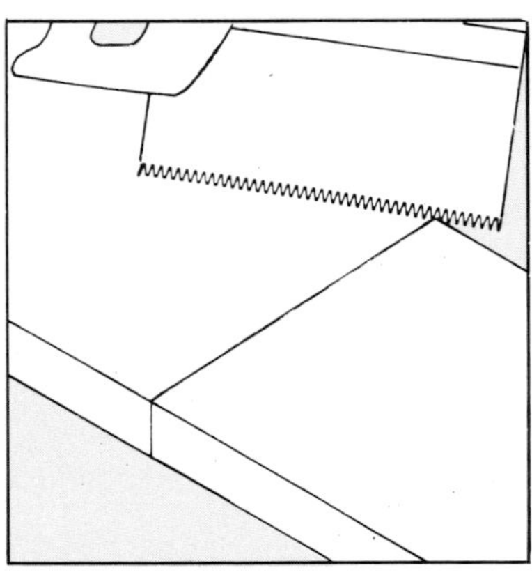

2 Saw both boards on score lines, being careful not to chip surface material. Clean up with sand paper.

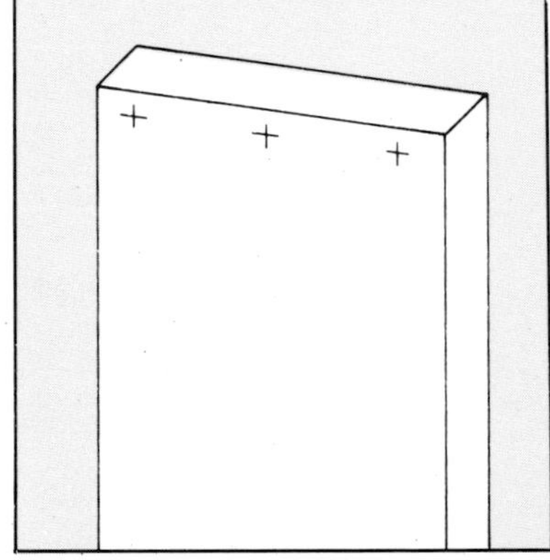

3 Mark positions for drilling on ends of both 36 inch lengths as indicated in diagram.

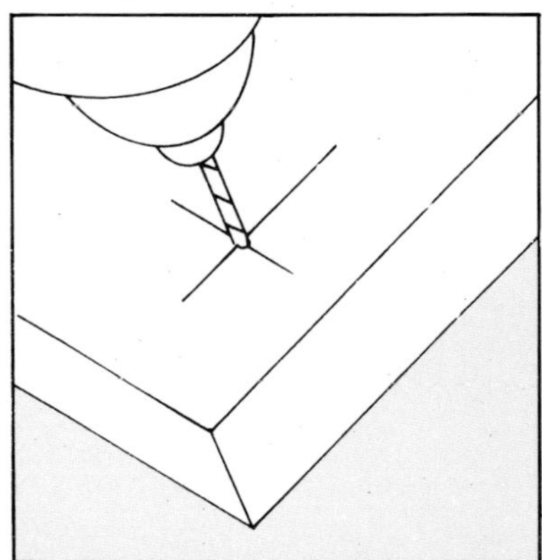

4 Drill twelve holes with a No. 8 drill.

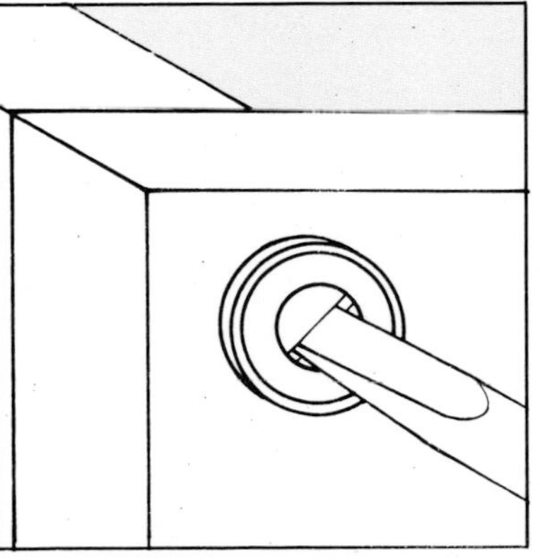

5 Hold 48 inch lengths of board at right angles to 36 inch length and screw in $1\frac{1}{4}$ inch screws.

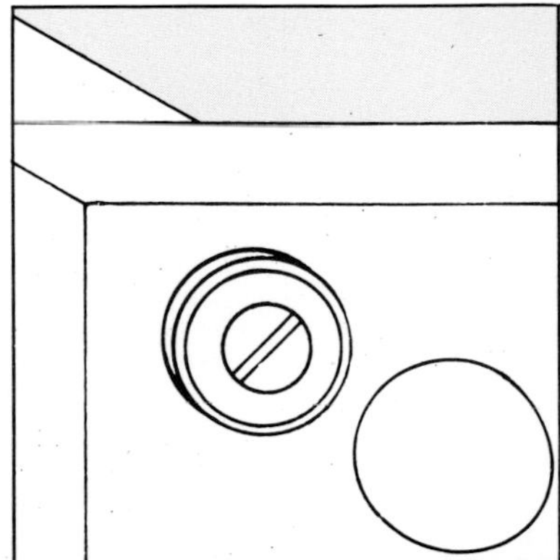

6 Screw the other edges together to form a box and cover screws with caps.

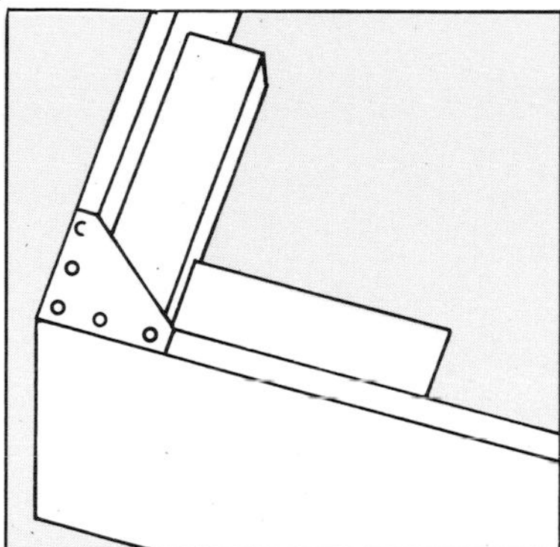

7 Check all corners for square and screw triangular plates to each corner, using 1 inch screws.

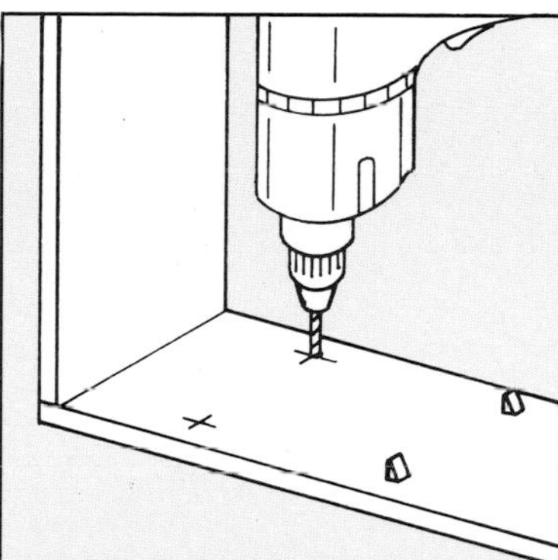

8 Mark and drill holes for shelf supports in required positions on inside of both 36 inch side pieces.

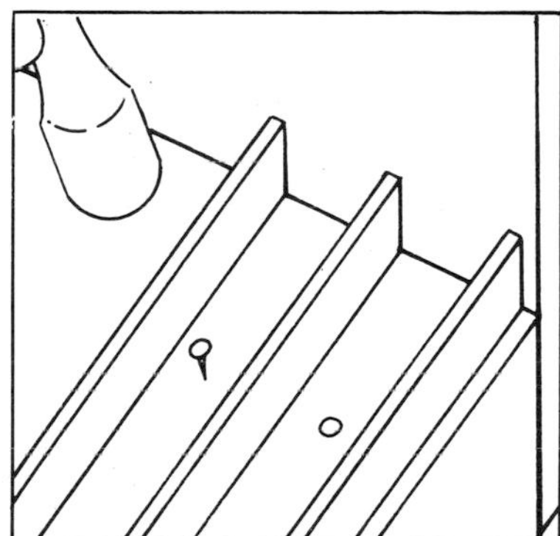

9 Nail sliding door runners in position on front edge of both 48 inch boards. Finally, fix the complete structure to the wall, position shelves on the supports and slot doors into runners.

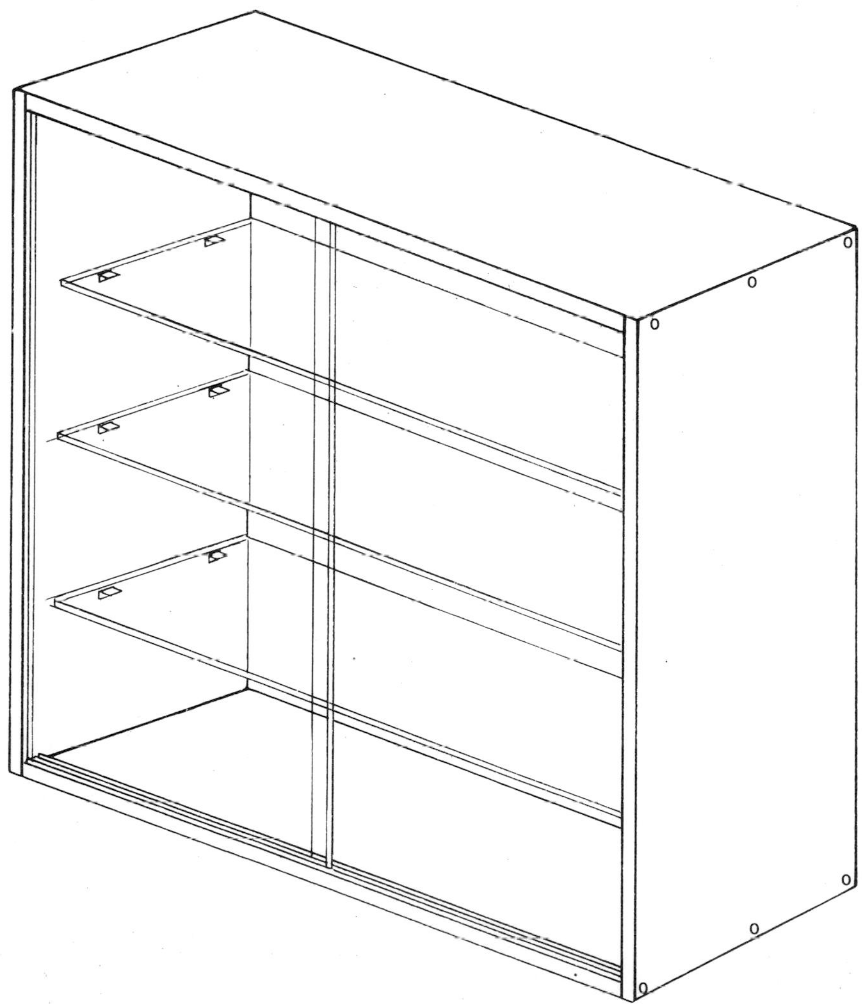

DRUMBEAT

Left three examples of commercially produced show cases made of perspex mounted on polished hardwood plinths.
Above a 1:32 scale Hellcat housed in its own individually-made glass display case.

and carpentry skills, a number of moderately priced alternatives are available. A basic kitchen wall cabinet in whitewood with sliding glass doors can look very presentable in domestic surroundings when painted or varnished. Sizes, prices, and storage capacities vary; but you can always fit extra shelves (offcuts from your local 'do-it-yourself' shop) if you are storing smaller scale models. A cabinet like this can be supported by angle brackets on a shelf, stood on a small table or chest of drawers, or hung on a wall.

Three-shelf bookcases with sliding glass doors are available in whitewood. Again, capacity can be increased by adding extra shelves. Study the various whitewood catalogues, as some manufacturers offer varied styles of cabinets which can be converted. Bookcases are not very deep and therefore natural light is usually sufficient illumination. Strip lighting units are available at most chain stores and are easy to fit provided a power point is nearby; alternatively, external spotlighting can be used.

Maintenance

Dust and rough, overeager or careless handling threaten models most. Dust obviously spoils the freshness and detail of a model, and cleaning means lifting and moving models. Covered storage does not completely eliminate cleaning in the long run but reduces it to a once- or twice-yearly operation. Models on open display probably need attention every week.

For cleaning a No. 5 brush, obtainable from art shops, is a valuable aid. The softest brush will enable you to dust all surfaces and rigging and rigging wires; a small paint brush may also be necessary for any models which have corners.

While dusting the models inspect them for defects such as missing or broken parts, rigging wires adrift and so on. Carry out repairs immediately and avoid a backlog of breakages. To avoid adding to the list of repairs, it's sensible to observe certain rules when picking models up. As a general rule, grip a model by its extremities, eg a ship by its bow and skin, an aircraft by its wing tips, with both hands. Cars are particularly fragile – bumpers, wheels and mudguards especially – so pick car models up under the 'belly'. Handle tanks in this way too. Plastic figures should be handled by the base.

PHOTOGRAPHY

Given a proper studio and sophisticated equipment, there is no limit to what can be done in the way of photographing small scale models. Most of us lack such facilities, however, so any model photography we do has to be carried out more simply.

Fortunately, if you own or have the use of fairly common sorts of camera you can still take quite acceptable model photographs. Taking photographs is not, of course, an essential part of model making, but it does add yet another dimension to the hobby. Many families these days own slide projectors, and there is no reason why you should not add a series of model pictures, the more colourful or realistic the better, to the family viewing programme. If you prefer colour or black and white prints, it is worth getting an album in which to keep them.

Apart from the fun of all this, a collection of model photos provides a useful record of your work. Even the most careful modeller loses some plastic models through breakage; others may be given away or replaced. But photography provides a permanent record of all that you have done.

In addition to all this, there are photography competitions from time to time, and you can send articles or photos to model magazines if you feel inclined – all

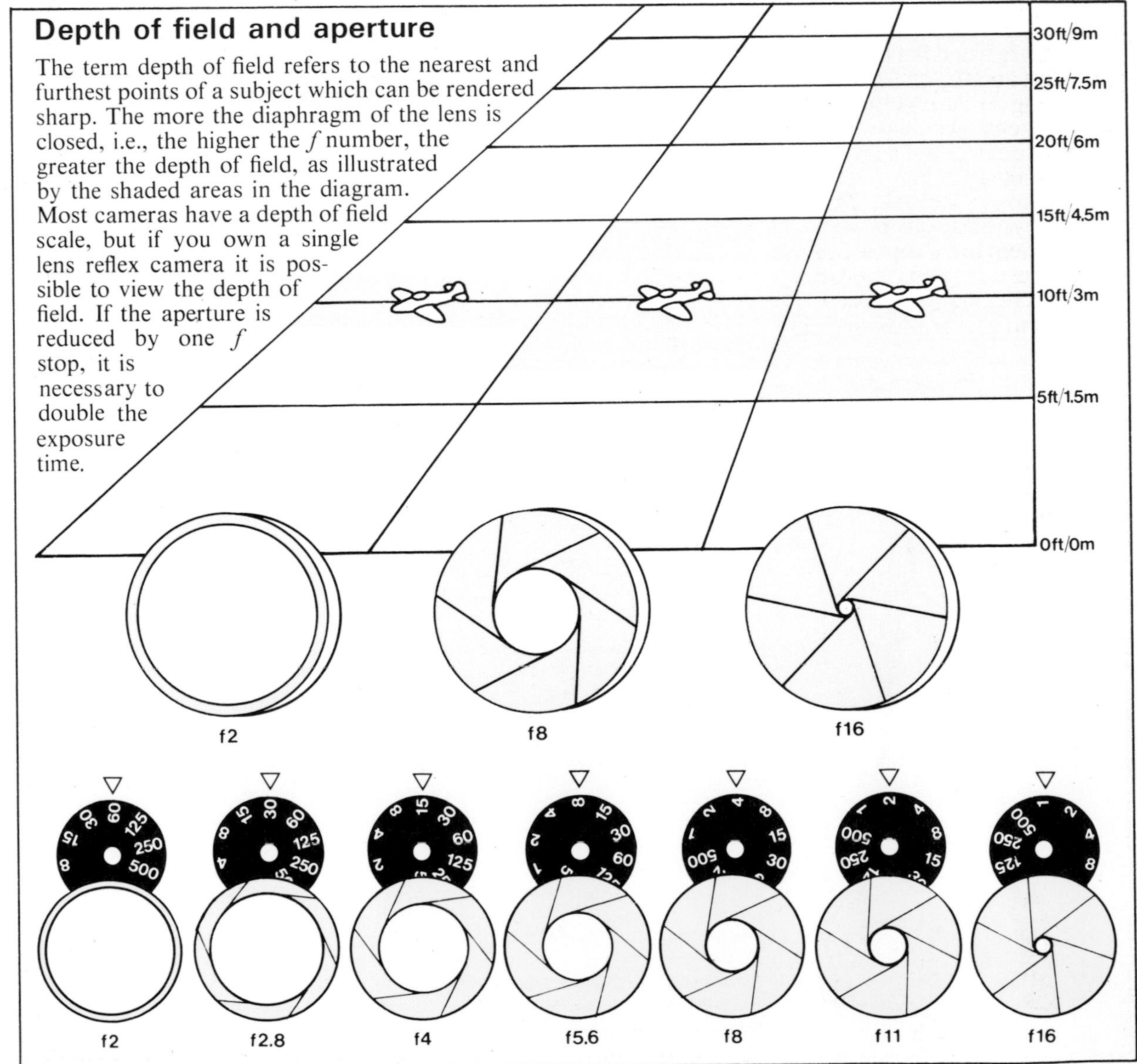

Depth of field and aperture

The term depth of field refers to the nearest and furthest points of a subject which can be rendered sharp. The more the diaphragm of the lens is closed, i.e., the higher the *f* number, the greater the depth of field, as illustrated by the shaded areas in the diagram. Most cameras have a depth of field scale, but if you own a single lens reflex camera it is possible to view the depth of field. If the aperture is reduced by one *f* stop, it is necessary to double the exposure time.

The ideal equipment

It is possible to photograph your models with the simplest of cameras, but the ideal camera is the 35mm single lens reflex. It enables you to view the subject through the lens, thus allowing an exact sight of what will appear on the film. The other advantage of this type of camera is the ability to change the lens to one of a different focal length. This facility also allows the use of extension tubes, (far right), which are fitted between the camera and the lens to allow focusing on close subjects. The extension bellows is a similar device, but has the advantage of being continuously variable. The other two basic pieces of equipment are a tripod and cable release, right, the latter being a flexible tube which is used to eliminate vibration.

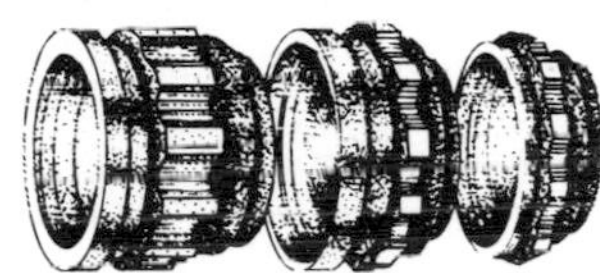

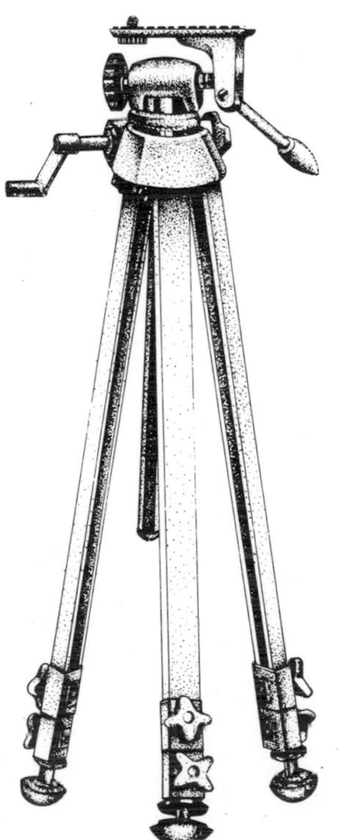

A simple photographic stand

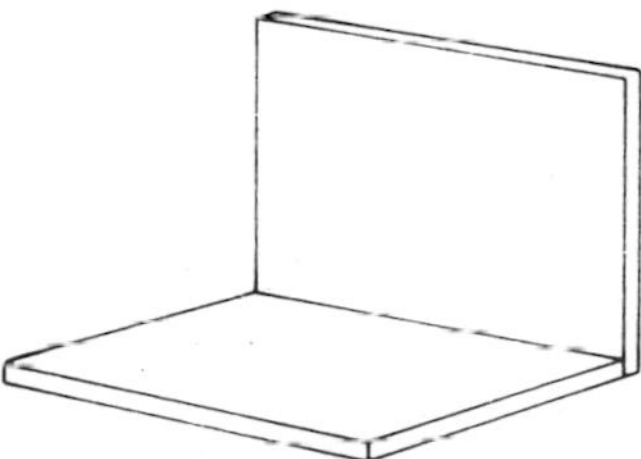

Nail or screw two pieces of board together at right angles. The size will depend on the model scale.

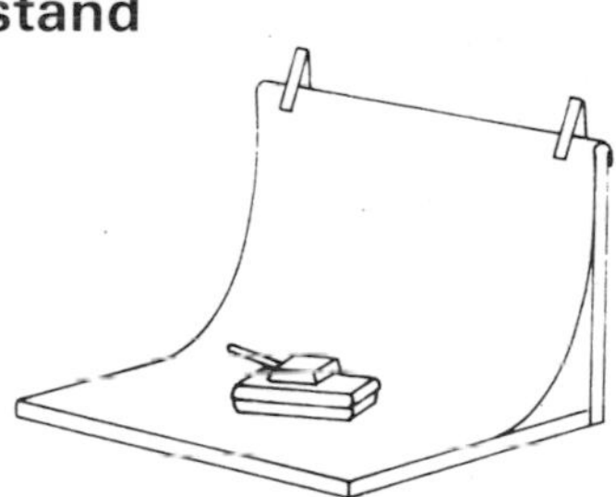

Peg a sheet of paper to the top and let it drop down in a gentle curve.

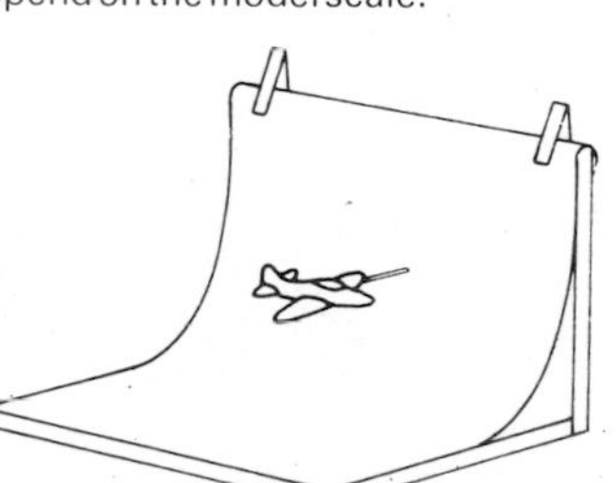

To photograph an aircraft in flight, drill a hole through the backboard and support the model on a piece of rod.

The same two pieces of board can be used to build a diorama on, with a photograph as a backdrop.

of which might lead to prizes or payment. So model photography is by no means time wasted.

If you are very careful and patient you can use old box cameras or simple fixed lens cameras for model photography. But you will need a 1, 2 or 3 dioptre close-up lens which fits your make of camera – by no means easy to find if the camera is obsolete – and then you will have to do a lot of old fashioned mathematics to work out focal lengths and depths of field. Experimentation like this uses up a lot of expensive film and success is in no way guaranteed. The real secret of model photography without tears is the modern type of SLR (single lens reflex) camera: this provides 'through the lens viewing', a close focusing lens, a good range of speeds and shutter apertures, and general convenience of use. SLR cameras mostly use 35 mm film, which is widely sold in cassettes. SLR cameras vary enormously in price and sophistication. Modellers need only an inexpensive type; the second-hand trade will yield a perfectly adequate camera for your needs at quite a modest price. If money is no object, however, highly complex cameras can be bought, packed with electronic facilities. Some, indeed, are fully automatic.

With an SLR camera you can choose both the shutter speed and the lens aperture, which means that, with the right speed say 1/125 second or faster, the camera can be hand held. But it pays to have time to think and study the model subject, so the next most useful item is a good firm tripod. Again, these may be bought second hand, but there are quite inexpensive new ones on the market too. Less vital but also useful is a cable release for the shutter when the camera is on the tripod; this saves the risk of displacing the camera.

This diorama was set up for photography on a sand table; a marble dropped into the sand provided the 'explosion'. The gun is 1:35, while the bomber is 1:144 to give an impression of distance.

Most SLR standard lenses focus down as close as 18 inches or a little more. With all but the smallest of models, this is completely sufficient. If you do make small scale soldiers or 1:144 aircraft you'll need either a supplementary (screw-on or press-on) close-up lens or a close-up extension set. The former is added to the lens front, the latter goes between the lens and camera body. A 2 dioptre supplementary lens is fine; it will enable you to focus down to 6 inches or less. The camera instruction book gives details of the type and size of close-up lens which will fit the front of the camera lens; be sure you get the correct fit for your make of

Above Matt paper in contrasting colours – a white disc for the moon, black for the ground – was used to obtain this striking view; the 'cloud' was sprayed on with an aerosol can.

Right 1:35 Panther tank posed against a photograph of a house printed up to a suitable size; the broken windows and 'smoke' were painted onto the background.

12

camera and lens. The same applies to close-up extension tubes.

Once you have this equipment you are well away. The model will fill the camera viewing screen and you'll get the picture you see in the viewfinder. Your final successful picture will of course depend on correct focus, depth of field, background arrangement and correct exposure.

Focus seems easy enough; but the closer the camera gets to its subject the more critical becomes what is called 'depth of field'. This simply means the distance from the camera at which the subject will appear sharply focused. Hence at a certain point everything between, say, 7 and 10 inches from the camera lens will be sharp. Objects closer than 7 inches or further than 10 inches will be progressively less sharp. To get maximum depth of field the aperture in the lens must be at its smallest. On most standard lenses this is f16, or occasionally f22. In practice f22, f16, f11, or f8 will yield suitable results, but aim for f16 or f11 as a general rule.

Exposure is determined by a separate or built-in light meter or by the manufacturers' exposure chart supplied with the film.

This is where the tripod and cable release come in. To get a sharp picture you need a small aperture, say f16. But with an aperture that small you need a longer exposure time, 1/60, 1/30 or 1/15 second. This is too slow for a hand-held camera but no problem if it is mounted on the tripod.

With a bit of practice you can work out 'depths of field' for yourself, simply by stopping down the lens until the desired effect is achieved. In other words you can choose whether to have the background sharply focused with the model, maybe for scenic effect, or whether to throw the background out of focus slightly to emphasize the sharply focused model. In the latter case you might open up the lens aperture to f8 or f5·6 and achieve the effect by reducing the depth of field.

Once you have grasped these basic principles, the rest is easy. Try them out first with an unloaded camera.

At its simplest you can do all your photography outdoors. Choose a good sunny day or a bright cloudy day, preferably with no wind. Any convenient table will do as a base for the model. One ideal accessory can be made at home which will greatly facilitate scene-setting. Just screw two pieces of chipboard together to form a

Realistic view of an Arado Ar 196 floatplane skimming over the waves. The 1:72 model, opposite, was posed in front of a large calendar picture of the sea and supported on a rod pushed through the backdrop and concealed by the plane's wing. The picture was taken with a hand-held SLR camera, right; floodlights have eliminated shadow, though on a bright day the picture could have been taken outdoors.

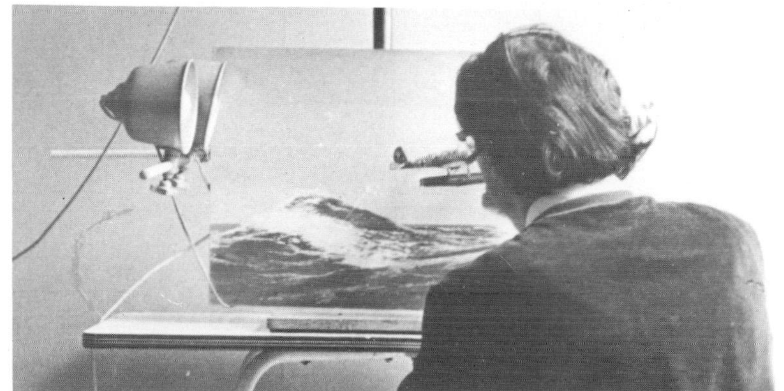

right angle. The back upright will support backsheets or scenes as required; if the gadget is painted pale matt blue, the backboard can be left uncovered to give a 'sky' background. Another rule to remember for effective model photography is to keep the camera at eye level to the model. Seen as a miniature man might look at them, most models look even more realistic than you might expect.

If you don't have a purpose-built stand, you'll need some other loose board which can be propped up to form a background holder.

For static record shots coloured paper can be clipped in place with clothes pegs and curved forward to clear the corner of the stand, eliminating the shadow that might otherwise be formed. Realistic 'atmosphere' pictures are more fun, however. With these, you can add a background illustration and place the models in more realistic positions. For a start, a simple background shot will suffice, but as you go on you can get more adventurous. Miniature trees, houses and other background items can be used – in fact you can make up what amounts to a temporary diorama. Background sheets of varied sorts can be bought at model shops, and judicious use of advertisements and prints, especially 'whole pages' cut from magazines, will make economical and unusual backgrounds. Sometimes travel agents will give away scenic posters which are always useful for this sort of work.

For 'air' shots of aircraft, a favourite trick is to find a good colour sheet depicting clouds or sky. Clip it in place, and then poke a knitting needle into some convenient hole in the underside of your model, embedding the other end of the needle in the backboard.

Apart from the quality of the modelling, one of the most important aspects of obtaining a realistic photograph is the angle of the shot. To give an impression of distance, the Stuka in this photograph is 1:72 scale, while the Fw 190 is 1:32.

How this picture was taken

The photograph on the opposite page shows a futuristic spacecraft orbiting Callisto, one of the moons of Jupiter. Although the techniques employed here are beyond the capability of most people, it is interesting to see just what can be achieved–given the right equipment and a lot of time and patience.

The model was made from various bits of plastic kits and given a matt finish by dusting lightly with talcum powder. It was suspended on a horizontal metal bar in front of a large piece of black velvet and lit by a single spotlight. Before photographing on a 5″ 4″ studio camera, an outline of the spacecraft was drawn on the ground glass screen on the back of the camera to indicate the position when adding the background. Three more exposures were made on the same piece of film using existing photographs of the surface of the moon, Jupiter and the stars to build up the background. These stages are shown in the four photographs below.

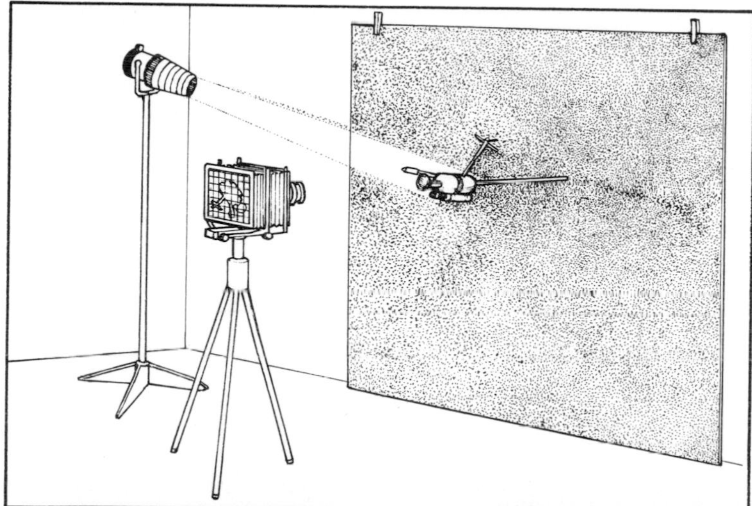

By adjusting the angle of the camera you can eliminate the needle from the finished picture. For an 'in flight' view, propellers should be moving. Flick or blow the propellers just before the shutter is fired, taking care not to dislodge the model. Professionals use an electric hair dryer to turn the propellers, holding it just outside camera range. There are many similar tricks; one favourite is to get a friend to blow smoke from a cigarette across a 'battle' scene just as the shutter is about to fire. Put a big sheet of white card reflecting towards the model to reduce shadow around it. Note how much lighter the deep shadows become.

There are some alternatives to a SLR camera. The older type of twin-lens reflex (TLR), for example, is excellent and can be bought second hand at reasonable prices. Though TLRs have less close focusing ability, 1, 2 and 3 dioptre close-up lenses including parallax correction in the viewfinder lens can be bought. TLRs mostly work on 120 size film which gives a 6 cm square negative.

The other camera very common today is the compact 35 mm, non-reflex type. Its shutter speeds are usually fully automatic. Certain makes have a close-up attachment as a standard accessory which is clipped or screwed over the lens of the camera and also incorporates a parallax-corrected viewfinder. The close-up attachment allows you to focus down to about 15 inches, which is adequate for most models. The angle of view of the compact camera lens is very wide, so the actual picture will show a larger area than a photo taken with the SLR.

In the winter months you may need to take your photographs indoors. For this you will require a floodlight. The 'clip-on' type can simply be placed above the models. Bring it as close as you can without intruding it into the picture. Shadows can be adjusted by moving the floodlight back and forth.

Appendix

Magazines and periodicals dealing with scale modelling subjects

These are all published monthly unless otherwise stated. While this list may not be exhaustive, it does include all known major publications. Most can be obtained or ordered from news stands. Many magazines published in one country can be obtained in another through specialist importers or hobby shops.

Almost without exception these magazines include modelling projects and ideas in every issue, lots of useful background and reference material (such as scale drawings) and news and reviews of new kits and model releases. So to keep really abreast of modelling ideas and developments, any keen modeller should try to obtain at least one or more magazines within his field of interest.

It should be pointed out here that this listing deals only with magazines which deal with conventional scale models. There are other publications, such as aviation magazines, which may include occasional or regular modelling articles, and some model magazines (eg, Radio Control Models) which are really very specialised and may include some scale coverage, but mainly this is secondary to technical coverage.

GREAT BRITAIN

Airfix Magazine
All types of scale model, mainly in plastic but also wood and metal and with the emphasis on converting or improving plastic kits

Scale Aircraft Modelling
Entirely devoted to aircraft modelling, mainly from plastic kits.

PAM News (PAM = Plastic Aircraft Modelling)
Entirely devoted to aircraft modelling, mainly from plastic kits.

Scale Models
All types of scale models with emphasis on aircraft, ships, road vehicles.

Military Modelling
All aspects of military models including tanks and soldiers and wargaming.

Model Soldier
All aspects of military modelling including tanks, guns, soldiers, and wargaming.

Model Mechanic
Sister journal of *Model Engineer* for the less advanced engineering modeller.

Kit Makers and Model Suppliers

The kit and model industry is in a constant state of flux, conditioned by such factors as production capacity, export markets, and changing public tastes. While the major manufacturers are very stable – but with model ranges changing from year to year – there are hundreds of small suppliers, some of whom flourish for only a short time. The current model magazines, carrying advertisements and kit reviews, are the best indicators of what is new or available at any given time. The following listing gives an indication of some brand names to look for in various categories of model and accessory.

Code of country of manufacture:
GB Great Britain; USA United States; URS Russia; P Poland; CZ Czechoslovakia; F France; WG West Germany; J Japan; C Canada; I Italy; SW Sweden; D Denmark; A Austria.

AIRCRAFT

Company	*Country*	*Scales*	*Remarks*
Airfix	GB/WG	1:144, 1:72, 1:48, 1:24	Plastic kits
Revell	USA/GB/WG	1:72, 1: 48, 1:32	Plastic kits
Monogram	USA	1:72, 1:48	Plastic kits
Tamiya	J	1:72, 1:48, 1:100	Plastic kits
Hasegawa	J	1:72, 1:48, 1:32	Plastic kits
Bandai	J	1:48, 1:24	Plastic kits
Heller	F	1:100, 1:125, 1:48, 1:50, 1:72	Plastic kits
Novo	URS	1:72, 1:96	Plastic kits
Crown	J	1:144	Plastic kits
Nichimo	J	1:48	Plastic kits
Otaki	J	1:144, 1:48	Plastic kits
LDM	GB	1:48	Metal kits
ESCI	I	1:48	Plastic kits
Italaeri	I	1:72	Plastic kits
Lifelike	USA	1:48	Plastic kits
Matchbox	GB	1:72, 1:32	Plastic kits
Lindbergh	USA	1:48, 1:96, 1:72	Plastic kits
KP	CZ	1:72	Plastic kits
Mikro	P	1:72, 1:144	Plastic kits
Contrail	GB	1:72	Vac-form kits
Rareplanes	GB	1:72	Vac-form kits
Airframe	C	1:72	Vac-form kits
Airmodel	WG	1:72	Vac-form kits
Pamela Veal	GB	1:48	Vac-form kits
Modeldecal	GB	All	Decals and markings only
Microscale	USA	All	Decals and markings only
Executive Display Models	GB	Various	GRP kits and assembled

FIGHTING VEHICLES

Company	*Country*	*Scales*	*Remarks*
Airfix	GB/WG	1:76, 1:32, 1:35	Plastic kits
Matchbox	GB	1:76	Plastic kits
ESCI	I	1:35, 1:72	Plastic kits
Italaeri	I	1:35	Plastic kits
Tamiya	J	1:48, 1:35, 1:16, 1:24	Plastic kits
Crown	J	1:48, 1:35	Plastic kits
Nichimo	J	1:35	Plastic kits
Monogram	USA	1:32	Plastic kits
Hasegawa	J	1:72	Plastic kits
Bandai	J	1:48, 1:24	Plastic kits
Heller	F	1:35	Plastic kits

MODEL FIGURES

Company	*Country*	*Scales*	*Remarks*
Airfix	GB	1:76, 1:32, 1:12	Plastic kits and complete plastic figures
Historex	F	1:32	Plastic kits
Britains	GB	1:32	Complete plastic figures (some metal)
Tamiya	J	1:35	Plastic kits
ESCI	I	1:35	Plastic kits
Italaeri	I	1:35	Plastic kits
Heller	F	1:35	Plastic kits
Hinchliffe	GB	1:25*, 1:76, 1:32	Metal kits
Rose	GB	1:32	Metal kits
Old Guard	USA/GB	1:32	Metal kits
Series 77	USA	1:25*	Metal kits
Ensign	GB	1:32	Metal kits
Phoenix	GB	1:64*, 1:32	Metal kits
Stadden	GB	1:32, 1:25*	Metal kits
Prinz August	SW	1:42*	Moulds for home casting
Zinnbrigade	WG	1:42*	Moulds for home casting
Soldiers	GB	1:32	Complete cast figures

*approximate scale - 75/77mm or 30/40mm high figures

Model Engineer (fortnightly)
Entirely devoted to mechanical models, mainly of the working or highly technical kind, requiring a home workshop.

Model Railways, Model Railway Constructor, Railway Modeller
These three journals, all from different publishers, give between them very full coverage of all aspects of model railways and associated subjects like scenery, model buildings, and some road transport.

UNITED STATES

Scale Modeler
All types of model with the emphasis on plastic kit models.

Military Modeler
Covers model fighting vehicles and soldiers of all sorts.

Campaigns (bi-monthly)
Covers model soldiers with the emphasis on historic periods.

Scale Aircraft Modeler
Covers all types of model aircraft, but mainly those made from plastic kits.

Model Railroader, Railroad Model Craftsman, Railroad Modeler
Three magazines from different publishers which give excellent coverage of American railroad modelling and associated subjects like model buildings and scenery.

FRANCE

RMF (Rail Miniature Flash), Loco Revue
Two magazines from different publishers which give good coverage to model railways French style, though they also cover other European nations.

POLAND

Modelarz
A well-produced magazine which gives good coverage to all types of scale modelling with the emphasis on East Europe.

HOLLAND

Miniatuur Banen
A good model railway journal covering Benelux, and other European interest.

WEST GERMANY

Modell Magazin
All types of scale model except trains, with the emphasis on converting kits.

Eisenbahn
Entirely devoted to German trains, with extensive coverage of both modelling and the real thing.

SHIPS

Company	Country	Scales	Remarks
Airfix	GB	1:1200, 1:600 (warships) –others various	Plastic kits
Matchbox	GB	1:700 (warships)	Plastic kits
Revell	USA/GB/WG	1:720, 1:500 (warships) –others various	Plastic kits
Tamiya	J	1:400, 1:700 (warships)	Plastic kits
Hasegawa	J	1:700 (warships)	Plastic kits
Aosima	J	1:700 (warships)	Plastic kits
Fujimi	J	1:700 (warships)	Plastic kits
Monogram	USA	1:500 (warships) –1:600	Plastic kits
Bandai	J	1:350 (sailing ships)	Plastic kits
Heller	F	1:400 (warships) –others various	Plastic kits
Novo	URS	1:500, 1:300 (warships)	Plastic kits
Billing	D	Various	Wood kits
Humbrol	GB	Various	Wood kits
Navis	WG	1:1250	Ready made models
Lifelike	USA	Various	Plastic kits
Hansa	WG	1:1250	Ready made models

CARS AND ROAD TRANSPORT (Inc. Motor Cycles)

Company	Country	Scales	Remarks
Airfix	GB	1:32, 1:24, 1:16	Plastic kits
Matchbox	GB	1:32, 1:24	Plastic kits
Revell	USA/GB/WG	1:32, 1:24, 1:16 1:8 etc	Plastic kits
Tamiya	J	1:24, 1:20, 1:16, 1:8	Plastic kits
Bandai	J	1:24, 1:20, 1:16, 1:8	Plastic kits
Protar	I	1:8	Motor cycles –plastic kits
Monogram	USA	1:32, 1:24	Plastic kits
ESCI	I	1:24	Plastic kits
Otaki	J	1:24	Plastic kits
Lifelike	USA	1:32	Plastic kits
Wills Firecast	GB	1:43, 1:32, 1:24	Metal kits
Western	GB	1:43	Metal kits
Varney	GB	1:48, 1:76 (buses)	Metal kits
LDM	GB	1:43, 1:32	Metal kits
Hubley	USA	1:24	Metal kits
Langley	GB	1:148, 1:76	Metal kits
Pirate	GB	1:76 (buses)	Metal kits

MODEL BUILDINGS AND MISCELLANEOUS

Company	Country	Scales	Remarks
Airfix	GB	1:76, 1:32	1:32 scale items are all military
Faller	WG	1:87, 1:43, 1:160	Plastic and/or card kits
Pola	WG	1:22, 1:87, 1:160	Plastic kits
Wiad	WG	1:87	Plastic kits
Vollmer	WG	1:87	Plastic kits
Heljan	D	1:87, 1:160	Plastic kits
Kibri	A	1:87, 1:160	Plastic kits
Bilteezi	GB	1:100, 1:148 1:76	Card kits
Builder Plus	GB	1:148, 1:76	Card kits
Superquick	GB	1:76	Card kits
Wilhelmshavener	WG	1:120, 1:87	Card kits
Linka	WG	1:87	Plaster kit
Campbell	USA	1:87	Wood kits

PAINTS AND ACCESSORIES

Company	Country	Remarks
Humbrol	GB	Paints, tools, adhesives, airbrushes
Testor	USA	Paints, tools, adhesives, airbrushes
Floquil	USA	Paints
X-acto	USA	Tools
Multicraft	GB	Tools
Gloy	GB	Paints, adhesives
Airfix	GB	Paints, tools
Joy	GB	Paints
Badger (Morris & Ingram)	USA/GB	Airbrush
Aerograph (De Villbis)	GB	Airbrush
Metalskin	USA/GB	Foil covering
Baremetal	USA	Foil covering
Plastruct	USA/GB	Constructional accessories
Slaters	GB	Plastic card and accessories

Index

Figures in italic refer to illustrations

R

S

T

V

W

Acknowledgements

The author and publishers would like to extend their thanks to the following individuals and companies for their help in supplying material for this book:

Airfix
M. Andress
Australian Information Service
A. F. J. Boyce
British Aircraft corporation
Builder Plus
Bundesarchiv
Alan Butler
Kai Choi
Christies
Helen Downton
Drumbeat Showcases
Simon Dunstan
T. P. Edwards
Faller
Mike Fear
Michael Freeman
R. Goldman
J. Groenveld
Clive Hayball
Historex Agents
Ian Howes
Humbrol
Imperial War Museum
Kardsmen/John Mackenzie
Keilkraft
Philip Lemon
Letraset
Matchbox
Metalskin
J. G. Moore
New Cavendish Books
Otaki
Keith Palmer
John Piper
Plastruct
Prototype Models
QED
Rareplanes
Revell
Riko/Tamiya
Gerald Scarborough
Seagull Models
Steve Small
Sothebys
Juliet Stanwell-Smith
Superquick
John W. R. and Michael Taylor
Les Whitehouse
Martin Woodford
Jon Wyand
John Wylie